T0305807

THE GREAT DEPRESSION

Its Origins in Acceleration and Electric Unit Drive

THE GREAT DEPRESSION

Its Origins in Acceleration and Electric Unit Drive

Bernard C. Beaudreau

Université Laval, Canada

World Scientific

NEW JERSEY · LONDON · SINGAPORE · BEIJING · SHANGHAI · HONG KONG · TAIPEI · CHENNAI · TOKYO

Published by

World Scientific Publishing Co. Pte. Ltd.

5 Toh Tuck Link, Singapore 596224

USA office: 27 Warren Street, Suite 401-402, Hackensack, NJ 07601

UK office: 57 Shelton Street, Covent Garden, London WC2H 9HE

Library of Congress Cataloging-in-Publication Data
Names: Beaudreau, Bernard C., 1955–   author.
Title: The Great Depression : its origins in acceleration and electric unit drive /
    Bernard C. Beaudreau, Université Laval, Canada.
Description: New Jersey : World Scientific, [2023] | Includes bibliographical references and index.
Identifiers: LCCN 2022034839 | ISBN 9789811264276 (hardcover) |
    ISBN 9789811264283 (ebook) | ISBN 9789811264290 (ebook other)
Subjects: LCSH: Depressions--1929--United States. | Industries--United States--History--
    20th century. | Electric driving--United States--History--20th century. |
    United States--Economic conditions--1918-1945.
Classification: LCC HB3717 1929 B33 2023 | DDC 330.973/0916--dc23/eng/20220721
LC record available at https://lccn.loc.gov/2022034839

British Library Cataloguing-in-Publication Data
A catalogue record for this book is available from the British Library.

For any available supplementary material, please visit
https://www.worldscientific.com/worldscibooks/10.1142/13083#t=suppl

Desk Editors: Nimal Koliyat/Geysilla Jean

Typeset by Stallion Press
Email: enquiries@stallionpress.com

Printed in Singapore

Acceleration rather than structural change is the key to an understanding of our recent economic developments. Gradually, the fact emerged during the course of this survey that the distinctive character of the years from 1922 to 1929 owes less to fundamental change than to intensified activity.

Report of the Committee on Recent Economic Changes
of the President's Conference on Unemployment, 1929

Preface

The year 2029 will mark the 100th anniversary of the start of the Great Depression, an event that remains shrouded in mystery despite decades of efforts to identify the cause(s). This book represents a new generation of work on this important period in U.S. and World history, one that provides a gestalt view of this far-reaching event, one that includes events before, during and after. Accordingly, it attempts to rationalize the Roaring Twenties, the Smoot–Hawley Tariff Bill, the Stock Market Boom and Crash of 1929, the Depression itself and the New Deal as parts of a greater whole, namely the massive increase in potential output that resulted from the wide-scale adoption of electric unit drive and its effects on the U.S. economy.

It brings together the findings of three research programs, each focusing on a specific aspect of the Great Depression. They are (i) an interest in the role of power drive technologies, specifically the introduction of electric unit drive, in increasing productivity and rated capacity throughout the 1920s and 1930s; (ii) the role of technology in the drafting of the Smoot–Hawley Tariff Act and the National Industrial Recovery Act, and (iii) the structural–as opposed to cyclical–policy objectives of these two policy measures.

The result is a historically and empirically consistent account of the Great Depression, one that offers a comprehensive view of this period. Hence, instead of being unrelated as is the current view, the many events/

developments of the 1920s and 1930s, including the Smoot–Hawley Tariff Act, the Stock Market Boom and Crash, and the National Industrial Recovery Act, are shown to be part of a bigger whole.

I would like to thank those who provided feedback and suggestions on earlier versions, especially Alex Field, Robert J. Gordon and Peter Temin.

About the Author

Bernard C. Beaudreau is Professor of Economics at Université Laval in Quebec City, Canada. He holds an M.A. and a Ph.D. in economics from Western University. His research interests include economic theory, economic history, the history of economic thought, international trade, and consilient science. He has published numerous articles in leading journals as well as a number of monographs, including *The Economics of Speed: Machine Speed as the Key Factor in Productivity* in 2021.

Contents

List of Figures

List of Tables

Chapter 1

Introduction

Characteristic of the period 1922–1929 was the rise in the use of power — three and three-quarters times faster than the growth of population — and the extent to which power has been made readily available not alone for driving tools of increasing size and capacity, but for a convenient diversity of purposes in the smallest business enterprise, on the farm and in the home. Factories no longer need to cluster about the source of power. Widespread interconnection between power plants, arising out of an increasing appreciation of the value of flexibility in power, and made possible by technical advances during recent years, has created huge reservoirs of power so that abnormal conditions in one locality need not stop the wheels of industry.

Report of the Committee on Recent Economic Changes
of the President's Conference on Unemployment, 1929

This book presents a novel view of the Great Depression, one according to which this epoch-defining event was the result of a massive technology shock that, despite a number of well-intentioned policy responses, went horribly wrong. More specifically, it is about how a new power-drive technology increased potential output of existing plant and equipment, about how this new potential failed to be realized, and about how as a result, the U.S. economy sank into the worse economic downturn ever. In short, it tells the story of how the Great Depression resulted from the inability of the U.S. economy to make a successful transition to a new, higher growth path, resulting in the worse economic catastrophe in the industrial era.

As will be shown, this is not the first time that scholars and analysts have pointed to technological change as the underlying cause. For example, Columbia University economics professor and New Dealer Rexford G. Tugwell, business executives Henry Ford and Edward A. Filene, MIT-trained economist Stuart Chase, engineer Howard Scott and countless others argued that excess, unused, surplus productive capacity was the root cause of the downturn. They maintained that the failure of wage income and expenditure in general to increase commensurately with potential output was the chief reason. What is novel about the argument presented here, however, are the structure and details it provides. Missing from this literature has been a theoretically and empirically consistent account of the shock itself, as well as the equations of motion of the failed transition. Until now, no one has succeeded in bringing these elements together to form a consistent whole, one that makes sense of the events before, during and after the onset–that is late 1929 and 1930. These include the Smoot–Hawley Tariff Act, the Stock Market Boom and Crash of 1929, the ensuing tariff war, and the Roosevelt Administration's radical blueprint for a new America, the National Industrial Recovery Act (NIRA).

The result is an integrated view of the events of the 1920s and 1930s, one which shows how the various policy measures by the Republicans and Democrats were attempts at resolving a growing problem, namely rapidly increasing U.S. potential output — in short, the increasing ability of the U.S. economy to generate wealth. Its main contribution, however, lies in identifying and describing the technology shock, namely acceleration/speed-ups resulting from the widespread adoption of electric unit drive. The conversion to electric unit drive posed a fundamental challenge to the economics profession, as it did to the engineering community, owing in large measure to the fact that it, as well as its effects, were poorly understood. Broad notions such as increased efficiency and lower costs were common in the literature. Just how electric unit drive contributed to increasing potential output throughout the U.S. economy was then and remains to this day somewhat of a mystery. After all, to the naked eye, nothing (i.e., labor and capital) appeared to have changed. In short, acceleration was the invisible X-factor in the 1920s and indeed, the 1930s. Double the speed of a machine or process and productivity and capacity double, yet nothing will have appeared to change.

As such, it will be shown that the seeds of the Great Depression were sown in the WWI and post-WWI period, when U.S. electricity-generating capacity soared, making the conversion to electric unit drive not only viable but profitable in the short and long runs. As Alfred Chandler, Warren Devine, Sidney Sonenblum and numerous others pointed out, productive capacity in this period increased largely as the result of greater process speeds and greater throughput rates. According to University of Wisconsin at Madison economics professor Harry Jerome:

> One generally observable trend in the character of mechanized equipment is the enlargement of the capacity of the machine unit, either by increasing the physical size of the machine or the speed at which its parts function. As such changes are frequently accompanied by less than proportionate increases in the operating crew and that this changes the ratio of equipment to workers, they may appropriately be described as increases in the mechanization of industry (Jerome, 1934, p. 245).

In short, acceleration was the key:

> The capacity of a machine may be enlarged by making the machine run faster than increasing its physical size. For example, the capacity of the auger type of brick molding machine has been enlarged with resorting to "design or larger dimensions of the barrel." These machines have almost exclusively rotary movements and more capacity has been obtained by greater speed or number of revolutions. "An auger shaft speed of 25–30 revolutions per minute in 1914 is now often from 40 to 50 revolutions per minute, without undue breakage of parts." ....
> One manufacturer of corrugated fibre-board products reported to us that by increasing the speed of his machines, he was able to "triple production since 1920 with approximately the same number of employees" (Jerome, 1934, p. 249).

The shift from earlier power-drive technologies (i.e., belting and shafting) occurred gradually but steadily, continuing throughout the 1920s and 1930s. The reason: greater operating speeds reduced labor and capital costs markedly. For example, a 40 percent increase in operating speeds reduces the cost per unit by an equivalent amount, at minimal cost. This made for a situation in which speeding-up production processes was a dominant strategy throughout the 1920s as well as the 1930s.

It is important to point out that electric unit drive-based productivity gains were not confined to the manufacturing sector, but were generalized across most sectors of the U.S. economy. For example, the use of electric motors in agriculture improved material handling processes, an example being the use of mechanized grain drills. It also ushered in innovations such as mechanized milking. Indirectly, by making tractors and other agriculture-related prime movers more affordable, it increased productivity by speeding up virtually all facets of agricultural activity. Moreover, the motorization of transportation and farming (i.e., the tractorization) liberated millions of acres that had until then been used to grow beast-of-burden feedstocks.[1]

It improved efficiency in mining, construction, transportation, communications and public utilities, and services in general. Electric-powered mining compressors and drilling equipment, electric-powered material handling processes in mining, and improved lighting combined to revolutionize the mining sector. Construction benefited from the introduction of power tools, as well as electric unit drive-powered winches, hoists and cranes, a good example of which was the flurry of skyscrapers erected in the late 1920s (e.g., the Chrysler building and the Empire State building in New York). In transportation, it contributed directly to increasing speeds on electric railroad lines. Indirectly, by making trucks more affordable, it revolutionized the transportation sector. The growing use of electric unit drive-powered material handing processes (e.g., conveyors, drills, etc.) increased efficiency and productivity (Douglas, 1927).[2]

In communications and public utilities, it contributed to increasing efficiency. Centralized water distribution systems and waste management systems, powered by electric motors, became the norm, providing clean

---

[1]According to the U.S. Department of Agriculture, the tractorization of agriculture and the motorization (trucks and automobiles) of transportation in the 1920s decreased the traction-based demand for grain and hay by 48,294,887 equivalent acres (Beaudreau, 2014, p. 1039).

[2]Among the causes of the increase in productivity, (Douglas, 1927) pointed to "the rapid development of American technical methods, including, as its most notable feature, the moving conveyor." "The moving assembly has indeed been the chief cause for the virtual trebling of output per man-hour which has occurred in the automobile industry during the thirteen years." "The principle of the moving conveyor is indeed the greatest technical contribution which America has made to industry during the last century" (Douglas, 1927, pp. 671–672).

water to all as well as improved sanitation. Lastly, all services, especially those requiring the use of force, benefited from improved efficiency. For example, laundromats and restaurants could now count on electric unit drive to power washing machines and dryers, as well as food-processing instruments such as blenders, mixers, etc.

Another non-electric unit drive-based development was the growing use of electric lighting which contributed to increasing the *de facto* rated capacity of U.S. industry by providing cheap, safe illumination, making the round-the-clock operation of factories possible. As the *Report of the Committee on Recent Economic Changes of the President's Conference on Unemployment* put it:

> The increased supply of power and its wider uses: the multiplication by man of his strength and skill through machinery, the expert division and arrangement of work in mines and factories, on the farms, and in the trades, so that production per man-hour of effort has risen to new heights: the quickening of these instrumentalities through capital provided from the surplus incomes of a constantly widening proportion of our people-all these represent an accumulation of forces which have long been at work (*Report of the Committee on Recent Economic Changes*, 1929).

The upshot of this work is relatively simple, namely that the Great Depression resulted from a massive, acceleration-based increase in potential GDP, a potential that failed to be realized, a potential that became the focus of subsequent government policies, including the Smoot–Hawley Tariff Act and the National Industrial Recovery Act, and a potential that would plunge the U.S. economy into the worst depression in modern history, its severity being directly proportional to the magnitude of the shock (i.e., the extent of the excess capacity).

To this end, the following eight chapters present evidence of the massive increase in potential U.S. GDP made possible by increasing throughput rates of existing plant and equipment in the 1920s, as well as providing an account of the various challenges it presented to analysts and policymakers. Chapter 2 presents a review of the relevant literature, which includes writings on (i) productivity gains throughout the 1920s; (ii) the Smoot–Hawley Tariff Act; (iii) the Stock Market Boom and Crash of 1929; (iv) the decrease in investment and the downturn; (v) the National Industrial Recovery Act, and (vi) the duration of the Depression. This is followed in Chapter 3 by a detailed discussion of power drive technologies with an emphasis on the conversion to electric unit drive and the increasing supply of what Yale University economics professor Irving Fisher referred to as purchased electricity. A formal macroeconomic model is then offered in Chapter 4 where the effects of acceleration on productivity are analyzed at the plant, firm and aggregate, economy-wide level. Evidence of the massive increase in U.S. potential GDP is also provided.

The emphasis shifts in Chapter 5 to the Republican Party's response to a widening output gap, namely the Smoot–Hawley Tariff Act. The focus is on the Kansas City national convention where the problem of growing productivity and generalized excess capacity was front and center. Chapter 6 examines Wall Street's response to the Party's proposed higher tariffs, greater market share for U.S. companies and the expected higher profits. Specifically, evidence is presented which shows how stock prices tracked tariff news throughout this period. Chapter 7 shows how a schism in the Party, with 13 senators crossing the floor and joining the Democrats to lower, not increase tariffs, led ultimately to the stock market crash, the drying up of investment expenditure and the slide into the worse downturn in history. In other words, the failure of the Senate to pass the much-anticipated Bill touched off the crash, followed by a massive decrease in investment expenditure and ultimately a spiraling downward of economic activity in general — ironically against a background of greater and greater acceleration-based rated capacity.

Next is Chapter 8 which presents the Roosevelt Administration's radical attempt at dealing with what it considered to be a structural problem (i.e., excess capacity) in the midst of the worse downturn in history, namely the National Industrial Recovery Act, which called for higher wages, government expenditure and a push for greater unionization. To most, the former made little sense at the time. However, it is shown why and how the Brains Trust drafted the controversial piece of legislation known as the National Industrial Recovery Act, and why it failed. Chapter 9 shows how and why ongoing conversion to electric unit drive-based acceleration throughout the 1930s contributed to prolonging the downturn. The fact that conversion to electric unit drive was profitable even in the downturn, combined with the increase in the availability of low-cost electric power, prompted in part by a number of New Deal programs, served to increase potential rated capacity in the depths of the depression thus prolonging the downturn. A summary of the book's main argument is then provided, along with a discussion of the reasons why the electric unit drive-based acceleration theory of the Great Depression was overlooked despite having gained significant traction in the 1920s and 1930s.

Appendix: *Report of the Committee on Recent Economic Changes of the President's Conference on Unemployment* — Selected Excerpts

This appendix presents the *Introduction, Table of Contents* and first chapter of the *Report of the Committee on Recent Economic Changes of the President's Conference on Unemployment* published in 1929. As the title indicates, it was established by President Herbert Hoover to examine the role of technology in the rising levels of unemployment in the late 1920s. Noteworthy are the following facts. First is the prominent role accorded to power and acceleration, both of which resulted from the on-going conversion of U.S. industry to electric unit drive. Second is the fact that the chapters dealing with this technology shock were written by engineers and not economists. Despite this, the analysis rarely goes beyond documenting the increase in horsepower at the industry level. Just exactly how the latter impacted productivity and potential output is not broached. Third is the emphasis on improving marketing techniques in order to close the gap between actual output-expenditure and the new-found potential. No mention is made of the trials and tribulations of increasing national income in response to greater productivity and potential output. Last, it illustrates the difficulty both the engineering and economics professions had at the time in understanding the nature and breadth of the changes brought about by the conversion to electric unit drive. This, we believe, owes to its non-material nature. Unlike plant and equipment, speed and acceleration are non-material in nature, making them more illusive.

Report of the Committee on Recent Economic Changes of the President's Conference on Unemployment

Section I Characteristics of 1922–1929

Acceleration rather than structural change is the key to an understanding of our recent economic developments. Gradually, the fact emerged during the course of this survey that the distinctive character of the years from

1922 to 1929 owes less to fundamental change than to intensified activity.

Forty years ago, David A. Wells wrote his *Recent Economic Changes*, showing that the quarter century which ended in 1889 was a period of "profound economic changes," which he described as "unquestionably more important and varied than during any former corresponding period of World history."

Each generation believes itself to be on the verge of a new era, an era of fundamental change, but the longer the committee deliberated, the more evident it became that the novelty of the period covered by the present survey rested chiefly in the fact that developments such as formerly affected our old industries have been recurring in our new industries. The changes have not been in structure but in speed and spread.

Invention is not a new art. Transportation and communication are not new services. The facilitating function of finance is older than coined currency. Agriculture is as ancient as history. Competition is not a new phenomenon. None of the changes in distribution on which emphasis has been laid in the last few years is basically new. Hand-to-mouth buying is old: sudden changes in style and demand are familiar: there is no new principle in installment selling: cooperative marketing is no discovery, the chain store movement dates back at least 25 years. But the breadth and scale and "tempo" of recent developments give them new importance.

The increased supply of power and its wider uses: the multiplication by man of his strength and skill through machinery, the expert division and arrangement of work in mines and factories, on the farms, and in the trades, so that production per man-hour of effort has risen to new heights: the quickening of these instrumentalities through capital provided from the surplus incomes of a constantly widening proportion of our people, all these represent an accumulation of forces which have long been at work.

The committee, like other observers, was early impressed by the degree of economic activity in these seven years. It was struck by the outpouring of energy which piled up skyscrapers in scores of cities: knit the 48 States together with 20,000 miles of airways: moved each year over railways and waterways more than a billion and a half tons of freight: thronged the highways with 25,000,000 motor cars: carried electricity to 17,000,000 homes: sent each year 3,750,000 children to high school and more than 1,000,000 young men and women to college: and fed, clothed, housed and amused the 120,000,000 persons who occupy our twentieth of the habitable area of the Earth.

But while the period from 1922 to 1929 has been one of intense activity, the committee noted that this activity has been "spotty." Certain groups have been more active than other groups: certain industries busier than their neighbor industries, and certain geographical areas more prosperous than other areas.

While rayon manufacturers have worked at top speed, cotton mills have been on part-time: While the silk hosiery industry, the women's shoe trad, and the fur business have been active, there has been depression in the woolen and worsted industry: while dairying has been prosperous, grain growers have been depressed. Coal mining has been in difficulties, and classes of wholesalers and retailers have been under grave economic pressure. Progress has been made toward more stable employment in seasonal industries, yet "technological" unemployment, resulting from the displacement of workers by improved machinery and methods, has attracted attention.

Geographical differences also were noted. The Pacific States have made an extraordinary advance: the South has rapidly developed as a manufacturing area: the East North Central Division has grown: while the New England States, and to some extent the Middle Atlantic section, have developed less rapidly and have experienced some difficulties in adapting their older industries to new conditions.

However, in spite of this variability, this difference in activity as between groups and areas and industries, the rising standard of living characteristic of this period was widespread and has reached the highest level in our national history.

Participation by the people as a whole in many of the benefits of increased productivity, which of itself varied as between different groups and geographical areas, has been one of the marked characteristics of the period. While industrial, agricultural, and commercial activity has been "spotty," the broad social advantages of our accelerated activity flowed out over the land. For example, the highway building programs throughout the nation were not limited to the intensely active areas: good roads were extended in all directions, serving the "whole population." The same might be said for educational advantages, radio entertainment, personal mobility made possible by low-priced motor cars, swift and dependable transportation and numerous other facilities and services making for comfort and well-being, beyond the elemental requirements of food, clothing and shelter.

This spread of higher living standards has been characteristic of our national life practically throughout our history. As a phenomenon, it is not new, but in its degree and scope it has taken on new importance.

The Speed Which Power Has Added to Production

Characteristic also has been the rise in the use of power — three and three-quarters times faster than the growth in population — and the extent to which power has been made readily available not alone for driving tools of increasing size and capacity, but for a convenient diversity of purposes in the smallest business enterprise and on the farm and in the home.

Factories no longer need to cluster about the sources of power. Widespread interconnection between power plants, arising out of an increasing appreciation of the value of flexibility in power, and made possible by technical advances during recent years, has created huge reservoirs of power so that abnormal conditions in one locality need not stop the wheels of industry.

The increasing flexibility with which electricity can be delivered for power has enabled manufacturers and farmers to meet high labor costs by the application of power-driven specialized machines: and power in this flexible form has penetrated into every section of the United States, including many rural areas. The survey shows that as a nation we now use as much electrical energy as all the rest of the world combined. Through the sub-division of power the unskilled worker has become a skilled operator, multiplying his effectiveness with specialized automatic machinery and processes. Thus, the unit cost of production has been reduced, the drudgery eliminated from much unskilled "work", and wages maintained or actually increased.

Production Increase and the Expansion of Human Wants

Partly as a result of this newly sensed principle of an accelerated cycle of production-consumption, and partly by reason of the development of a stream of credit and an abundance of flexible power made broadly, the years 1922–1929 witnessed a marked increase in the physical volume of production. Some years stand out. More conspicuously than others: two — 1924 and 1927 — show minor recessions: but the period as a whole has been notably consistent.

Since 1922 primary production has been increasing 2.5 percent a year: manufacturing, 4 percent: and transportation, 4 percent. Taking 1919 — a year of fair harvests — as a base, crop production in 1922 was 102: in 1925, 104: in 1927, 106.

There have been prosperous periods in the past which may have surpassed these rates of increase, but none so far as the committee can learn which has shown such a striking increase in productivity per man hour. Notwithstanding the reductions in hours of labor, per capita productivity is nearly 60 percent greater than it was toward the close of the nineteenth century: the increase in per capita productivity in manufacturing from 1922 to 1925 was 35 percent: the productivity of farm workers has increased at a rate probably never seen before. And these increases in productivity have been joined to a corresponding increase in the consuming power of the American people. Here has been demonstrated on a grand scale the expansibility of human wants and desires.

Economists have long declared that consumption, the satisfaction of wants, would expand with little evidence of satiation if we could so adjust our economic processes as to make dormant demands effective. Such an expansion has been going on since the beginning of the Industrial Revolution. It is not a phenomenon of the postwar period, except in degree. But it is this degree of economic activity, this almost insatiable appetite for goods and services, this abounding production of all things which almost any man can want, which is so striking a characteristic of the period covered by the survey.

Our Natural Advantages

It is obvious, of course, that the economic position of this nation is in no slight degree due to our possession of abundant raw materials and sources of power, to the fact that our domestic market is so large, and that there are no trade barriers between the States of our Union. We can exchange goods without stopping them for inspection or the payment of duties between States. We can effect their transfer without the barriers of differing languages or customs. Advertising is peculiarly effective because we have so great an area with a common language which enables us to talk to all the people and to develop national consumption habits, which in turn make possible large-scale production.

This fortuitous situation should be borne in mind as an important factor in both the speed and the spread which have characterized our recent economic development.

The balance which has been maintained between consumption and production is nowhere better shown than in the fact that wages have been rising, and that there has been no striking increase of unemployment in a period marked by the broadest technological advancement which we have yet known.

Perhaps the deepest economic significance of the new situation lies not in the rapidity with which the service industries have grown and have become integrated, nor in the universality of their spread, but in the fact that the situation which they have created is reciprocal. Our increasing standard of living is not participated in only by those who produce our food, clothing and shelter, but has flowed back to those in the service industries. The population as a whole can enjoy the rising standard of living — the music which comes in over the radio, the press, the automobile and good roads, the schools, the colleges, parks, play grounds and the myriad other facilities for comfortable existence and cultural development.

Our ancestors came to these shores with few tools and little organization to fight nature for a livelihood. Their descendants have developed a new and peculiarly American type of civilization in which services have come to rank with other forms of production as a major economic factor.

Chapter 2

Literature Review

2.1 Introduction

As mentioned, this book presents an integrated view of the events of 1920s and 1930s, combining several developments, from productivity growth in the 1920s (i.e., the Roaring Twenties) to the Smoot–Hawley Tariff Bill, to the stock market boom and crash, to the precipitous fall in investment in the early 1930s, to the Great Depression, to the New Deal signature piece of legislation, the National Industrial Recovery Act and, finally, to the slow recovery. More to the point, it sets out to demonstrate how all of these events were related in what can best be described as a cascade of developments in response to what the *Report of the Committee on Recent Economic Changes of the President's Conference on Unemployment* referred to as the acceleration of the U.S. economy. In this chapter, the existing literature on these developments is presented and critiqued. It is shown that, for the most part, they are viewed as being largely unrelated. The following topics will be reviewed (i) the productivity growth in the 1920s (i.e., the Roaring Twenties) (ii) the Smoot–Hawley Tariff Act of 1930 (iii) the stock market boom and crash (iv) the onset of the Great Depression (v) the National Industrial Recovery Act and (vi) the slow recovery of the 1930s.

2.2 Productivity Growth in the 1920s (The Roaring Twenties)

Today, a century after the fact, the Roaring Twenties remain somewhat of an enigma, productivity-wise. After all, output and productivity exploded, yet the cause or causes remain shrouded in mystery. Referring to Table 2.1 which presents a non-exhaustive list of the various works, both period and more recent, three factors stand out, namely the introduction of a new power source in the form of electric power, the mechanization of many production lines and organizational innovations.

As shown, most period writers pointed to electric power as the key innovation, without however being able to make the link between it and productivity. A good example is Irving Fisher who, in his defense of the stock market boom, pointed to the increase in purchased electrical power, (see Figure 2.1) which he used as a proxy for the ongoing conversion to electric unit drive. It bears noting as Warren Devine (1983) pointed out, that electricity was replacing steam in manufacturing, not adding to the overall level of power consumed. Just how and why this would lead to greater productivity is not clear. Some pointed to the resulting improved

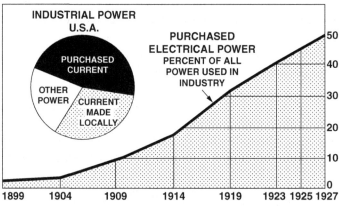

CHART 15 – Total primary factory power applied through electric motors increased, 1919–1927, from 55 percent to 78 percent.
Inset: 50 percent purchased, 28 percent made locally.

Figure 2.1.   Irving Fisher, Purchased Electrical Power and Electric Unit Drive
Source: Fisher (1930, p. 132).

Table 2.1. The Roaring Twenties: Period and More Recent Literature

Author	Cause
Period Works	
Filene (1923)	Mass production
Ford (1926a)	Mass production, electric power, speed and accuracy
Foster and Catchings (1927)	Our greatly increased productive capacity
Tugwell (1927)	Electric power
Tryon (1927)	New power sources
Thomas (1928)	Large-scale production
Report of the Committee on Recent Economic Changes of the President's Conference on Unemployment (1929)	Acceleration of existing plant and equipment
Fisher (1930)	Purchased electric power, new products and improved management
Brookings (1932)	Mass production
Scott (1933)	Increasing use of power
Polakov (1933)	Power production, the new power age
Chase (1934)	The new technique of mass production
Bohn and Ely (1935)	Production and transmission of electricity for light and power
Recent Works	
Soule (1947)	Electric unit drive
Giedion (1948)	Automation (e.g., bread in the 1920s)
Lorant (1967)	Technological change (ex. chemical industry Weizman fermentation process)
Chandler (1977)	Process speed, increased throughput rates
Devine (1983)	Electric power, increased flow of production as the result of plant layout
Cohen (1984)	Increasingly sophisticated use of electric power in pulp and paper manufacturing processes
Oshima (1984)	Increase in price of unskilled labor leading to mechanization
Wright (1990)	Increased utilization of America's endowment of natural resources
Field (2003)	Greater total factor productivity (TFP)

factory designs, others pointed to improved flow through. Still, others pointed to the resulting automation.

While not referring to electric unit drive *per se*, Harvard Business School business historian Alfred D. Chandler (1977) was one of the few to invoke greater process speed. As he put it, "In modern mass production, as in modern mass distribution and modern transportation and communications, economies resulted more from speed than from size. It was not the size of the manufacturing establishment in terms of the number of workers and the amount and value of productive equipment, but the velocity of throughput and the resulting increase in volume that permitted economies that lowered costs and increased output per worker and machine (Chandler, 1977, p. 244). Walter Polakov (1933) referred to something he called the rate of production, which can be understood as a reference to acceleration and speed. Specifically, output was an increasing function of time, the number of employees and the rate of production.[1]

The failure to identify electric power-based acceleration or speed-ups as the key innovation in the 1920s can be attributed, in large part, to the very state of production theory both in economics and engineering. As a number of these writers pointed out, electric unit drive ushered in an age of speed, when material processes were accelerated, resulting in greater output per unit labor and capital. Process speed and acceleration, however, were absent from neoclassical production theory and process engineering. Neoclassical production theory at the time focused on broadly defined capital and labor. While process engineers were at the heart of the age of speed, their formalizations of industrial processes were, for the most part, devoid of this key element.

This oversight has made for a situation in which the most recent literature (Field, 2003; Bakker *et al.*, 2015) attributed the phenomenal growth in the 1920s and 1930s to increases in total factor productivity (TFP), which in many ways represents a setback relative to period writers who focused, for the most part, on electrification, mass production and new power sources (see Tables 2.2 and 2.3). While the latter were unable to identify, describe and formalize the exact transmission mechanism, they were nonetheless on the right track. The most recent literature, on the other hand, contented itself with references to innovation in general (i.e., the Solow residual, or TFP).

---

[1] Output = $T \times E \times R$, where T = time, E = employees, and R = rate of production, or machine speed.

Table 2.2. Compound Annual Average Growth Rates of Output per Hour, Private Domestic and Private Non-Farm Economy, United States, 1919–1948

	Private Domestic Economy	**Private Non-Farm Economy**
1919–1929	2.36	2.27
1929–1941	2.48	2.35
1941–1948	2.17	1.71

Source: Field (2003, p. 1409).

Table 2.3. TFP Growth Sector and Industry 1919–1929, 1929–1941

	1919–1929	**1919–1929**	**1929–1941**	**1929–1941**
	TFP Growth	**Contribution**	**TFP Growth**	**Contribution**
Private domestic economy	1.7	1.68	1.9	1.87
Manufacturing	4.5	1.18	2.3	0.61
Non-manufacturing	0.6		1.8	1.26
One big wave sectors	2.6	0.60	3.1	0.74
Chemicals	7.6	0.21	0.70	0.02
Chemicals	7.1	0.08	2.1	0.03
Petroleum, coal products	8.2	0.10	–1.1	–0.01
Rubber products	7.3	0.03	1.5	0.01
Electricity	2.6	0.07	4.9	0.15
Electric machinery	3.1	0.03	4.6	0.05
Electric utilities	2.3	0.04	0.51	0.10
Internal combustion engine	1.9	0.30	3.30	0.54
Transport equipment	7.9	0.14	3.5	0.07
Local transit	3.6	0.04	0.4	0.00
Distribution	0.9	0.12	3.4	0.46
Communications	2.0	0.02	2.5	0.04
Telephone	1.1	0.01	1.4	0.01
Spectator equipment	3.2	0.02	4.4	0.02

Source: Bakker *et al.* (2015).

2.3 The Smoot–Hawley Tariff Act

The Smoot–Hawley Tariff Act is undoubtedly the most infamous of all tariff acts, being enacted in the first months of the Great Depression and having

Table 2.4.   Origins of Smoot–Hawley Tariff Act

Taussig (1930)	Agricultural tariff hikes plus log-rolling and pork-barreling
Schattschneider (1935)	Agricultural and industrial lobbying
Pastor (1980)	Party politics and 1928 election results
Eichengreen (1989)	Coalition of northern farmers and light industries
Callahan *et al.* (1994)	No evidence of log-rolling. Rather, a party measure
Irwin (2011)	Political ploy-appease mid-west

triggered the only full-fledged all-out tariff war in history. Why the U.S. chose to double tariffs a mere seven years after having enacted the prohibitive Fordney–McCumber Tariff Act is still very much an open question.

The general consensus (see Table 2.4) is that it started off as a limited tariff bill focused on agriculture which, via log-rolling and pork-barreling, turned into a generalized bill affecting industry as well as agriculture.

The interesting thing about this literature is the lack of context. To Taussig, Schattschneider, Eichengreen and Irwin, the tariff initiative was motivated by politics, specifically a will on the part of the Party to assuage Mid-Western voters. However, a more careful reading of the record, specifically of the 1928 Republican National Convention in Kansas City, Missouri, paints an altogether different picture and rationale. Specifically, the Party officials, with Senator Reed Smoot as the key figure, called for a generalized, upwards revision of the tariff schedule with an emphasis on manufactures. This was based on the view that many lines of business were suffering from excess capacity and that higher tariffs, by reducing imports, would create more room for domestic firms.

2.4 The Stock Market Boom and Crash of 1929

Like the literature on the Smoot–Hawley Tariff Act, the literature on the stock market boom and crash is highly impressionistic. Other than the rare reference to fundamentals, the consensus (see Table 2.5) is that the boom and crash was a speculative bubble aided and abetted by Wall Street banks, specifically by the proliferation of margin buying. Not helping matters was the fact that those who pointed to fundamentals as the basis for the boom were unable to explain the crash. This was the case of Irving

Table 2.5. Stock Market Boom and Crash — Cause(s)

Fisher (1930)	Boom: Improved fundamentals; crash: Speculation, margin-buying
Dice (1929)	Mass production and modern management
Sirkin (1975)	Greater expected earnings
Galbraith (1954)	Speculative bubble
Wanniski (1976)	Crash: Smoot–Hawley–Thomas amendment
Pecora (1939)	Crash: Banks' stock market investments
Shiller (2000)	Irrational exuberance
McGrattan and Prescott (2004)	Boom: Fundamentals (intangible assets)

Fisher, who in the aftermath of the crash, was unable to provide a consistent, let alone convincing, explanation of the crash, thus throwing doubt on his explanation of the boom, which he attributed to fundamentals, including an increase in purchased electrical power, new management techniques and new products.

Non-standard approaches to the crash include Jude Wanniski's (1976), who pointed to the deliberations in the Senate over the proposed Smoot–Hawley tariff bill. Specifically, he argued that the defeat of the Thomas amendment on October 20, 1929, an amendment that called for a limited tariff bill (to the agricultural sector), was the deciding factor as it signaled to the market that tariffs on manufactures would rise, provoking a tariff war and a decrease in world trade. Eugene White, however, cast considerable doubt on this view by showing that all stocks, irrespective of whether or not they were in the export sector, were equally affected (White, 1990).

The upshot of this literature is relatively straightforward: the stock market boom and crash of 1928–1929 was a speculative bubble begotten, in large measure, by what appeared to be uncontrolled margin-buying (White, 1990).

2.5 The Decrease in Investment and the Start of the Great Depression

The precipitous decline in investment expenditure in the fall of 1929 and throughout 1930 is seen by many as the event that led to the

Table 2.6.   The Cause of the Fall in Investment Expenditure

Robinson (1937)	Animal spirits
Keynes (1936)	Falling marginal efficiency of investment (MEI)
Friedman and Schwartz (1963)	Bank failures leading to a decrease in money supply
Gordon (1961)	Most investment opportunities exploited
Hansen (1977)	Lack of investment opportunities
Szostak (1996)	Lack of new product innovations

Great Depression. Over the course of the following 24 months, it decreased from $7.78 billion to $620 million in 1932, prompting a downward spiral in income and expenditure. By 1933, U.S. GDP had decreased by 47 percent and employment by 25 percent.

Not surprisingly, much has been written about the role of investment expenditure in the downturn. Hypotheses and theories abound (see Table 2.6), from the stock market crash, to secular stagnation, to animal spirits, to the Smoot–Hawley Tariff Act, to higher interest rates.

2.6   The National Industrial Recovery Act

By the time Franklin D. Roosevelt took office in 1933 and proposed a New Deal to the American people, the economics profession had been literally shell-shocked. Starting with the Roaring Twenties which appeared to defy explanation, to the Smoot–Hawley Tariff Act that made little sense and openly violated the basic principles of trade theory, to the stock market crash which came out of nowhere, to the sudden precipitous decrease in investment expenditure which in combination with the ongoing tariff war ushered in the worse downturn in history, the world appeared to be coming unhinged. After all, the U.S. went from riding the crest of an unprecedented wave of optimism to the depths of despair.

So, when Roosevelt and the Brains Trust released their blueprint for a radical overhaul of wage and price-setting, the profession was, for the most part, mute. While raising wages at a time of record unemployment appeared, to most, to be pure folly, little criticism ensued.

The NIRA was passed in May 1933 and declared unconstitutional in June 1935, ending what was a two-year policy experiment. Given its ephemeral history, little was said or written in its aftermath.

The National Industrial Recovery Act of 1933 was and remains to this day the most ambitious piece of economic reform legislation ever conceived of in the Western world. Never before in peacetime had a government attempted to set wages and prices throughout the economy, alter the dynamics of the worker-management relationship and increase government expenditure. Coming as it did in the wake of the Roaring Twenties, the stock market boom and crash, the Smoot–Hawley Tariff Act and the downturn, it was, intellectually speaking, overwhelming. The established order had, as it were, come apart. And with the election of Franklin Roosevelt in 1932 came a whole new — radical — way of thinking about the world.

Not surprisingly, the first impressions were not favorable (see Table 2.7). After all, Roosevelt was attempting to alter fundamentally the workings of the free-market U.S. economy, one whose foundations were intricately tied to the very notions of freedom and liberty.

While the NIRA was billed as a recovery measure, it was first and foremost intended as a structural measure. Roosevelt, Wagner and

Table 2.7.   The Underlying Rationale for the NIRA as Seen in the Literature

Author	No Mention of a Rationale	Cut-Throat	Progressive Ideas	Halting Business Failures	Deflationary Shock	Insufficient Purchasing Power
Lyon *et al.* (1935)		X	X	X		
Friedman and Schwartz (1963)	X					
Weinstein (1980)	X					
Bernanke (1986)	X					
Beaudreau (1996, 2005)						X
Alexander (1997)				X		
Powell (2003)	X					
Cole and Ohanian (2004)	X					
Taylor (2011)		X				
Eggertsson (2008)					X	

Tugwell were of the view that the downturn was the result of a structural imbalance, namely excess capacity. In short, America's ability to produce wealth exceeded its ability to generate income and expenditure — in short, underconsumption. In their view, only by addressing the structural imbalances could recovery occur and long-term growth follow.

This very fact was lost on both the academic community and the public at large. The events of 1929–1933 had overshadowed the question of fundamentals, which engendered an overwhelming sense of derision in the minds of many. After all, to most observers, the problem was getting the economy back on track, of increasing employment and output. And higher wages appeared to most as counterintuitive.

This dichotomy (structural versus contractionary) characterizes most of the literature on the NIRA.

2.7 The Slow Recovery

One of the distinguishing features of the Great Depression was its duration, namely nearly a decade. Up until then, downturns had lasted on average 18 months (peak to peak). This begs the question why? Why was the U.S. economy mired in a downturn for the good part of the decade? The consensus view (see Table 2.8), put forward initially by Milton Friedman and Anna Schwartz (1963), points to the wage and price provisions of the National Industrial Recovery Act of 1933 and the wage provisions of the National Labor Relations Act of 1935, both of which served to either maintain or increase wages and freeze prices, thus preventing the needed downward adjustment. In short, government policy was the leading cause.

Table 2.8.   Causes of the Slow Recovery

Author	Cause
Friedman and Schwartz (1963)	National Industrial Recovery Act/National Labor Relations Act — Higher Wages
Eichengreen (1992a,b)	Gold standard-delay in suspending convertibility
Cole and Ohanian (2004)	National Industrial Recovery Act/National Labor Relations Act — Higher Wages
Vedder and Galloway (1993)	National Industrial Recovery Act/National Labor Relations Act — Market Rigidity

University of California–Berkeley economics professor Barry Eichengreen (1992a,b) pointed to another cause, namely the failure on the part of the Federal Reserve to suspend the gold standard, the argument being that by failing to follow the lead of most other European nations, the U.S. could not engage in expansionary monetary policy. However, as it turned out, Roosevelt did suspend the gold standard in 1934, and depreciated the value of the dollar. Yet, the U.S. economy would languish in depression for the next five years.

2.8 Summary and Conclusions

This chapter has presented a review of the relevant literature, from the Smoot–Hawley Tariff Act, to the duration of the Great Depression itself. One of the distinguishing features of this literature is the extent to which it is fractured. Each of these events is viewed as being independent, having little-to-no bearing on the others. Taken together, the overall view of the 1920s and 1930s that emerges is one of a period characterized by (i) irrational tariff policy (ii) irrational behavior on the part of investors and bankers (iii) irrational firms (iv) irrational wage and price legislation and (v) irrational labor legislation. It is as if the U.S. economy and government were overcome by a wave of collective irrationality. Add to this the fact that all of this came on the heels of the most productive decade in all of history. In the following chapters, we intend to show how these events are related, and how they are all, in actual fact, the result of what analysts and observers of the time referred to as the lack of balance (equilibrium) set against a paradigm power drive-related technology shock in the form of electric unit drive.

Chapter 3

Electric Unit Drive and Interconnected Power Grids

The speed with which electricity was adopted may be readily indicated. Electric motors accounted for less than five percent of total installed horsepower in American manufacturing in 1899. The growth in the first years of the 20th century was such that by 1909, their share of manufacturing horsepower was 25 percent. Ten years later, the share rose to 55 percent, and by 1929, electric motors completely dominated the manufacturing sector by providing over 80 percent of total installed horsepower. The sharp rise in productivity in the American economy, in the years after World War I, doubtlessly owed a great deal, both directly and indirectly, to the electrification of manufacturing.

Nathan Rosenberg (1972)

3.1 Introduction

The key element in our narrative of the Great Depression is the introduction and widespread adoption of a new power drive technology, known as the electric unit drive. The increasing conversion to and use of electric unit drive were made possible in large measure by the increasing availability of low-cost electricity in the 1920s which prompted one of the most spectacular increases in wealth in history, namely the near doubling of potential output in many industries. To set the stage, this chapter focuses on power drive technologies in general which, by definition, consist of (i) the power source and (ii) the transmission mechanism, and on the electric unit drive in particular. The transmission mechanism is, by definition, the apparatus that delivers the power to the relevant tool, which in turn performs the work that ultimately creates wealth.[1] While electrification has a history in U.S. manufacturing dating back to the late 19th century when it powered a drive technology known as belting and shafting, it was only with the introduction of conversion to unit drive that productivity soared, owing in large measure to the resulting acceleration of machine operating speeds.

3.2 The Role of Power Drive Technologies in Industrialization

Power drive technologies were the defining feature of the industrial revolution. James Watt and Matthew Boulton's reciprocating steam engine, patented in 1800, increased throughput rates (machine speed) and, in so doing, led to the first industrial revolution.[2] Technically speaking, they increased the amount of force/power than could be delivered to a tool per unit of time, which according to the laws of kinetics resulted in greater speeds or, simply put, acceleration. This was achieved by simply increasing the speed at which the shaft from the engine to the tool/machine was turning. Put differently, the first industrial revolution was, first and foremost, about speed — a manifold increase in the speed of the machine throughput.[3] In light of the integral role power drive technologies played and play in the creation of wealth, each element will be examined in detail.

3.2.1 *Power sources*

Power sources should be regarded as the ultimate source of power or energy. Among these are hydraulic, wind, chemical, nuclear, and solar

---

[1] This view is consistent with Beaudreau (1998, 2020) according to whom wealth creation, like all known material processes, is an increasing function of work, which, in turn, is an increasing function of energy use.

[2] In fact, one could include John Kay's Spinning Jenny in the category of power drive technologies as a single individual could now drive multiple spindles.

[3] It is important to note that the industrial revolution witnessed no new products *per se* rather existing material processes (largely artisanal) were speeded up/accelerated.

Table 3.1. Power Sources

Source	Application
Hydraulic	Water wheels, water turbines
Wind	Windmills
Chemical	Fossil fuels, wood
Nuclear/atomic	Nuclear reactors
Solar	Solar panels

energy. Each can be defined in terms of its ability to do or perform work. Hydraulic power refers to a combination of water (H_2O) and gravity. Ultimately, the force at work is gravity. Wind power refers to temperature gradients that result in pressure differences and ultimately in a source of work. Chemical energy refers to the heat energy that is released in a chemical reaction. Nuclear energy refers to the energy released in an atomic reaction or put simply, the ability to do work that results from such a reaction. Solar energy refers to the ability of solar radiation to do work.

Ultimately, these six power sources (Table 3.1) are tributary of the four fundamental fields/forces in theoretical physics (strong and weak force, gravity, and electromagnetic force). The story of civilization, it could be argued, is the story of a species, *homo sapiens sapiens*, and its increasing ability to direct/use/exploit increasing quanta of the earth's available energy. Among the key breakthroughs were the Neolithic revolution which witnessed the development of large-scale agriculture and the increasing use of fire to fashion tools, the industrial revolution that was marked by the large-scale use of coal and coke to power material processes, and the nuclear age, where *homo sapiens sapiens* tapped into the energy stored in atoms.

3.2.2 Transmission mechanisms

By definition, transmission mechanisms (Table 3.2) transmit the energy source to the tool which ultimately performs the work. A windmill is a good example of a transmission mechanism which transmits wind energy (temperature gradient) into power/force which drives the grinding stones and thus mills the various grains. It consists of a series of shafts, gears, and, in some cases, pulleys. Transmission mechanisms, in general, range

Table 3.2.   Transmission Mechanisms

Shafts of wooden, iron, and steel
Gearing of wooden, iron, and steel
Belting
Dynamos and electric motors unit versus group drive (achieved with a combination of shafts, gears, and belts)

from shafts and belts to dynamos and electric motors. In the latter case, the source of energy is transformed into electromagnetic force, which powers AC or DC motors, which in turn powers various tools.

3.3   Power Drive Technologies in U.S. Industry: A Timeline

Figure 3.1 shows the timeline of the various drive technologies in U.S. manufacturing from 1869 to 1939. What stands out is the extent to which, by 1939, the electric unit drive had displaced steam and water-powered belting and shafting as the prime mover in U.S. manufacturing. With this shift came a decrease in capital intensity as electric unit drive dispensed with the cumbersome — and costly — shafting and belting technology that had characterized mechanical drive (see Figure 3.2). More importantly, however, was the fact that it removed what had been, for decades, an upper limit on machine speed, thus opening the way to acceleration-based productivity and capacity increases.

As shown in Figure 3.3, the shift to electric unit drive, as measured by purchased electric energy, gained momentum in the 1920s, as both the level and share of purchased electric energy increased markedly, going from less than 10 million horsepower in 1919 to roughly 23 million horsepower in 1929. This represented 55 percent of total horsepower in 1919 and 78 percent in 1927. According to Louis Hunter and Lynwood Bryant:

> The initiative in this change did not originally come from the central-station industry, but rather from the makers of electrical equipment and

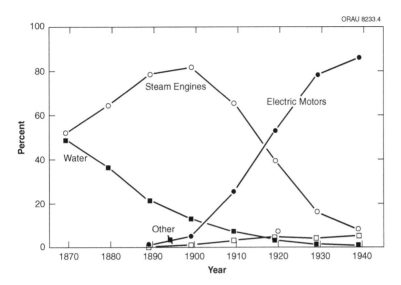

Figure 3.1. Evolution of Mechanical Drive in U.S. Manufacturing Establishments 1869–1939

Source: Devine (1983, p. 349).

the consulting engineers, who were interested in guiding the enlightened factory owner in the process of adapting his machinery to electric drive and converting his direct-drive power plant to the generation of electric current (Hunter and Bryant, 1991, p. 307).

3.4 Electric Unit Drive: A Revolution in Power Drive Technology

The key feature of a power drive technology is the quantity of energy it can transmit to/deliver to a tool per period of time. The more the kinetic energy/force, the greater the speed of operation, and the more work that can be achieved, again per period of time. Primitive wooden gears and shafts were limited speed-wise (measured in rpm), largely as the result of high tolerances. Complex belting and shafting technology was also limited. As it turned out, the greatest innovation or revolution in power drive technologies occurred with the introduction of an electric unit drive (see Figure 3.2). Previously, power within plants was distributed via a single shaft which powered a series of smaller shafts, which in turn powered a

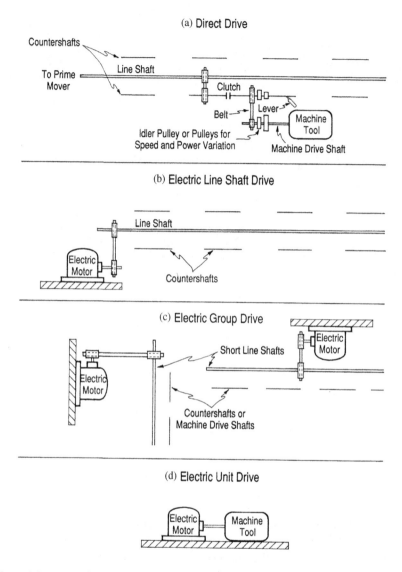

Figure 3.2.   Evolution of Power Transmission Technologies
Source: Devine (1983, p. 353).

number of belts which ultimately powered the various tools. In addition to being cumbersome and prone to breakdown, this configuration placed an upper limit on speeds. In addition, a good part of the force generated by the prime mover (steam engine or electric motor) was used to drive the

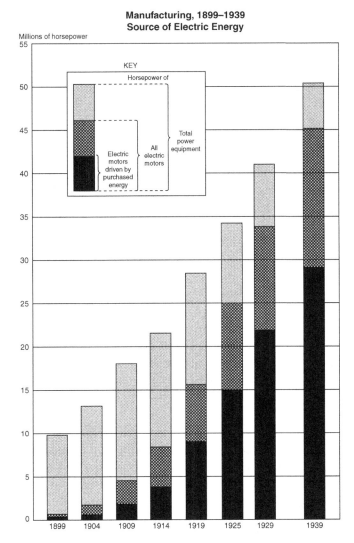

Figure 3.3.   The Electrification of Manufacturing 1899–1929

Source: Hunter and Bryant (1991, p. 308).

various gears, shafts, and belts and thus was not delivered to the tools, those being lost productivity-wise.[4]

---

[4]A good analogy is the drive technology in electric automobiles, namely as having dispensed of the traditional drive technology of internal combustion engines (transmission, drive shaft, differential, and axles).

All of this changed with the introduction of electric unit drive which as its name implies is a drive technology consisting of individual electric motors each driving a specific tool. According to Warren Devine (1983):

> It is found that the output of manufacturing establishments is materially increased in most cases by the use of electric driving. It is often found that the gain actually amounts to 20 to 30 percent or even more, with the same floor space, machinery, and number of workers. This is the most important advantage of all because it secures an increase in income without an increase in the investment, labor, or expense, except perhaps for material. In many cases, the output is raised, and at the same time, the labor item is reduced (Devine, 1990, p. 32).

Sidney Sonenblum (1990) made a similar point:

> During these years, the focus of management attention shifted from enlarging the scale of operations to increasing operating efficiency by speeding up the rate of throughput in the plant. High priority was assigned to modifications of factory design and layout in order to better integrate worker and machine tasks. Advances in the electrification of machine drive were indispensable to the realization of these new objectives and, indeed, may have served to stimulate the new managerial perspective that emerged (Sonenblum, 1990, p. 291).

As it turns out, the resulting acceleration-based increase in aggregate wealth was nothing new, as speed had been the key element in the first industrial revolution. More specifically, the Boulton–Watt reciprocating, high-pressure steam engine, by increasing the rated capacity of the existing plant and equipment, was single-handedly responsible for the manifold increase in U.K. wealth in the 19th century. Material processes that had been powered by human and animal muscles were speeded up and operated 24 hours per day, seven days a week. This led notable British economist David Ricardo and businessman and social reformer Robert Owen to estimate the increase in British GDP to be in the order of between 40- and 100-fold.

Throughout the early 20th century, U.S. engineers reveled in the advantages of electric unit drive, the most important of which was machine and process acceleration. Table 3.3 presents a sample of these.

Table 3.3. Electric Unit Drive and Acceleration: Period Views

Oberlin Smith (1901)	The problem talked much about until quite recently has been whether we should put in motors at all because we did not know whether they were going to take more power or not — that is a point of very little importance, compared with the total expenses of the shop. It doesn't matter if it is 5 or 10 or 20 percent, considering the great advantages we are going to get in all these other ways (Crocker, 1901, p. 427)
S. M. Vauclain, Baldwin Locomotive Works (1901)	In conclusion, while the question of the saving in power which the adoption of electric motors permitted was of importance, it was by no means the deciding factor: I would have put in electric driving systems not only if they saved no power but also even if they required several times the power of a shaft and belting system to operate them (Crocker, 1901, p. 8)
Crocker-Wheeler Electric Company (1901)	There were many factories which introduced electric power because we engaged to save from 20 to 60 percent of their coal bills, but such savings as these are not what has caused the tremendous activity in electric power equipment that is today spreading all over this country — those who first introduced electric power on this basis found that they were making other savings than those that had been promised, which might be called indirect savings (Crocker, 1901, p. 9)
F. B. Crocker, V. M. Benedikt, and A. F. Ormsbee (1895)	The great advantage of the electric system as here used (the Dunnell Cotton Manufacturing Company, Pawtucket, Rhode Island) is not so much in the saving of power as in the convenience to the workmen, and hence the increased production — the increase in the production amounted to more than 25 percent, and the quantity of "seconds" (inferior product) was also considerably reduced (Crocker *et al.*, 1895, pp. 412–413)
W. H. Tapley (1899)	Advantage to be gained from changing over from belting to individual electric motors for printing-press work is not alone in power saved, but, most of all, an increased product. Output of the Government Printing Office pressroom has been increased 15 percent — $45,000, a sum that makes the saving in motive power dwindle into insignificance. A few years will pay for the entire electric equipment, including the lighting (Tapley, 1899, p. 278)

(Continued)

Table 3.3.   (*Continued*)

Charles Day (1904)	We have similar machines running side by side, one being operated by belt and the other by motor. The belt-driven machine has every advantage which we could give it, but experience would indicate that, under average working conditions, metal could be removed at least twice as fast as was originally possible (Day, 1904, p. 329)
F. B. Crocker (1901)	It is found that the output of manufacturing establishments is materially increased in most cases by the use of electric driving. It is often found that this gain actually amounts to 20 or 30 percent or even more, with the same floor space, machinery, and number of workmen. This is the most important advantage of all because it secures an increase in income without any increase in investment, labor, or expense, except perhaps for material. In many cases, the output is raised, and at the same time, the labor item is reduced (Crocker, 1901, pp. 6–7)

3.5   Report of the *Committee on Recent Economic Changes*: Estimates of Conversion to Electric Unit Drive

As pointed out in the *Introduction*, the one theme that stands out to the point in defining the *Report of the Committee on Recent Economic Changes of the President's Conference on Unemployment* was the emphasis placed on power in general and on electric unit drive in particular. Chapter after chapter, section after section, author after author made reference to the increasing use of electric power as the driving force behind the exceptional growth in the period under consideration, namely 1921–1927. Here are excerpts taken from the three chapters that dealt specifically with this new technology: electric unit drive.

3.5.1   Section 1 — Characteristics of the years 1922–1929

Invention is not a new art … … But the breadth and scale and "tempo" of recent developments give them new importance.

The increased supply of power and its wider uses: the multiplication by man of his strength and skill through machinery.

The Speed Which Power Has Added to Production. Characteristic also has been the rise and use of power — three and three-quarters times faster than the growth in population — and the extent to which power has been made readily available not alone for driving tools of increasing size and capacity but for a convenient diversity of purposes in the smallest business enterprise and on the farm and the home (Report of the Committee on Recent Economic Changes, 1929, p. xi).

3.5.2 *Part 2 — Technical changes in manufacturing industries, L. P. Alford*

In a preceding part of this report, it has been shown that the increasing primary power available to each worker in manufacturing establishments is one of the most important and significant changes which have taken place since 1919. This is not the only significant change to power utilization. There have been increases in the installation of electric motors to supply mechanical power in manufacturing in the amount of power purchased instead of generated by manufacturing establishments, in the efficiency of prime movers. The first of these trends accounts, in part, for the rapid development of electric public utility companies. The increase in the capacity of prime movers which supply power to manufacturing establishments is a rough measure of the increased use of machinery by those establishments.

Increase in Electric Motor Power. The electric motor first appeared as a factor in industrial power in 1899, the amount of power purchased at the time and applied through electric motors being but 1.8 percent. So rapid has been the increase, however, that in 1927, the last year for which we have statistics, nearly 50 percent of the power applied in manufacture, was by means of electric motors operating on purchased power (Report of the Committee on Recent Economic Changes, 1929, p. 126).

3.5.3 *Part 3 — The changing structure of industry, Willard L. Thorp*

Scale of Production in Terms of Horsepower. The record for horsepower per establishment offers a much clearer picture of growth. The census figures refer to the total rated horsepower capacity of engines, motors, and other prime movers. Motors run by power generated within the establishment are excluded as involving duplication, since the power producer which runs the generator is already included. Because the figures refer to total rated capacity, they are considerably larger than if they were the amount of power in actual daily use.

As one might expect the range of power capacity among the industries is tremendous. The hairwork industry, with 87 establishments, reports but 13 horsepower in total, or less than 0.15 per establishment. At the other extreme is the copper smelting industry with 26 establishments and a total of 326,509 horsepower per establishment.

The average values for the industries emphasize the steadiness and degree of the advance. That this tendency is general is indicated by the fact that in 1925, five-sixths of the industries showed increased horsepower over 1914.

If one keeps in mind the fact that horsepower is gaining on average much more than wage earners, Table 8 can be accepted as a clear demonstration of the interrelation between the two devices which have been used to measure size. There are cases where horsepower is gaining and wage earners are declining (Report of the Committee on Recent Economic Changes, 1929, p. 179).

However, it was only after two important developments had taken place that it *de facto* revolutionized power drive in the United States and indeed, throughout the rest of the world, namely the development of alternating current (AC) and the spread of large-scale, integrated electrical utilities.

3.6 Alternating Current and the Emergence of Large-Scale Utilities

While electric unit drive held out great promise in so far as power drive technologies were concerned, it had one important disadvantage, namely the power source. Moving from steam-powered belting and shafting to electric unit drive required an on-site power plant, complete with an extensive distribution network delivering power throughout the plant. Clearly, the cost, including the dismantling of the cumbersome shafting and belting equipment in place (and the steam plant), would be prohibitive.

As it turned out, a number of developments in the 1910s would change all of this, making electric unit drive the preferred power drive technology. These included the development of AC power which could be transmitted over long distances, the development of large-scale electrical utilities, and interconnection (grids). All three combined to not only lower the cost of power but also make it available literally wherever and whenever it was needed. Firms no longer had to invest in generating and transmitting power. Instead, they could concentrate on the tasks at hand, namely creating wealth. According to Hunter and Bryant (1991):

> The rise of the electric power industry in the years 1900–1925 was based on two technical innovations — alternating current and the steam turbine — that made long-distance production of this new form of energy possible. The general adoption of steam turbines coupled to alternators supplied the means for an open-ended increase in the scale and economy of energy production, which continued apparently without limit for half a century and more (Hunter and Bryant, 1991, p. 243).

This section describes these developments and their impact on material processes, the most important of which was acceleration. Unshackled from the physical limits of belting and shafting, process speeds increased, thus increasing productivity. In short, with the same tools and supervision (labor), more could be produced per period of time.

3.6.1 *Alternating current versus direct current*

The development of three-phase AC was a key development in the electric power revolution. Direct current (DC) had the unfortunate disadvantage of not being transmissible beyond a certain distance, beyond which it would lose much of its force. This made for a situation in which the power had to be generated at or near the point of use/consumption. Put differently, companies had to generate DC electricity on site.

All of this changed with the development of three-phase AC by Nikolai Tesla and George Westinghouse. Now, electricity could be produced and distributed over long distances. Transmission losses were minimal in comparison to direct current. Large-scale power-generation plants could now be built. Extensive distribution networks could now be built. Companies could now purchase electric power at a fraction of the cost of generating it. More importantly, these same companies could now distribute power throughout their plants with little to no loss — compared to the cumbersome belting and shafting of yore.

3.6.2 *Large-scale electrical utilities*

The introduction of AC paved the way for the development of large-scale power utilities. In the early years, the most prevalent type consisted of thermal power-generating stations consuming coal (e.g., Edison's New York City Pearl Street plant). However, in little time, hydraulic power-generating stations entered the fray. Turbines that had up until then powered belting and shafting were converted to AC electric power-generating stations. Throughout this period, the cost of electric power measured in $/kWh decreased monotonically, as shown in Figure 3.4.

3.6.3 *Interconnection*

The second key development/innovation in this period was interconnection, by which should be understood the integrating/pooling of the various prime movers in the form of electrical utility networks (see Figures 3.5–3.7). Given important variations in the demand for power across users and across time, interconnection offered the possibility of offering power on a

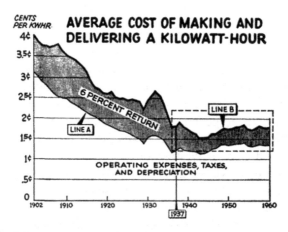

Figure 3.4.   Average Cost of Making and Delivering a Kilowatt Hour

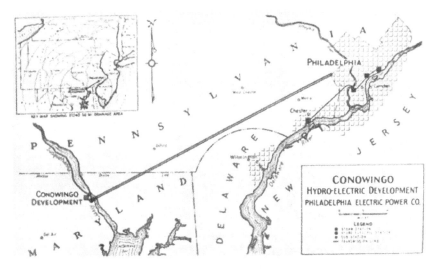

Figure 3.5.   Conowingo Hydroelectric Dam 1927

grid, where non-synchronous users could make use of the power, at a discount. The end result was a manifold increase in power availability and a marked decrease in price, the latter owing to the reduced cost of operating thermal plants on a continuous basis, as opposed to an on-off basis. Furthermore, the possibility of selling surplus power in the grid undoubtedly precipitated investment decisions by increasing the rate of return.

According to Thomas Hughes (1983):

> The developments that took place in electric supply systems in the 1920s are comparable to those that occurred in railway systems in the second half of the nineteenth century. Major railroad systems were then interconnected and standardized with respect to gauge and equipment. As a result, the major traffic centers and routes of regional and national systems were identified. The principal routes were then upgraded, traffic nexus and switching yards were laid out, and the trunk lines of the regional and national systems were further developed.
>
> The post-World War I rationalization of electric supply took many forms, but it is generally categorized as having been either evolutionary or planned. In a subsequent section, consideration will be given to the way in which the well-established, large-area utilities with relatively long histories evolved into regional systems integrated by high-voltage transmission networks. In this section, emphasis is placed on the new

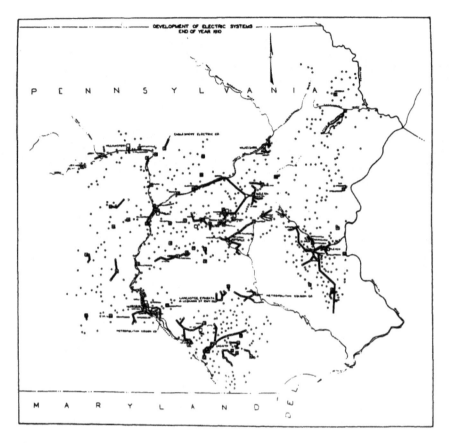

Figure 3.6.   Electrical Utility Interconnection Pennsylvania 1920
Source: Hughes (1983, p. 10)

systems that were established according to master plans. The purpose of these new systems was to knit together, on a regional scale, utilities that had formerly evolved independently.

The planned networks, or grids, usually took the form of high-voltage lines ringing a supply region, or polygon, the sections of which met at major load centers. They differed from the evolving networks, which, because of the generally less orderly character of historical change, usually were more complex in form. The planned grids represented the pooling of energy from utilities that preserved their legal identities, primarily as distributors of the pooled energy. In some instances, a separate corporate entity owned and managed the grid: in others, the utilities presided over the grid, or pool, using a committee structure. Since the

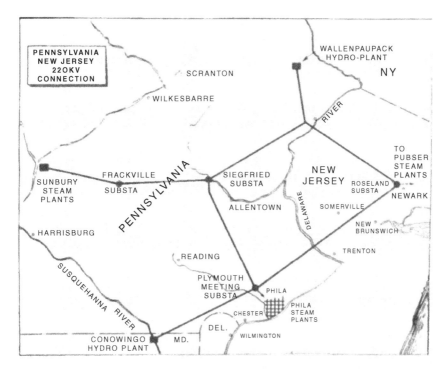

Figure 3.7.   The Pennsylvania–New Jersey Interconnection
Source: Hughes (1983, p. 327).

participating utilities preserved their corporate identities and often negotiated decisions about the operation of the power pool, such grids were
analogous to confederations of nation-states. Under some plans, the utilities or power companies fed the pool from their own power plants. Under
others, the grid took power both from its own plants and from the plants
of participating utilities (Hughes, 1983, p. 325).

3.6.4 *Interconnectivity: The role of the War Industries Board*

A key impetus in the drive to interconnectivity was the War Industries
Board (WIB) created by President Woodrow Wilson in 1918, whose main
purpose was to increase America's capacity to produce armaments in wartime. By the 1910s, a key input in the production of armaments was nitrogen (for explosives). A new process for extracting/fixing this element from
atmospheric oxygen had been developed in Germany (known as the
Haber–Bosch process), a process that required abundant supplies of energy.

Since the U.S. production of nitrogen had fallen behind that of Germany, the WIB recommended the creation, by the government, of a plant in Sterling, Georgia, with the express purpose of closing the gap. The corresponding electric power would be supplied ultimately by the development of the Muscle Shoals river basin and by increasing interconnectivity. In other words, parochial interests would be sacrificed for the national good. According to Hughes (1983):

> The technology of electric power systems that was introduced during World War I not only caused perturbations in trends but also carried into peacetime certain aspects of the wartime environment. The extremely large electric generating stations that were built to fill the pressing and unusual needs for electric power during World War I survived the war and became, in a sense, a solution in search of a problem. Another, less obvious case, is the large number of interconnections of electric light and power systems that were made during the emergencies of wartime and carried over into peacetime (Hughes, 1983, p. 286).

As Warren Devine (1983) pointed out, this was a key development in the widespread conversion to electric unit drive:

> The third reason for believing that unit drive was not widespread until the 1920s is that electricity did not become widely available until the rise of the electric utilities. In 1909, electric drive accounted for slightly less than 25 percent of total capacity for driving machinery: by 1919, electric motors represented over 53 percent of the total horsepower used for this purpose. This major transition was concurrent with changes in the supply of electricity. In 1909, 64 percent of the motor capacity in manufacturing establishments was powered by electricity generated on: ten years later 57 percent of the capacity was driven by electricity purchased from electric utilities. Although electric generating capacity in manufacturing continued to increase over this period, electric utilities were expanding so fast that after about 1914 their generating capacity exceeded that in all other industrial establishments combined (Devine, 1983, p. 370).

As mentioned, the WIB of 1917 was created by executive order with the mandate to oversee government procurement of war supplies. More specifically, its role was to "coordinate the purchase of war supplies between the War Department (Department of the Army) and the Navy Department. Since the United States Department of Defense (the

Pentagon) would only come into existence in 1947, this was an *ad hoc* construction to promote cooperation between the Army and the Navy (with regard to procurement); it was founded by the Council of National Defense (which on its turn came into existence by the appropriation bill of August 1916)." In addition to coordinating the purchase of war supplies, it was also active on a number of policy fronts, notably in (i) encouraging U.S. industry to adopt the mass production techniques made famous by the Ford Motor Company and (ii) investing heavily in the nitrate and cyanamide industries (National Defense Act of 1916). The latter would employ the newly developed Haber–Bosch process which was energy-intensive, specifically electricity-intensive. A nitrate plant was built in Sheffield, Alabama, and a cyanamide plant in Muscle Shoals. To supply power to the latter, a hydroelectric station and dam were to be completed at Muscle Shoals.

Throughout its brief history, the WIB openly promoted the construction of large-scale electricity-generating facilities, in part to power the various war-related industries. One such facility was the Wilson hydroelectric dam built on the Muscle Shoals section of the Tennessee river, begun in 1918 and completed in 1925 (Figure 3.8). This had the effect of

Figure 3.8.   The WIB-Sponsored Wilson Hydroelectric Dam (Tennessee River, Alabama)

increasing the availability of relatively cheap electric power, which in turn accelerated the conversion to electric unit drive. Formally, it acted on both the demand and supply sides of the market, increasing the demand for war supplies and openly encouraging firms to increase supply.

3.7 Power Generation and Interconnectivity as Seen by Herbert Hoover's Committee on Recent Economic Changes

The *Report of the Committee on Recent Economic Changes of the President's Conference on Unemployment* was adamant: innovations in power use and generation were the driving force behind the astonishing growth of the 1920s. Regarding the power generation, it pointed out the following:

Table 3.4.   Electricity Generated 1912–1930 (million kWh)

Year	Total — Utilities and Industrial Establishments	Utilities	Industrial Establishments	Hydro	Steam and Internal Combustion
1912	24,752	11,569	13,183	7,337	17,365
1917	43,427	25,438	17,991	13,948	29,481
1920	56,559	39,405	17,154	20,311	36,248
1921	53,125	37,180	15,945	18,732	34,393
1922	61,204	43,632	17,572	21,262	39,942
1923	71,399	51,229	20,170	23,421	47,978
1924	75,892	54,662	21,230	24,138	51,754
1925	84,666	61,451	23,215	26,112	58,554
1926	94,222	69,353	24,869	30,355	63,867
1927	101,390	75,418	25,972	32,924	68,466
1928	108,069	82,794	25,275	37,297	70,772
1929	116,747	92,180	24,567	37,038	79,709
1930	114,637	91,112	23,525	34,874	79,768

Source: U.S. Department of Commerce (1975), Historical Statistics of the United States, S-32–43.

The growth of the size of central station machinery should be noted. The first large turbo-generator built by General Electric Co. about 1900 was of 5,000-kilowatt capacity. Today, single units of 50,000 kilowatts are common, combined units of 100,000 kilowatts not unusual and one of 208,000-kilowatt capacity is under construction. The new State Line Power House of the Chicago Edison Co. will have a final capacity of 1,000,000 kilowatts, and there is no apparent diminution to the growth of such plants, either as to size or number. A survey of our public utilities in the Blakemore Analytic Reports, dated December 20, 1926, gives the total horsepower of prime movers in this industry as 3,000,000 in 1902: 12,000,000 in 1912, 24,000,000 in 1922, and a prospective 30,000,000 in 1930 (Report of the Committee on Recent Economic Changes, 1929, p. 91).

Referring to Table 3.4, we see that electricity generation in the U.S. increased rapidly throughout the 1920s, nearly doubling in a span of five years (1921–1926). Most of the increase came from utilities as opposed to industrial establishments. Referring to Columns 5 and 6, we see that both hydroelectric generation and conventional steam and combustion increased markedly throughout this period.

3.8 Summary and Conclusions

Despite being the underlying cause of the first and second industrial revolutions and, indeed, of the manifold increases in wealth that define the industrial age, power drive technologies and innovations to these technologies have been a largely overlooked feature of production theory. References to the steam engine and the electric motor notwithstanding the role of power in wealth and growth have been largely ignored.[5] This chapter has examined power drive technologies, in general, and electric unit drive, in particular, the latter being the key factor that increased the potential rated capacity of U.S. industry throughout the 1920s and 1930s and being the source of the Roaring Twenties.

A number of things stand out, not the least of which is the stealth-like nature of electric unit drive. Acceleration or speed-ups are largely imperceptible to even the seasoned observer. After all, the only thing that will

---

[5] For more on this, see Beaudreau (1999).

have changed is the speed at which material processes operate. This explains in part both the dearth of work and writing on it, as well as the difficulty analysts in general had in describing the changes in the 1920s, referring to it cryptically as acceleration (Report on Recent Economic Changes 1929). That machine speed and acceleration were not part of production theory either in the engineering or economics literature explains this oversight.

Nonetheless, the fact of the matter is that machine/process speeds were increasing throughout the 1920s, increasing conventionally defined productivity and vastly increasing the rated capacity of existing labor and capital. To reiterate Harvard University's Alfred D. Chandler's perspicacious observation:

> In modern mass production, as in modern mass distribution and modern transportation and communications, economies resulted more from speed than from size. It was not the size of the manufacturing establishment in terms of the number of workers and the amount and value of productive equipment but the velocity of throughput and the resulting increase in volume that permitted economies that lowered costs and increased output per worker and per machine (Chandler, 1977, p. 244).

How companies would respond to these changes is the subject of the next chapter. How governments responded to their responses will be the subject of subsequent chapters.

Chapter 4

Assessing the Impact of Electric Unit Drive-Based Acceleration on Productivity and Rated Capacity: The Case of the 1920s and 1930s*

But after 1919, something happened. The implications of which are not yet sufficiently gauged. It was of enough significance to cause President Hoover's Committee on Recent Economic Changes to remark that "acceleration rather than structural change is the key to an understanding of our recent economic developments." The committee added: "But the breadth and the tempo of recent developments give them new importance." What happened was indicated by the fact that in the United States, 8.3 million workers produced in 1925 one quarter more than 9 million workers turned out in 1919. The new indexes of the Federal Reserve Board measuring production record this gratifying advance which reflects an increase in the American standard of living ... The general volume of production had increased between 1919 and 1927 by 46.5 percent: primary power by 22 percent, primary power per wage

*This chapter is based on Beaudreau, Bernard C. The Economies of Speed, KE = 1/2mv² and the Productivity Slowdown, *Energy* Vol. 124, April 2017, 100–113 and Beaudreau, Bernard C. *The Economics of Speed: Machine Speed as the Key Factor in Productivity Growth*. Switzerland: Springer International, 2019.

earner by 30.9 percent (between 1919 and 1925) and productivity per wage worker by 53.5 percent.

Irving Fisher, *The Stock Market Crash and After,* 1930

4.1 Introduction

As Irving Fisher highlighted in this excerpt taken from *The Stock Market Crash and After,* President Herbert Hoover's *Committee on Recent Economic Changes,* formed in 1929, concluded that something had happened after 1919, something whose breadth was as overwhelming as its cause, something it referred to as acceleration, not conventional structural change. In other words, it had little to do with more capital and/or labor, and more to do with speed or acceleration. Years later, *The General Electric Company,* a 1937 short film, would refer to this something as "the magic hand of speed." Machine speeds had increased throughout U.S. industry, resulting in a marked increase in conventionally measured productivity and output. More specifically, with greater speeds, the rated capacity of the existing capital stock had increased, in some cases even doubling.

According to Nathan Rosenberg, the acceleration in question took place over a period of decades, with the 1920s witnessing the greatest increase.

The speed with which electricity was adopted may be readily indicated. Electric motors accounted for less than 5 percent of total installed horsepower in American manufacturing in 1899. The growth in the first years of the 20th century was such that by 1909, their share of manufacturing horsepower was 25 percent. Ten years later the share rose to 55 percent and by 1929 electric motors completely dominate the manufacturing sector by providing over 80 percent of total installed horsepower. The sharp rise in productivity in the American economy, in the years after World War I, doubtless owed a great deal, both directly and indirectly, to the electrification of manufacturing (Rosenberg, 1972, p. 124).

This chapter examines the role of machine speed or acceleration in material processes — aka production processes. It does so by drawing from Beaudreau (2017a, 2020), who formalized the role of machine or process speed in the theory of production. Specifically, a kinetics-based microeconomic model of material processes is presented, one that is able to explicitly account for the changes described by President Hoover's *Committee on Recent Economic Changes*, notably machine speed.[1] The result is then incorporated into a macroeconomic model, which will then be used to chronicle and analyze the acceleration-based developments in the post-1919 period, a period known as the Roaring Twenties.

4.2 Theoretical Framework

The role of speed in material processes has been and continues to be largely ignored–both in engineering and economics. Material processes in economics are generally defined in terms of labor and capital. Energy and energy intensity are often ignored, or at best, assigned to the technology scaler. As such, it comes as little surprise that members of President Herbert Hoover's committee were unable to grasp not only the breadth of the changes acting on the U.S. economy in the 1910s and 1920s, but the underlying mechanics. In this section, a microeconomic model of material processes is presented in which speed and its energy equivalent, kinetic energy, are incorporated. This is achieved by integrating the basic law of kinetics, $KE = 1/2mv^2$, into a two-factor model, the other factor being capital (plant and equipment). It then introduces the result into a macroeconomic model, which is used throughout the book to chronicle and analyze the various acceleration-based developments in the 1920s and 1930s.

4.2.1 *A microeconomic model of production with acceleration*

The first and second industrial revolutions were first and foremost about speed, machine speed to be precise. In the case of the first industrial revolution, the simple and complex tools of the pre-industrial era were converted to the new power drive technology that was the Watt–Boulton reciprocating steam engine. Processes that had been powered by human or animal muscles were converted to steam power. Consider the case of carding and spinning, which had been done by hand, but which was mechanized at the start of the 18th century by John Lombe, Lewis Paul and Richard Arkwright. As few new goods/services were introduced in this period, it stands to reason that the first industrial revolution was

---

[1] By machine speed, it should be understood the speed of all power-based material processes, not exclusively those in manufacturing.

essentially about acceleration. A good example is the railroads, where the previous technology (rails, wagons and horses) was converted to steam, thus increasing speed–and lowering the costs.

The defining feature of the second industrial revolution was also speed. Material processes that had been powered by steam engines or electric motors in a group configuration of shafting and belting were now driven by individual electric motors (direct drive). It is important to note that this change was subtle, and thus far from obvious both in the 19th and 20th centuries. The tools in question remained essentially the same, as did the workers (machine operatives). It is therefore little surprise that acceleration both in the 19th and 20th centuries would have eluded even the most perspicacious of observers, including most political economists.

4.2.1.1 *Speed and acceleration in economic thought*

Early political economists struggled with the concepts of speed and acceleration, starting with Adam Smith who referred to the source of the acceleration he witnessed first-hand at Matthew Boulton's Soho Manufactory in Birmingham as "fire power." In Chapter 1 of the *Wealth of Nations,* where he lays out his basic model of wealth, he identified three sources of steam engine-based greater productivity, namely (i) specialization (ii) reduced downtime from changing tasks and (iii) machinery. Just how machinery increased productivity was not well described, other than a reference to "fire power."[2] The upshot, however, is that wealth was increasing in labor. This soon became the standard in early 19th century classical economists. While in actual fact steam engine-based acceleration was the source of the productivity gains, it was largely ignored in the formal literature.

There were, however, a number of exceptions, including the writings of Charles Babbage who in his *On the Economy of Machinery and Manufactures* provided detailed descriptions of the new technology. Consider, for example, the following excerpt where classical mechanics is used to illustrate the contribution of wind, water and steam.

---

[2]According to classical mechanics, a tool (read machinery) cannot increase work as it is not a source of energy. Its role consists solely of increasing second-law efficiency.

Of those machines by which we produce power, it may be observed that although they are to us immense acquisitions, yet in regard to two of the sources of this power, the force of wind and of water, we merely make use of bodies in a state of motion by nature: we change the directions of their movement in order to render them subservient to our purposes, but we neither add to nor diminish the quantity of motion in existence. When we expose the sails of a windmill obliquely to the gale, we check the velocity of a small portion of the atmosphere, and convert its own rectilinear motion into one of rotation in the sails: we thus change the direction of force, but we create no power …. The force of vapour is another fertile source of moving power: but even in this case it cannot be maintained that power is created. Water is converted into elastic vapour by the combination of fuel (Babbage, 1832, p. 15).

Interestingly, he devoted a whole chapter to speed or what he referred to as "velocity." Chapter 4, titled "Increase and Diminution of Velocity," showcases using industry-specific examples the role of increased speed as a key feature of mechanization.

In turning from the smaller instruments in frequent use to the larger and more important machines, the economy arising from the increase in velocity becomes more striking. In converting cast into wrought iron, a mass of metal, of about a hundred in weight, is heated almost to white heat and placed under a heavy hammer moved by water or steam power. This is raised by a projection on a revolving axis: and if the hammer derived its momentum only from the space through which it fell, it would require a considerably greater time to give a blow. But it is important that the softened mass of red-hot iron should receive as many blows as possible before it cools, the form of the cam or projection on the axis is such that the hammer, instead of being lifted to a small height, is thrown up with a jerk, and almost the instant after it strikes a large beam, which acts as a powerful spring, and drives it down on the iron with such velocity that by these means about the double the number of strokes can be made in a given time (Babbage, 1832, p. 26).

Another surprising exception was German-born British political economist, Karl Marx. It is often thought or believed that of all the non-mainstream economists, there was none greater than Karl Marx. After all, he is credited with single-handedly changing the course of political economy, especially distribution theory. A careful reading of the first seven chapters of *Das Kapital*, published in 1867, reveals what is a characteristically classical approach to wealth, putting labor at the core of production and hence of wealth. Like his classical forebearers, he held labor to be at the center of all wealth creation. However, if one takes the time to read *Das Kapital* from cover to cover (which few do), in Chapter 15 one discovers a more compelling description of wealth creation in the age of machinery, one that is based on classical mechanics.

Mathematicians and mechanicians, and in this they are followed by a few English economists, call a tool a simple machine, and a machine a complex tool. They see no essential difference between them, and even give the name of machine to the simple mechanical powers, the lever, the inclined plane, the screw, the wedge, etc.

As a matter of fact, every machine is a combination of those simple powers, no matter how they may be disguised. From the economic standpoint this explanation is worth nothing, because the historical element is wanting. Another explanation of the difference between tool and machine is that in the case of a tool, man is the motive power, while the motive power of a machine is something different from man, as, for instance, an animal, water, wind, and so on. According to this, a plough drawn by oxen, which is a contrivance common to the most different epochs, would be a machine, while Claussens circular loom, which, worked by a single labourer, weaves 96,000 picks per minute, would be a mere tool. Nay, this very loom, though a tool when worked by hand, would, if worked by steam, be a machine. And since the application of animal power is one of man's earliest inventions, production by machinery would have preceded production by handicrafts. When in 1735, John Wyatt brought out his spinning machine, and began the industrial revolution of the 18th century, not a word did he say about an ass driving it instead of a man, and yet this part fell to the ass. He described it as a machine to spin without fingers.

All fully developed machinery consists of three essentially different parts, the motor mechanism, the transmitting mechanism, and finally the tool or working machine. The motor mechanism is that which puts the whole in motion. It either generates its own motive power, like the steam-engine, the caloric engine, the electromagnetic machine, etc., or it receives its impulse from some already existing natural force, like the water-wheel from a head of water, the wind-mill from wind, etc. The transmitting mechanism, composed of fly-wheels, shafting, toothed wheels, pulleys, straps, ropes, bands, pinions, and gearing of the most varied kinds, regulates the motion, changes its form where necessary, as for instance, from linear to circular, and divides and distributes it among the working machines. These two first parts of the whole mechanism are there, solely for putting the working machines in motion, by means of which motion the subject of labour is seized upon and modified as desired. The tool or working machine is that part of the machinery with which the industrial revolution of the 18th century started. And to this day it constantly serves as such a starting-point, whenever a handicraft, or a manufacture, is turned into an industry carried on by machinery (Marx, 1867, p. 321).

Clearly, there was more to Marx's thinking than the simple labor theory of value. In fact, these excerpts indicate that he was well aware of the basic principles of classical mechanics, specifically of the role of force in material processes, not to mention the role of tools in material processes.

Perhaps the most influential of 19th century iconoclasts — in large part, much in spite of himself — was William Stanley Jevons, the father of neoclassical production theory. In *The Theory of Political Economy* published in 1871, he outlined what was to become neoclassical production theory, namely that wealth is an increasing, continuous, twice-differentiable function of homogeneous labor and capital. A lesser known, but equally important contribution, of his was *The Coal Question, An Inquiry Concerning the Progress of the Nation, and the Probable Exhaustion of Our Coal-Mines*, published in 1865 in which he addressed the question of Great Britain's dwindling coal reserves. In the opening salvo, he declared:

Day by day it becomes more evident that the Coal we happily possess in excellent quality and abundance is the mainspring of modern material civilization. As the source of fire, it is the source at once of mechanical motion and of chemical change. Accordingly, it is the chief agent in almost every improvement or discovery in the arts which the present age brings forth. It is to us indispensable for domestic purposes, and it has of late years been found to yield a series of organic substances, which puzzle us by their complexity, please us by their beautiful colours, and serve us by their various utility.

And as the source especially of steam and iron, coal is all powerful. This age has been called the Iron Age, and it is true that iron is the material of most great novelties. By its strength, endurance, and wide range of qualities, this metal is fitted to be the fulcrum and lever of great works, while steam is the motive power. But coal alone can command in sufficient abundance either the iron or the steam: and coal, therefore, commands this age — the Age of Coal.

Coal in truth stands not beside but entirely above all other commodities. It is the material energy of the country — the universal aid — the factor in everything we do. With coal almost any feat is possible or easy: without it, we are thrown back into the laborious poverty of early times (Jevons, 1865, p. xi).

Paradoxically, some six years later (i.e., in 1871), coal or the energy input had disappeared completely from what is largely considered to be his magnum opus, namely *The Theory of Political Economy*, where capital is included in the production function and, more importantly, is assumed to be physically productive. In short, both labor and capital were assumed to be physically productive and more importantly, were interchangeable/substitutable. One could argue that internal validity (i.e., vis-à-vis the debate over the role of capital in wealth) is what prevented Jevons from incorporating energy into the corpus of neoclassical analysis.

By far, the greatest of British iconoclasts was Nobel-prize laureate chemist Frederick Soddy, who after his pioneering work with Ernest Rutherford on atomic transmutation turned his attention to economics, largely in response to the alleged "misspecification" of production theory, more to the point, to the absence of energy from the analysis. The gist of his critique can be found in the following allegory:

At the risk of being redundant, let me illustrate what I mean by the question, How do men live? by asking what makes a railway train go. In one sense or another the credit for the achievement may be claimed by the so-called engine-driver, the guard, the signalman, the manager, the capitalist, or share-holder, or, again, by the scientific pioneers who discovered the nature of fire, by the inventors who harnessed it, by Labour which built the railway and the train. The fact remains than all of them by their united efforts could not drive the train. The real engine-driver is the coal. So, in the present state of science, the answer to the question how men live, or how anything lives, or how inanimate nature lives, in the sense in which we speak of the life of a waterfall or of any other manifestation of continued liveliness, is, with few and unimportant exceptions, By sunshine. Switch off the sun and a world would result lifeless, not only in the sense of animate life, but also in respect of by far the greater part of the life of inanimate nature. The volcanoes, as now, might occasionally erupt, the tides would ebb and flow on an otherwise stagnant ocean, and the newly discovered phenomena of radioactivity would persist. But it is sunshine which provides the power not only of the winds and waters but also of every form of life yet known. The starting point of Cartesian economics is thus the well-known laws of the conservation and transformation of energy, usually referred to as the first and second laws of thermodynamics (Soddy, 1922, p. xi).

In short, according to Soddy, energy was the cornerstone of all human activity, including production. Labor, capital, information, technology, etc. are all accessory inputs, necessary for but not the actual source of wealth. Despite much promise, the proposed Cartesian economics, based on the laws of basic physics (mechanics and thermodynamics) failed to make inroads into mainstream economics.

As it turned out, the torch of production theory-related iconoclastic thought would soon cross the ocean, arriving in North America. However, the resulting strain would be less ideological and more practical. Specifically, the late 19th century conversion from belting and shafting to electric unit drive (i.e., individual electrical motors integrated in machinery) had witnessed a non-negligible increase in energy use in U.S. manufacturing, one that produced a sizable increase in output against a backdrop of lower capital expenditure/stock. The latter owed to the fact that electric generators and motors were less costly than the elaborate shafting and belting they replaced.

With the passage of time, it became increasingly obvious that energy use in general, and electric power in particular, had become the driving force, increasing output and wealth. Frederick G. Tryon of the Institute of Economics (Brookings Institution) was among the first to point to the incongruity between production processes as modeled in economics and those he observed in early 20th century America.

Anything as important in industrial life as power deserves more attention than it has yet received by economists. The industrial position of a nation may be gauged by its use of power. The great advance in material standards of life in the last century was made possible by an enormous increase in the consumption of energy, and the prospect of repeating the achievement in the next century turns perhaps more than on anything else on making energy cheaper and more abundant. A theory of production that will really explain how wealth is produced must analyze the contribution of this element of energy.

These considerations have prompted the Institute of Economics to undertake a reconnaissance in the field of power as a factor of production. One of the first problems uncovered has been the need of a long-time index of power, comparable with the indices of employment, of the volume of production and trade, of monetary phenomena, that will trace the growth of the factor of power in our national development (Tryon, 1927, p. 281).

One year later (i.e., in 1928), Woodlief Thomas of the Division of Research and Statistics of the Federal Reserve Board, published an article in the *American Economic Review* titled "The Economic Significance of the Increased Efficiency of American Industry," in which he attributed the "striking changes in American industry" to power-related developments:

Large-scale production is dependent upon the machine process, and the increasing use of machinery and power and labor-saving devices has accompanied the growth in size of productive units. The growing use of power in manufacturing, for example, is reflected in the increase in horsepower of installed prime movers. This does not tell the whole story, moreover, for owing to increased use of electricity, the type of power used is now more efficient — requiring less fuel and labor for its production. Out of a total installed horsepower in factories of 36 million in 1925, 26 million or 72 percent was transmitted to machines by means of electric motors, as compared with 55 percent in 1919, 30 percent in 1909, and only 2 percent in 1899. Between 1899 and 1925 horsepower per person employed in factories increased by 90 percent and horsepower per unit of product increased by 30 percent. Power has been substituted for labor not only through machines of production but also in the form of automatic conveying and loading devices (Thomas, 1928, p. 130).

In little time, this oversight reached academia, specifically Columbia University where a group of engineers, known as *The Technocracy Alliance,* outright rejected mainstream approaches to understanding wealth (essentially neoclassical production theory), arguing that they ignored mechanics, thermodynamics, process engineering and the state of the art regarding material processes in general.

4.2.1.2 *The critics: Big on principles, small on specifics*

What is abundantly clear, judging from these quotations, was the growing realization of the need to incorporate energy into the core of economic analysis, specifically in production theory. However, as is often the case, the devil was in the details. How could/would this be done? By simply appending a new variable, say $e(t)$, to the standard neoclassical production function? Accordingly, an increase in energy, *ceteris paribus*, will increase output. But how and why? What form of energy? And just how does energy enter production? The answer according to many observers was through kinetics or movement — that is, through machine speed. Greater energy consumption resulted in greater machine speeds and greater output, a fact made abundantly clear by Henry Ford in his description of mass production.

> Mass production is not merely quantity production for this may be had with none of the requisites of mass production. Nor is it merely machine production, which also may exist without a resemblance to mass production. Mass production is the focusing upon a manufacturing project of the principles of power, accuracy, economy, system, continuity and speed (Ford, 1926b, p. 821).

The General Electric Company, one of the chief architects of the electric-unit-drive revolution, pointed to increased machine speed–controlled machine speed–as one of the defining features of modernity and of productivity growth. Under the title of *Today is the Day of Speed*, it maintained that:

> Our transportation systems, our industrial processes, our factory machinery — all these have felt the magic hand of speed — controlled speed that has given us more things to enjoy and more time in which to enjoy them: that has produced more goods for more people at less cost and that has created a better standard of living for the average man. These are the benefits of ever-increasing speed and accurate control (General Electric Company, 1937).

Graham Laing, in *Towards Technocracy*, pointed to machine speed as a key factor behind the unprecedented productivity gains in the 1920s and 1930s.

Industrial processes have been speeded up, new inventions are being added to manufacturing, new economies of personnel and of management have been made in industry. The 1929 production can undoubtedly be achieved with thousands, and probably millions, fewer workers (Laing, 1933, p. 23).

George Soule, in his 1947 classic work, *Prosperity Decade: From War to Depression, 1917–1929*, pointed to the conversion from belting and shafting to electric unit drive:

A basic element in technical progress was the increase in the use of power as a substitute for human muscle, and the enhanced economy and flexibility in the employment of power itself. In earlier years the typical individual factory had bought its coal, made its steam in a hand-fired boiler, and carried the power to the workplaces by a series of steam engine, shafts, pulleys, and belts. The substitution of individual electric motors on the machines was a great advance in flexibility. In 1929 about 70 percent of manufacture was electrified, against 30 percent in 1914. More factories bought their power from the utility company; this in turn produced it more economically (Soule, 1947, p. 128).

Alfred Chandler, in his classic work on early 20th century U.S. business organizations, echoed this view, generalizing it to the U.S. economy as a whole.

In modern mass production, as in modern mass distribution and modern transportation and communications, economies resulted more from speed than from size. It was not the size of the manufacturing establishment in terms of the number of workers and the amount and value of productive equipment, but the velocity of throughput and the resulting increase in volume that permitted economies that lowered costs and increased output per worker and per machine (Chandler, 1977, p. 244).

Sidney Sonenblum, in his extensive work on electrification and productivity growth in manufacturing, also pointed to speed, specifically accelerating the rate of throughput as a key element in productivity growth:

> During these years, the focus of managerial attention shifted from enlarging the scale of operations to increasing operating efficiency by speeding up the rate of throughput in the plant. High priority was assigned to modifications of factory design and layout in order to better integrate worker and machine tasks. Advances in the electrification of machine drive were indispensable to the realization of these new objectives and may, indeed, have served to stimulate the new managerial perspectives that emerged (Sonenblum, 1990, p. 291).

Running through each of these accounts of speed and its role in productivity is the notion of control. General Electric referred to "accurate control," while Ford referred to "accuracy, system and continuity." Hence, speed and control are to be understood as complementary inputs. Theoretically, control can be defined in terms of four functions (i) constancy of speed (ii) minimal breakdown-related downtime, (iii) sub-process coordination and (iv) machine programming. Put differently, the better able is the firm/engineer at maintaining a constant speed, the greater the output. The same holds for machine breakdown. As not all machines/sub-processes operate at the same speed, it is essential — in order to avoid bottlenecks — to coordinate speeds throughout the plant. Lastly, because firms typically produce many different goods/models of goods with the same machinery, it stands to reason that more efficient machine programming will reduce downtime and, hence, increase the average operating speed per period of time.

According to Warren D. Devine, control technologies underwent a series of innovations in the 20th century that were instrumental in increasing machine speed. In a nutshell, hydraulic drive and control mechanisms gave way to servomechanisms, which in the 1950s, gave way to numerical control, which reduced machine downtime considerably. Not only would productivity rise as the result of greater machine speeds (i.e., owing to greater energy use), the machines themselves would be more fully utilized in any given time period. He noted:

> Numerically-controlled machinery had a number of advantages over conventional manually controlled machinery. The time required to get a newly designed part into production — the machine setup time — was sometimes as much as 65–75 percent less with numerical control (Devine, 1990, p. 50).

In a 1966 report titled *Technological Trends in Major American Industries,* the U.S. Department of Labor pointed to control technologies in the form of the computerization of data processing and increased mechanization (read: faster speeds) as the leading innovations of the post-WWII period. Under the heading of "Trend Toward Increased Mechanization," it pointed out that:

> Improvements in machinery that do not involve drastic departure from conventional design will continue to be an important factor in raising productivity in many industries. Faster operation, larger size, automatic loading and unloading devices and automatic lubrication significantly reduce the amount of labor required per unit of output. The integration of a number of separate operations into one large specialized machine which performs a long cycle of operations with a minimum of intervention by the machine tender constitutes a more advanced type of mechanization.
>
> Examples of greater mechanization are found in many industries: faster textile machine speeds with larger packages of stock: continuous steel casting machines that require one-half the number of steps of traditional ingot casting: machinery in meatpacking for continuous production of frankfurters: tape controlled line casting machines in printing: faster, larger capacity machines in tire and tube manufacture. Other examples are mechanical "lumberjacks" to cut trees in the lumber industry: larger capacity stripping equipment in copper mining: greater use of continuous coal mining machines: and a machine that combines a number of operations in shirt making.
>
> As fabricating operations become highly mechanized, new ways are sought to achieve labor savings in moving goods and materials from one plant operation to the next. Mechanized material handling often is introduced or improved to utilize more fully the high speed and large capacity of modernizing fabricating equipment (U.S. Department of Labor, 1966, p. 5).

Clearly, machine speed and its relationship to energy use, specifically, to electric power use, were the key elements in raising overall productivity. In the next section, an attempt to formalize this both in terms of a theoretically consilient and empirically consistent model of output is made. The term theoretically consilient refers to the property of being consistent or in-keeping with the principles of related fields such as classical mechanics, thermodynamics and process engineering. The term empirically consistent refers to the property of being consistent with the data — that is, is confirmed by the data. Put differently, models of production should at the very least be able to confirm the relevant underlying laws of physics in material processes.

4.2.1.3 *Understanding acceleration*

In physics, acceleration and speed are formalized in terms of the laws of kinetics: speed is an increasing function of kinetic energy, or energy/power/force. In other words, acceleration is the result of greater kinetic energy. Hence, it stands to reason that an understanding of the role of acceleration in wealth creation would require, first and foremost, a model of production that incorporates speed and thus energy/power/force. Following Beaudreau (1998) who classified inputs in terms of two main categories, namely broadly defined energy and organization, a two-tiered approach to understanding production is presented. The first tier is purely physical and is governed by the laws of physics, specifically, the laws of machine and chemical kinetics. Neither tools and/or equipment nor conventionally defined labor (supervisors) is physically productive, and hence are parametric to this tier. Tier I is universal in its application and breadth, accessible to industrial engineers, to physicists as well as to economists and production specialists, thus ensuring both internal and external validity. The second tier is the organization tier which focuses on the creation and supervision of first tier material processes. It focuses on creating and the overseeing — in short, the organization — of machines. Alfred Marshall referred to the latter in 1890 as "machine operatives." It is important to point out that such operatives are not a source of power/energy and hence are not physically productive: hence they cannot be substituted for primary power. Traditional factor substitution is, as such, rendered unfeasible and theoretically impossible across our two tiers. Machinery, equipment and machine operatives, not being sources of power, cannot be substituted for energy.[3]

---

[3] While this result will appear to be counterintuitive to economists, it will come as no surprise to applied physicists, process engineers and material scientists, highlighting the chasm between the these groups who nonetheless share the same goal, that of describing and understanding production processes.

Table 4.1.   Manufacturing Processes and the Corresponding Kinetics

Type	Kinetic Law	Examples	Acceleration
Mechanical-translational	Translational kinetics $KE = 1/2mv^2$	Material handling transportation	Higher speed
Mechanical-rotational	Rotational kinetics $KE = 1/2mi^2$	Grinding, shaping, assembling, reducing	Higher speed
Chemical/Thermal	Chemical kinetics $k(t) = Ae^{-Ea/RT}$	Refining, electrolysis cracking	Higher temperature Higher voltage

4.2.1.4 *Tier I: Machine and chemical kinetics at the process and plant levels*

A firm will be defined as a series of n sub-processes $y_i^j(t)$, $j = m,c$ which can be of two types, namely mechanical (n^m) and chemical (n^c) (Equation (4.1)). These are described in detail in Table 4.1. Formally, overall output is defined as the minimum of the $y_i^j(t)$, $j = m,c$ sub-processes. Mechanical sub-processes are governed by the laws of translational and rotational kinetics, while chemical sub-processes are governed by the laws of chemical kinetics. Included in the mechanical sub-processes category are the material handling processes (pumps, conveyor belts, etc.) between the various sub-processes. That is, in sequential production processes, the output of one sub-process becomes the input for the next sub-process.

$$y(t) = \min\left[y_i^m(t)\forall i = 1,2,\ldots\ldots,n^m : y_i^c(t)\forall i = 1,2,\ldots\ldots,n^c\right] \quad (4.1)$$

Mechanical sub-processes are assumed to be governed by the laws of basic machine kinetics (translational and rotational), according to which output $y_i^m(t)$ is an increasing function of operating speed(s) $s_i^m(t)$ and the machines themselves, denoted by $k_i^m(t)$. The measured individual n machine speeds, defined as the machine rates of output per unit time, are governed by translational/rotational kinetics $e = 1/2mv^2$, where $e =$ kinetic energy, $\mu =$ mass and $v =$ velocity. Thus, $v(t) = s(t) = [2e_i^m(t)/\mu]^{0.5}$, which can be reduced to $e_i^m(t)^{0.5}$. As a result, in the absence of machine downtime, the effect of an increase in energy use on operating speed, and hence on output, will be determined by the law of translational/rotational kinetics.

$$y_i^m(t) = s_i^m(t)k_i^m(t) = e_i^m(t)^{0.5} k_i^m(t) \quad (4.2)$$

However, in the presence of machine downtime, the statistical or measured relationship between energy (e) and output $y_i^m(t)$ will be described by Equation (4.2) where $\gamma_i^m(t) \forall i = 1, 2, 3, \ldots, n^m$ where $0 \leq \gamma_i^m(t) \leq 0.5$ is an adjustment factor. Translational kinetics defines operating speed (e.g., revolutions per minute, feet per minute) for a given mass (m) and kinetic energy (e).[4] Machine downtime can be the result of either (i) maintenance (ii) idleness due to lack of coordination between sub-processes or (iii) retooling for a new product. To capture these effects, statistical operating speed will be defined in terms of Equation (4.3) where $\gamma_i^m(t) \ni [0 < \gamma_i^m(t) < 0.5]$ captures sub-process i downtime in period t.[5] The closer $\gamma_i^m(t)$ is to 0.5, the higher is average downtime per t, and hence the higher will be the resulting output elasticity.[6]

$$s_i^m(t) = e_i^m(t)^{0.5+\gamma_i^m(t)} \forall i = 1, 2, 3, \ldots, n^m \qquad (4.3)$$

Thermal and chemical sub-processes (see Table 4.1) are governed by the laws of chemical kinetics (e.g., Arrhenius Equation) according to which chemical reaction rates are an increasing function of temperature T_i^c which in turn is a function of energy consumption E_i^c being activation energy and R being the activation energy constant (8.314) (Equation (3)).

$$s_i^c(t) = \left[A_i^c exp^{-E_i^c/RT(e_i^c(t))}, \gamma_i^c(t) \right] \forall i = 1, 2, \ldots, n^c \qquad (4.4)$$

As in the previous case, temperature T is increasing energy use $e_i^c(t)$, which will result in a higher reaction rate, which in our analysis is akin to an increase in machine speed.

$$y_i^c(t) = k_i^c(t) \left[A_i^c exp^{-E_i^c/RT(e_i^c(t))} \right] \forall i = 1, 2, \ldots, n^c \qquad (4.5)$$

As was the case with mechanical sub-processes, the effect of increased energy use on operating speed (reaction rates) will be

---

[4]Machine speed can be defined either in time or in number of product (i.e. maximum speed is 10 seconds per product, maximum speed is six products per minute).

[5]In the case in which energy per machine remains constant, a one percent increase in downtime will increase output by one percent. Electric use will rise by one percent as a result. We capture this process via $\gamma(t)$.

[6]This owes to the fact that the increased energy use from restarting idle machines will result in more output than increasing energy use (i.e. increasing speed) of operating machines.

determined by two factors, namely chemical kinetics (Arrhenius's Law), and by machine downtime $\gamma_i^c(t) \forall i = 1, 2, 3, \ldots, n^c$ where $0 \leq \gamma_i^c(t) \leq 0.5$.

The more downtime there is, the more linear will be the relationship, and vice versa. Equations (4.3) and (4.4) describe the two types of sub-process production functions, the first for rotational and translational-based processes, and the second for chemical and thermal-based processes.

Assume that $s_i^m(t)$ and $s_i^c(t)$ are bounded from above. In other words, for each sub-process, there exists a maximum speed.[7] It can be defined as a combination of (i) translational/rotational chemical kinetics (ii) material tolerances and (iii) average downtime (owing to maintenance, retooling, etc).

Equations (4.2) and (4.3) define the sub-process/process technologies of a firm at time t. What is immediately obvious is that the speed of production at the plant level — and hence, the overall measured productivity — will depend on the n^c and n^m sub-process machine speeds — and in particular on the slowest (i.e., minimum) of these sub-process speeds.[8] They also illustrate a key result, notably the explicit relationship between energy use and the corresponding process speeds/reaction rates. Specifically, it increases quadratically — that is, doubling speed will quadruple energy consumption.[9]

These equations provide a formalization of the West's experience with energy-based technologies in the early 20th century. As indicated by the quotations in Section 4.2, rising productivity was associated with greater energy use per unit of capital, with the latter operating on the former via the increased operating speeds made possible by electric unit drive. As Alfred Chandler pointed out, the productivity gains of the early 20th century owed in large measure to increasing machine speeds (Jerome (1934), Chandler (1977), Devine (1983)). As early as 1901, Professor F.B. Crocker summarized the effect of electric unit drive on productivity and output as follows:

---

[7] $s_i(t)^{max} = \bar{s}_i$ can be viewed as a combination of the asymptote of $s_i(t) = e_i(t)^{0.5 + \gamma_i(t)}$ $\forall i = 1, 2, 3, \ldots, n$, and the physical upper limits of machine speed/chemical reaction rates.

[8] In this case, machine speed defines total factor productivity — or capital productivity. It is important to keep in mind that in modern material processes, labor is a supervisory input. Hence, faster machines will raise output per unit labor (supervisory) input, despite what is essentially a constant effort on its part.

[9] This is also the case for chemical and thermal processes, where increasing operating temperatures will increase the rate of output, but at a decreasing rate.

It is found that the output of manufacturing establishments is materially increased in most cases by the use of electric driving. It is often found that the gain actually amounts to 20–30 percent or even more, with the same floor space, machinery, and number of workmen. This is the most important advantage of all, because it secures an increase in income without an increase in investment, labor, or expense except perhaps for materials. In many cases, the output is raised and at the same time, the labor item is reduced (Devine, 1990, p. 32).

Sidney Sonenblum described the shift to electric unit drive from 1920 to 1948 as a period of "accelerating the rate of throughput."

During these years the focus of managerial attention shifted from enlarging the scale of operations to increasing operating efficiency by speeding up the rate of throughput in the plant. High priority was assigned to modifications of factory design and layout in order to better integrate worker and machine tasks. Advances in the electrification of machine drive were indispensable to the realization of these new objectives and may, indeed, have served to stimulate the new managerial perspectives that emerged (Sonenblum, 1990, p. 291).

4.2.1.5 *The kinetics approach to production: The evidence*

As indicated, the kinetics approach to material processes is based on the law of kinetics, namely that energy use increases at the square of velocity/speed. Or, conversely, velocity/speed increases at the square root of energy use. Tables 4.1–4.3, taken from Beaudreau (2020), list the various estimates of the output elasticity of energy use, whether at the aggregate or industry level. As can be seen, the majority are not statistically different from the predicted theoretical value of 0.50.[10] Thus, regardless of the country, the period or the industry, material processes appear to behave according to the laws of physics, notably the law of kinetics.

---

[10] It is important to note that the greater the downtime, the greater the estimate. As such, the output elasticity has to fall in the interval of 0.5 and 1.

Table 4.2.   Estimates of the Electricity-Use Output Elasticity-Manufacturing

Method	Source	Country and Period	Estimate (*t*-stat)
OLS	Beaudreau (1995)	U.S. (1950–1984)	0.5330 (10.791)
OLS	Beaudreau (1998)	U.S. (1958–1984)	0.4483 (12.469)
		Germany (1962–1988)	0.7474 (3.135)
		Japan (1962–1988)	0.6055 (3.017)
LINEX	Kummel *et al.* (2002)[a]	Germany	0.64
		U.S. (1960–1993)	0.51
		Japan (1965–1992)	0.61
		U.S.-Total (1960–1993)	0.30
		Germany-Total (1960–1989)	0.44
Cointegration	Stresing *et al.* (2008)	Germany (1960–1989)	0.517
		Japan (1965–1992)	0.350
		U.S. (1960–1978)	0.663

Note: [a]No standard errors or *t*-statistics are provided in Kummel *et al.* (2002) and Stresing *et al.* (2008).
Source: Beaudreau (2020).

4.2.1.6 *Tier II: Organization and the demand for machine supervision and tools*

While early models of production (i.e., classical production theory) viewed labor as being physically productive (e.g., classical theory of value), by the end of the century, most mainstream economists, including neoclassical writers, viewed labor for what it had become, namely what Alfred Marshall referred to as "machine operatives." Take, for example, the following excerpt from Alfred Marshall's *Principles of Economics* where he refers to workers (conventional labor) as "managers":

> We may now pass to the effects which machinery has in relieving that excessive muscular strain which a few generations ago was the common lot of more than half the working men even in such a country as England … in other trades, machinery has lightened man's labours. The house carpenters, for instance, make things of the same kind as those used by our forefathers, with much less toil for themselves … Nothing could be more narrow or monotonous than the occupation of a weaver of plain

Table 4.3.   2-Digit SIC Industry Electric Power Output Elasticities 1947–1984

SIC	Industry	Elasticity-I (*t*-stat.)	Elasticity-II (*t*-stat.)	Elasticity-III (*t*-stat.)
20	Food and kindred products	0.610 (30.873)	0.552 (13.074)	0.586 (26.239)
21	Tobacco products	0.386 (12.604)	0.399	(13.315)
22	Textile mill products	0.401 (5.243)	0.301 (5.154)	0.490 (11.897)
23	Apparel and other textile products	0.142 (7.800)	0.200 (7.489)	0.164 (8.7221)
24	Lumber and wood products	0.518 (17.614)	0.474 (10.923)	0.493 (17.966)
25	Furniture and fixtures	0.227 (5.785)	0.490 (13.566)	0.359 (11.568)
26	Paper and allied products	0.5937 (17.55)	0.673 (32.139)	0.616 (28.6918)
27	Printing and publishing	0.156 (3.3158)	0.458 (14.599)	0.341 (11.686)
28	Chemicals and allied products	0.519 (9.651)	0.595 (9.475)	0.560 (9.380)
29	Petroleum and allied products	1.153 (8.486)	0.658 (9.161)	0.733 (15.109)
30	Rubber and misc. products	0.247 (1.822)	0.804 (24.828)	0.550 (9.437)
31	Leather and leather products	0.382 (7.373)	0.048 (0.8439)	0.323 (14.970)
32	Stone, clay and glass products	0.627 (11.702)	0.769 (22.983)	0.728 (20.323)
33	Primary metal industries	0.607 (16.826)	0.552 (13.074)	0.571 (17.622)
34	Fabricated metal products	0.480 (11.841)	0.603 (28.612)	0.489 (22.141)
35	Machinery, except electrical	0.624 (18.007)	0.624 (18.007)	0.622 (20.763)
36	Electric and electronic equipment	0.403 (6.740	0.744 (23.012)	0.583 (15.339)
37	Transportation equipment	0.737 (20.826)	0.791 (19.149)	0.749 (19.692)
38	Instruments and related products	0.662 (15.220)	0.812 (37.508)	0.725 (28.350)
	Average	0.493	0.543	0.550

stuffs in the old time. But now, one woman will manage four or more looms, each of which does many times as much work in the course of a day as the old hand loom did: and her work is much less monotonous and calls for much more judgment than his did (Marshall, 1890, p. 218).

This change was echoed in official statistics. For example, the U.K. Board of Trade, in its *Censuses of Production*, no longer referred to workers or production workers, but rather to operatives. The concept of labor productivity, it therefore follows, took on a new meaning, specifically as a measure of output per machine manager or operative. Theoretically, labor was not physically responsible for/involved in generating wealth, but rather was responsible for overseeing/managing the corresponding machines. To formalize this, the demand for supervision/machine operatives is modeled as a function of output, specifically desired output. The greater the desired or targeted level of output on the part of firms, the greater the demand for supervision and supervisors.

As machine operatives are involved in all n-sub-processes defined by Equation (4.1), it stands to reason that the demand for supervision will depend on a number of considerations, from the individual sub-process supervision technology, to average overall machine speed, to the overall scale of operation. For example, if a company automates a given sub-process, then it would stand to reason that the demand for supervision per unit of output would fall as a result. The same would hold for an increase in machine speed in which case machine operatives would be overseeing what is a faster machine. Only with an increase in the overall scale of operations (i.e., all sub-processes are increased by the same factor) will the demand for supervision per unit of output stay the same.

$$n(t) = \alpha \left[s(t), i(t) \right] y(t) \qquad (4.6)$$

The firm level demand for supervision can be formalized as Equation (4.6), where n_t refers to the number of machine operatives or supervisors, and α refers to the demand for supervision per unit y_t, which is a function of $s(t)$, average machine speed at time t, and $i(t)$, the level of automation at time t.[11] As such, an increase in s_t, machine speed, will result in an increase in $y(t)$ per unit $n(t)$. However, it bears reminding that such an increase owes in no measure to labor's intrinsic properties or productivity, but rather to greater machine speed and more output per unit capital (i.e., machinery) and supervision.[12]

---

[11] In this section, we chose to examine the demand for supervision at the more aggregate level — that is, not at the individual sub-process level.

[12] As such, it is by no means clear that labor's remuneration should rise as a result. If anything, there is reason to believe that it would decrease globally as less supervision is required for a given level of output.

Similarly, innovations in ICT-based technological change will affect labor demand. Specifically, innovations in machine control technology will, in general, reduce α, thus reducing the demand for supervision per unit output — in some cases, reducing it to zero (i.e., the case of total factory automation). Measured output per machine operative will, consequently, rise, again in no part due to the intrinsic contribution of conventionally defined labor.

$$k(t) = \beta\big[s(t), \eta(t)\big]\, y(t) \tag{4.7}$$

Like the supervisory input, tools (capital) are considered to be an organizational input, one that defines a given material process, but not one that is physically productive. According to classical mechanics, tools provide mechanical advantage, which is defined as the advantage gained by the use of a mechanism in transmitting force: specifically, the ratio of the force that performs the useful work of a machine to the force that is applied to the machine. The demand for tools can, as such, be modeled analogously to that of supervision — that is, as a function of projected output, $y(t)$. According to Equation (4.7), the demand for tools is an increasing function of the latter variable, with $\beta[s(t),\eta(t)]$ being the corresponding scaler. As can be seen, the per-unit output demand for tools (capital) is a decreasing function of machine speed, and of $\eta(t)$, the level of second-law efficiency (in short, the productivity of energy). The more efficient the energy input, the less capital required per unit output.

4.2.2 *A macroeconomic model of the U.S. economy with acceleration*

In this section, a macroeconomic model that incorporates acceleration-based increases in the rated capacity of existing plant and equipment is developed and used to estimate U.S. potential GDP for the period under study (1920s and 1930s). To capture the notion of machine/process speed-related increases in aggregate potential output (Polakov, 1933; Jerome 1934; Chandler, 1977), the left-hand side of the standard national income accounting equation was modified as shown in Equation (4.8), where the value of aggregate output (GDP) is defined as the product of $p(t)$, the price level, $s(t)$, average economy-wide machine speed per hour (units per hour), $k(t)$, aggregate capital (plant and equipment) and $h(t)$ the average number of hours the machine/unit aggregate capital operates.[13] Average machine speed is by definition an average of economy-wide individual machine speeds. Machines in this case include all material processes, from those in the manufacturing sector, to those in the transportation sector, to those in the construction sector, and to those in the service sector. As labor and capital are not physically productive inputs (Beaudreau, 1998), but rather are organizational in nature, it will be assumed that regardless of $s(t)$, each unit of capital $k(t)$ requires one unit of labor $n(t)$. In other words, each unit of capital requires a supervisor.[14] $h(t)$, the average number of hours worked, is as such a measure of capacity utilization, with 24 being the maximum $(\bar{h})$ it can take on.

The right-hand side of the equation defines aggregate expenditure.[15] To simplify the analysis, it is assumed that all of wage income is consumed and all of profit income is invested. Purchasing power is defined as the product of $w(t)$, the average wage, $h(t)$ and $k(t)$. If capital is fully employed, $h(t)$ would be 24, which is the equivalent of three eight-hour shifts. Overall profits $\pi^i(t)$ are defined as the sum of $\pi^v(t)$, profits that are used to finance planned investment expenditure, and $\pi^s(t)$, as excess profits that are saved. Put differently, investment expenditure is assumed to be exogenous, being determined at the beginning of time t $(\pi^v(t))$. Another way of seeing this is that any additional profit income (unanticipated) is not automatically invested. Last, a discretionary expenditure variable φ is included for analytical purposes — that is, to allow for the analysis of discretionary government policy measures such as commercial policy or expenditure policy.

$$p(t)s(t)k(t)h(t) = w(t)k(t)h(t) + \pi^v(t) + \varphi \qquad (4.8)$$

$$h(t) = \frac{1}{[p(t)s(t) - w(t)k(t)]}[\pi^v(t) + \varphi] \qquad (4.9)$$

---

[13] Polakov (1933) outlined a similar model, as follows: Output = T × E × R, where T = time, E = employees, and R = rate of production, or machine speed.

[14] Accordingly, $k(t)h(t)$ defines the aggregate number of hours worked per day. Equivalent monthly and yearly levels can be obtained by simply scaling $k(t)h(t)$ up by the number of days (30 and 365, respectively).

[15] Implicitly, we assume a variant of Say's Law, namely that money income equals money expenditure. However, income is not always equal to potential output as defined by the left-hand side of Equation (1).

Solving Equation (4.8) for $h(t)$ yields Equation (4.9), where the equilibrium number of hours (out of 24) per machine (i.e., unit of $k(t)$) is decreasing in $p(t)$ and $s(t)$, but increasing in $w(t)$. An increase in $s(t)$, the average economy-wide machine speed, will *ceteris paribus* decrease $h(t)$, the average number of hours worked (Equation (4.9)).[16] This follows from the fact that increased productivity in the face of unchanged expenditure ($w(t)$ is fixed) will force firms to cut the number of hours their plants operate, thus reducing the demand for labor.[17] However, if the same increase in $s(t)$ is accompanied by a commensurate increase in $w(t)$, then there exists the possibility that $h(t)$ would not be affected. Wage income will increase as will profit income. If investors increase planned investment, then overall expenditure would have increased in proportion to the increase in productive capacity.

As in the standard macroeconomic model, a decrease in planned expenditure (i.e., $[\pi^v(t) + \varphi]$) will decrease $h(t)$ via the acceleration-adjusted multiplier (i.e., $\frac{1}{[p(t)s(t) - w(t)k(t)]}$. According to the latter, an increase in $s(t)$ will diminish the efficacy of fiscal policy as every additional dollar spent will require fewer hours given the greater machine speed. Also, the acceleration-adjusted multiplier is decreasing in $w(t)$. Thus, lowering wages/falling wages in a downturn will hamper expenditure-based efforts to increase employment, which could explain why President Herbert Hoover was opposed to a decrease in wages to restore employment in 1930. It also sheds light on Hoover and Roosevelt's high-wage doctrine as higher wages increase the acceleration-adjusted multiplier.[18]

4.2.2.1 *Acceleration, disequilibrium and policy*

How acceleration (i.e., an increase in $s(t)$) affects output and employment will depend on a number of factors, the most important of which is whether firms choose to (i) produce at the new, higher accelerated level of

---

[16]This version of the multiplier is akin to Richard F. Kahn's 1931 original employment multiplier. See Kahn (1931).

[17]By definition, the aggregate level of hours is simply the product of $h(t)$ and $k(t)$.

[18]This we maintain captures Keynes's argument that a decrease in wages could potentially decrease output.

output or (ii) operate plant and equipment at the new, accelerated speed but reduce the utilization rate.[19] Each is now examined.

4.2.2.1.1 Acceleration and full capacity utilization

In this case, companies operate their plants at full capacity, which entails $h(t) = 24$ and maximum speed (i.e., $s(t)$). Hence, the left-hand side of Equation (4.8) increases, thus creating a disequilibrium (imbalance according to President Hoover's *Committee on Recent Economic Changes*). Given that wages and profits have not changed, it stands to reason that product markets in general will find themselves with excess supply — that is, unsold products. Not surprisingly, this is an unlikely outcome for a number of reasons, not the least of which is the fact that firms are more likely to reduce hours than flood the market with their products.[20]

4.2.2.1.2 Acceleration and constrained capacity utilization

In this case, firms operate their plants at the accelerated speeds, but reduce capacity utilization (i.e., $h(t)$).[21] In so doing, they reduce their variable costs by roughly the same percentage as the increase in speed. For example, if speed accelerates by 20 percent, then the current level of output can be produced with an 80 percent utilization rate. In this case, $h(t)$ falls, which translates into weakening in employment and in the labor market in general. Thorstein Veblen referred to this response as a form of sabotage on the part of companies as it pre-empted the full utilization of the new-found potential.

---

[19]A third possibility would be to maintain pre-conversion machine speeds — that is, the status quo. This possibility is not considered.

[20]President Herbert Hoover's *Committee on Recent Economic Changes* was well aware of this scenario, which prompted it to focus attention on new ways in which to market goods and services.

It stopped short of calling for higher wages, but did devote two chapters to the question of restoring balance.

[21]Unlike DC motors, AC motors cannot be speeded up or slowed down. Hence, newly installed AC motors would have been operated at their rated speed (i.e., rpm).

4.2.2.2 *Acceleration and underincome*

Generalized machine speed-ups/acceleration present important challenges in so far as their income equivalents are concerned, owing in large measure to the fundamental nature of income creation/generation. More specifically, as mentioned the resulting productivity and output gains have, according to the laws of kinetics, nothing to do with either labor or capital. Existing plant and equipment are simply speeded up, and workers simply oversee what are faster operating machines. Ultimately, the productivity gains are the result of the increased energy consumed (i.e., according to the laws of kinetics). One way of seeing this is that energy (i.e., kWh) creates rents which, for a successful transition to the new higher macroeconomic equilibrium, need to be (i) assigned/attributed and (ii) monetized. Theoretically, this can be achieved by either increasing wages and/or increasing profits. The problem with the former lies in the fact that it cannot be justified by workers' contribution to productivity (labor being a supervisory input), making for a situation in which managers will, in general, have a tendency to not increase wages — or resist increasing wages on technical grounds. Put differently, as workers' tasks will not have changed, there would be no legitimate reason in the eyes of managers to increase wages. Increasing profits is also problematic as profits — returns to capital — are a residual form of factor payment, paid out *ex-post* and not *ex-ante*. Put differently, firms do not pay the owners of capital a "wage" prior to the sale of the product.

4.2.2.2.1 Acceleration-based disequilibrium: A numerical example

In this numerical example (Table 4.4), acceleration increases $s(t)$ from 5 per hour to 7 per hour, a 40 percent increase in period 1. Initial GDP is 1,200, with wage income of 840 and profit income of 360. In the first iteration, output rises to 1,680, which is not sustainable given income and expenditure of 1,200, thus forcing companies to readjust, decreasing $h(t)$ in the second iteration to 17.14, which brings the level of output back down to 1,200. However, in so doing, it reduces the wage bill to 600, thus decreasing overall expenditure to 960. In the next iteration, firms decrease $h(t)$ to 13.71 in the hope of equilibrating or balancing the product market. However, in so doing, wage income decreases to 480, thus forcing yet another cut in $h(t)$. This process continues until Period 10 when equilibrium is reestablished as output, income and expenditure are all equal.

Table 4.4.   Acceleration-Based Disequilibrium: A Numerical Example[a]

Period	$h(t)$	$p(t)s(t)h(t)k(t)$	$w(t)h(t)k(t)$	$\pi^v(t)$	$\pi^s(t)$
0	24	1,200	840	360	0
1	24	1,680	840	360	0
2	17.14	1,200	600	360	240
3	13,71	960	480	360	120
4	12	840	420	360	60
5	11.14	780	390	360	30
6	10.71	750	375	360	25
7	10.50	735	367	360	8
8	10.40	728	363	360	5
9	10.33	724	361	360	3
10	10.31	722	360	360	2

Notes: [a]All values are in constant dollars. $p(t) = 1$, $s(t) = 5$, $k(t) = 10$, $h(t) = 24$, $w(t) = 3.5$, $\pi(t) = 360$.

This example assumes that investment expenditure is fixed and thus not affected by the downward spiral. It also highlights the fact that in the process, firms will earn higher profits (Column 6) as labor costs per hour ($w(t) = 3.5$) are constant despite productivity gains of 40 percent (see Column 6).

4.2.2.3 *Policy options*

This raises the question of possible policy options. How could a fully-informed government (third party) close an acceleration-based output gap? In other words, what policies could such a government put into place to close the gap? Consider the following options. The first option would be to legislate an increase in real wages, either by forcing across-the-board wage increases or price decreases (or a combination thereof). Of course, this assumes the existence of a certain degree of homogeneity in so far as the productivity gains are concerned — namely that the increase be generalized and of similar magnitude across firms and industries. A second option would be to increase central bank-financed government expenditure in an amount of the output gap (i.e., 480). Understandably, there are problems with this approach. First, it would serve to increase profits (residual) without increasing wages. Profits would increase as firms produce at the new, higher level of output, raising the question whether the resulting excess savings would be invested, and in so doing raise the overall level of expenditure. If not, then the increase in government expenditure would have to be recurrent. Year in, year out, it would need to maintain the higher level of expenditure via increased money-supply-based expenditure levels. This in turn would raise other issues such as the resulting increased liquidity in the banking system (owing to increased profits) and its effects on the economy.

Clearly, the policy options available to a government are relatively limited, other than decreeing an across-the-board increase in wages, assuming of course that the speed-ups are generalized across the industries and sectors of the economy. The problem comes down to the non-proprietary nature of the resulting energy/speed rents. Acceleration increases potential output without increasing costs and hence national income, making for a macroeconomic disequilibrium — or what the *Committee on Recent Economic Changes* referred to as imbalance. Neither labor nor capital can legitimately lay claim to these rents, yet in order to maintain full-employment, they must somehow be assigned/attributed/monetized. That is, the right-hand side of Equation (4.8) must be equal to the left-hand side for a value of $h(t) = 24$.

4.3 Machine Speed, Acceleration and Rated Capacity in the 1920s: The Evidence

In this section, evidence of the acceleration-based increase in productivity and potential output in the 1920s is presented. To begin with, it is important to point out that owing to the nature of the new drive technology, there are no actual data (reported data) on potential output/rated capacity at the firm, industry or economy-wide levels for the 1920s and 1930s. As pointed out, acceleration increases the potential rated capacity of existing capital without necessarily increasing actual output. Second, the diffusion of electric unit drive throughout the U.S. was not instantaneous. Not all firms within a given industry or sector adopted the new technology in the 1920s. In fact, the evidence shows that the conversion to electric unit drive occurred throughout the 1920s and 1930s. The estimates presented here consist of a combination of survey results as well as indirect measures of overall productivity growth based on conventional measures, such as reported labor productivity.

4.3.1 *Estimates of output gap/definition of rated capacity*

Throughout the 1920s, there were numerous references to the purported widening gap between potential and actual output (see Table 4.5). Few, however, provided actual estimates. Was potential output 20, 30 or 40 percent greater than actual output? By how much had electric unit drive increased firms' ability to produce? As it turned out, only a decade later,

Table 4.5. Pre-Crash Excess Capacity as Seen in the Literature

Howard Scott (1933)	The United States of our forefathers, with 12,000,000 inhabitants, performed its necessary work in almost entire dependence upon the human engine, which, as its chief means of energy conversion, was aided and abetted only by domestic animals and a few water wheels. The United States today has over one billion installed horsepower. In 1929, these engines of energy conversion, though operated only to partial capacity, nevertheless had an output that represented approximately 50 percent of the total work of the world (Scott, 1933, p. 54).
Paul Douglas (1927)	The second factor which has contributed to our prosperity has been our development of automatic and efficient machinery and of effective technical processes (Douglas, 1927, p. 26).
Irving Fisher (1930)	"Acceleration rather than structural change is the key to an understanding of our recent economic developments" (Fisher, 1930, p. 3). "But the breadth and the tempo of recent developments gives them new importance."
Rexford Tugwell (1927)	"Revolution underway in U.S. industry." Foremost among the "technical causes" of increased productivity, he argued, was "the bringing into use of new and better power resources more suited to our technique, more flexible and less wasteful: and continued progress in the technique of generating and applying power" (Tugwell, 1927, p. 180).
Stuart Chase (1934)	A point at which consumption becomes a greater problem than production. Circa 1920. "Our economy" says F. L. Ackerman, "is so set up that it produces goods at a higher rate than it produces income with which to purchase them" (Chase, 1934, p. 11).
Harold Loeb (1935)	"The budget total $135,516,000,000, an increase of some $43 billion, over the actual production of 1929. The goods and services represented by this consist of desired goods and services which the people of the United States could produce but do not produce" (Loeb, 1935, p. 238).

in the depths of the depression, would estimates of the excess capacity be published, first by the Brookings Institution and then by Harold Loeb and the New York Housing Authority.

4.3.1.1 *The Brookings Institution*

The first systematic set of estimates of excess capacity was provided by the Brookings Institution, founded and headed by Robert S. Brookings. In what was an extremely ambitious project, it set out in the early 1930s to estimate what it referred to as "America's Ability to Produce." As potential output is just that, a potential, it was decided that a survey of the nation's manufacturers would be undertaken. More specifically, a survey of production managers was carried out where the focus was on providing estimates of potential as opposed to actual output. Put simply, they were asked to estimate potential output whether or not they had ever produced at that level. The results were reported in a series of volumes in the mid-1930s. Table 4.6, taken from Nourse *et al.* (1934) shows that the output gap stood at roughly 17 percent throughout the 1920s.

4.3.1.2 *Harold Loeb and the New York housing authority*

A similar attempt was made by writer Harold Loeb and the New York Housing Authority in 1935. In a report titled "The Chart of Plenty:

Table 4.6. The Brookings Institution Estimates of Excess Productive Capacity 1922–1929 (billion)

Year	Potential Productive Capacity	Actual GDP	Gap (%)
1922	75.5	63.4	16
1923	83.2	69.9	17
1924	85.1	71.5	17
1925	89.6	75.3	16
1926	91.9	77.2	16
1927	93.2	78.3	17
1928	94.9	79.7	16
1929	97.5	81.9	17

Source: Nourse (1934, p. 176).

A Study of America's Product Capacity Based on the Finding of the National Survey of Potential Product Capacity," he and his associates provided estimates of excess capacity based on survey data. The gist of both the study and its findings can be found in the following quote:

> *Practicability of Capacity Production.* It might be contended that higher speeds of operation would lead to breakdowns of both plant and personnel. Fifty years ago, this might have been true. Then, most of the labor was purely physical, of a repetitive nature, hard on the worker and destructive of his morale and well-being. Today, as industrial electrification has progressed, controls are becoming simple, a matter of push-button manipulation and entirely automatic: and labor, when it is not carried out along primitive lines such as digging, plastering and similar operations, has in many cases assumed a supervisory character. As a result, the attainment of higher speeds of output does not wear out the labor force as it once did (Loeb, 1935, p. xxiii).

The upshot of the report can be summarized in Table 4.7 where, according to the study, potential GDP in 1929 was 45 percent greater than the actual output of $93 billion. This gap would, over the subsequent years, reach 135 percent in 1932, the depth of the downturn. The cumulative loss of wealth to the nation was $287 billion over this five-year period.

Mordecai Ezekiel (1936), in his study of population and unemployment, provided the estimates of productivity growth reported in

Table 4.7.   Statement of Losses to the American People (billion 1929 dollars)

Year	Budget	National Income	Annual Loss to Consumer
1929	$135	$93	$42
1930	$137	$86	$51
1931	$138	$79	$59
1932	$139	$59	$70
1933	$141	$75	$65
	Total Loss to Consumer	(1929–1933)	$287

Source: Loeb (1935, p. 125).

Table 4.8.   Physical Productivity (Efficiency) Per Worker by
Census Periods 1870–1930 (1900 = 100)

Census Year	Agriculture	Manufacturing	Mining
1870	58	64	36
1880	77	75	56
1890	82	93	84
1900	100	100	100
1910	100	117	104
1920	119	131	139
1930	141	163	147

Table 4.8 from 1870 to 1930. As he put it: "In all three lines of physical production — farming, mining and manufacturing — there has been a rapid and continuous increase in output per worker occupied, The increase has been steadiest in manufacturing ….. Mining shows the most rapid rate of increase in productivity through most of the period ….. From 1920 to 1930, the gain in output per worker was 41 percent in agriculture and 39 percent in manufacturing" (Ezekiel, 1936, p. 232).

4.3.1.3 *Backward induction*

In Beaudreau (1996), potential output in the 1920s was estimated using basic growth theory, known as backward extrapolation. According to standard growth theory, gross national product grows at rate $n + \tau$, where n is the rate of labor force growth and τ is the rate of technological change — in this case, the percentage rate of acceleration-based productivity growth. As pointed out, since acceleration does not necessarily translate into output growth, actual GNP data will fail to capture potential output. To get around this, backward extrapolation makes the strong assumption that it will over time work itself into the growth rate and, hence, into actual GNP. By identifying that point in time, estimates of potential GNP for the preceding years can be obtained by extrapolating actual GNP for the year in question back in time at the rate of growth of the labor supply.

For example, suppose that the U.S. economy was producing at its potential in 1944. That is, by 1944 in the depth of World War II, companies throughout the U.S. economy were producing at their new, higher-rated capacity. Potential GNP for the years prior to 1944 can then be estimated by simply discounting 1944 actual GNP by the rate of growth of the labor force — that is, the rate at which the economy would grow in the absence of technological change. In 1944, U.S. GNP stood at $361.3 billion. The rate of growth of the U.S. non-agricultural labor force from 1910 to 1950 was estimated at 1.85 percent per annum. Potential 1925 GNP, it therefore follows, can be obtained by dividing $361.3 billion by 1.4166404 (i.e., $(1.0185)^{19}$), the appropriate discount factor, which yields $255.0 billion. Dividing the former by the level of actual 1925 U.S. GNP of $179.4 billion yields a value for electric unit drive-based productivity growth of 0.4216. That is, the resulting estimate of τ, the electric unit drive-based technology shock, in this case would be 42.1 percent.

The first set of estimates of potential U.S. GNP and the resulting values for τ (in parentheses) is presented in Table 4.9. Two base years (i.e., t'), 1944 and 1943, and three target years (i.e., t''), 1925, 1927 and 1929, were chosen. In 1943, real U.S. GNP was $337.1 billion (constant 1958 dollars), which, extrapolated backward to 1925 at an annual rate of 1.85 percent, yields a value for potential U.S. GNP in 1925 of $242.3 billion (see Figure 4.1). That is, actual 1925 U.S. GNP of $242.3 billion growing at an annual rate of 1.85 percent, the rate of growth of the labor force over this period, yields a level of 1943 U.S. GNP of $337.1 billion. Dividing this figure by reported actual 1925 GNP of $179.4 billion (constant 1958 dollars) yields a value of τ, the rate of technological change, of 0.3508 (reported in parentheses). By choosing

Table 4.9.   Backward Extrapolation Estimates of Potential U.S. Gross National Product — Unweighted

Target Year (t'')/ Base Year (t')	1925	1927	1929
1943	$242.3	$251.4	$260.7
	(0.3508)	(0.3245)	(0.2809)
1944	$255.0	$264.5	$274.4
	(0.4216)	(0.3938)	(0.3164)

Notes: 1. Base and target years are reversed owing to the nature of the corresponding estimates (i.e., backward looking).
2. Actual U.S. GNP/$(1+n)$1.015(20).
3. Potential U.S. GNP/actual U.S. GNP-1 (billion constant 1958 dollars).
Source: Beaudreau (1996, p. 93).

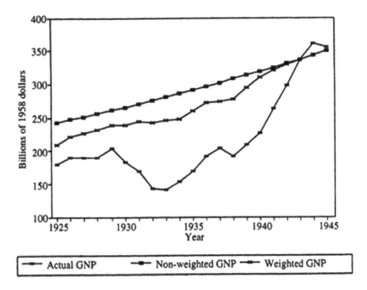

Figure 4.1. Actual and Potential U.S. Gross National Product, 1925–1945 (Non-Weighted and Weighted)

Source: Beaudreau (1996, p. 96).

1944 as the relevant base year, potential 1925 U.S. GNP increases to $255.3 billion, which corresponds to a value for τ of 0.4216.

Thus, potential U.S. GNP, as defined by electric unit drive-based accelerated speed in 1925 (i.e., mass production), was between 35 ($t' = 1943$) and 42 ($t' = 1944$) percent greater than actual GNP (see Figure 4.1). Similarly, potential U.S. GNP in 1927 was between 23 ($t' = 1943$) and 39 ($t' = 1944$) percent greater than actual GNP, and lastly, potential GNP in 1929 was between 23 ($t'= 1943$) and 34 ($t' = 1944$) percent greater than actual GNP.

4.3.1.4 *Weighted estimates*

This set of estimates assumes that the adoption of electric unit drive by all sectors of the economy was instantaneous. In other words, there were no diffusion lags (David, 1990). However, in actual fact there are a number of reasons why this was typically not the case. First, firms may delay the adoption of a new technology to coincide with their investment cycle. Second, they may find themselves constrained on product markets, which

Table 4.10.　Backward Extrapolation Estimates of Potential U.S. Gross National Product — Weighted

Target Year (t'')/ Base Year (t')	1925	1927	1929
1943	$209.4	$227.3	$238.8
	(0.1675)	(0.1979)	(0.1729)
1944	$215.5	$235.3	$247.2
	(0.2013)	(0.2402)	(0.2141)

Notes: 1. Base and target years are reversed owing to the nature of the corresponding estimates (i.e., backward looking).
2. Actual U.S. GNP/$(1+n)^{1.085(20)}$.
3. Potential U.S. GNP/actual U.S. GNP-1 (billion constant 1958 dollars).

will also lead to delayed adoption. Third, they may adopt the new technology, but not produce at the new, higher potential.

In light of this, a second set of estimates of potential GNP and τ, the technology shock was generated. Using a diffusion index based on the level of electric power consumed per worker (1925–1945), the set of weighted potential U.S. GNP values and τ values provided in Table 4.10 was generated. Unweighted potential 1925 U.S. GNP was estimated to be $255.0 billion, which yields a τ value of 0.4216. According to the diffusion index, electric unit drive in 1925 had been adopted by roughly 47.7 percent of firms in the U.S. industry. Multiplying the former by the latter results in a weighted estimate of τ of 0.20. Not surprisingly, lower estimates of potential GNP and τ now result. Weighted potential GNP in 1925 (base year 1944) was $215.5 billion ($\tau$ = 0.2013) as opposed to $255.0 billion ($\tau$ = 0.4216). Potential U.S. GNP, as defined by the penetration of electric unit drive in 1925, was between 16.7 (t' = 1943) and 20.1 (t' = 1944) percent greater than actual GNP.[22] Similarly, potential U.S. GNP in 1927 was between 19.7 (t' = 1943) and 24.2 (t' = 1944) percent greater than actual GNP, and lastly, potential GNP in 1929 was between 17.2 (t' = 1943) and 21.4 (t' = 1944) percent greater than actual GNP (see Figure 4.2).

---

[22]These estimates are consistent with those reported by the Brookings Institution (see Moulton, 1935).

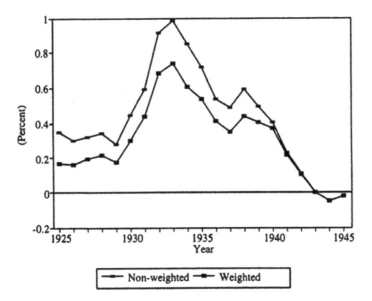

Figure 4.2. Estimates of the Gap between Actual and Potential U.S. Gross National Product, 1925–1945

4.3.1.5 *Productivity-based estimates of* τ

The logic of backward extrapolation can also be used to estimate aggregate and sector-specific values for τ: from reported labor productivity data for the base and target years. In this case, it is assumed that electric unit drive-based acceleration was a Hicks-neutral technological shock.[23] As a result, estimates of τ were obtained by simply differencing labor productivity at times t' and t''.

The resulting set of estimates of τ for $t'' = 1924$, 1925 and 1926, based on labor productivity growth data from 1924 to 1944, is provided in Table 4.11, where values range from 80.3 percent (end-of-base year 1923 to end-of-target year 1944) to 58.9 percent (end-of-base year 1925 to end-of-target year 1944). For the U.S. economy as a whole, they range from 57.3 percent (1924–1944) to 51.0 percent (1926–1944).

---

[23]The use of the Hicks-neutral nomenclature is for expository purposes as, in this case, neither labor nor capital is physically productive. Hence, conventional productivity data should be understood as a metric of output per worker or supervisor and not a measure of the latter's productivity.

4.3.1.6   *Labor market-based estimates of* τ

As pointed out earlier, electric unit drive-based acceleration increased productivity by speeding up existing production processes. Workers, however, were not the source of the increase. Nonetheless, wages did in fact increase over the course of the 1920s, 1930s and 1940s. By assuming that these increases were in keeping with productivity, estimates of τ can nonetheless be obtained by comparing real wages in the mid-1940s with those in the 1920s.

First, the real wage in manufacturing in 1944 was compared to the real wage in 1924 (end-of-year 1923 data). Referring to Table 8.5 in Chapter 8, the real wage in manufacturing between 1923 and 1944 increased 71 percent, resulting in an estimate of τ of 0.71. The real wage in U.S. manufacturing at the end of 1923 stood at $1.01 (constant 1958 dollars): in 1944, it had increased to $1.73 (constant 1958 dollars). What is particularly interesting to note is the fact that the bulk of the increase came via an increase in the nominal wage, which increased from $0.52 in 1923 to $1.01 in 1944, indicating a greater willingness to pay on the part of companies. The price level (1958 = 100) increased from 51.3 in 1923 to 58.2 in 1944.

Table 4.11.   Labor Productivity-Based Estimates of τ

Target Year (t')/ Base Year (t'')	Total 1924	Man. 1924	Total 1925	Man. 1925	Total 1926	Man. 1926
1926	7.03	15.67	2.46	8.84	2.69	1.97
1928	8.89	23.63	4.26	16.12	4.49	8.99
1930	9.60	30.39	4.93	22.19	5.16	14.69
1932	6.32	25.62	1.79	17.99	2.02	10.74
1934	14.75	42.78	9.86	23.44	10.11	25.87
1936	24.59	53.23	19.28	43.92	19.55	35.08
1938	28.10	49.00	22.64	39.95	22.92	31.35
1940	37.00	70.89	31.16	61.51	31.46	50.65
1942	45.19	80.09	39.01	69.15	39.32	58.77
1944	57.37	80.34	50.67	69.39	51.01	58.99

Notes: 1. End-of-year data.
2. ((Output per man-hour at t'-output per man-hour at t'')/output per man-hour at t'').
Source: U.S. Department of Commerce (1975), Series D86 and D685.

Table 4.12. Fabricant's National Bureau of Economic Research (NBER) Indexes of Employment Per Unit of Output

Year	Wage Earners-Man (1899 = 100)	Man-Hours-Man (1899 = 100)	Agriculture (1900 = 100)	Railroads (1929 = 100)	Mining (1929 = 100)
1919	84	74	84	124	135
1920	78	67	83	120	128
1921	74	61	82	130	130
1922	64	55	81	119	119
1923	65	56	79	114	116
1924	64	53	76	114	118
1925	59	50	74	108	112
1926	57	48	71	105	112
1927	55	47	70	106	108
1928	53	44	68	102	103
1929	51	42	67	100	100

Source: Soule (1947, p. 121).

Solomon Fabricant provided various estimates of labor productivity growth from 1919 to 1929 reported in Soule (1947) and reproduced in Table 4.12. According to George Soule, "For the decade between 1919 and 1929, the output per person employed, as well as the output per man-hour, increased with unusual rapidity. In manufacturing, the index of number of wage earners per unit of output was reduced from 84 in 1919 to 51 in 1929. The man-hours per unit fell in the same period from an index number of 74 to 42, or 43 percent (Soule, 1947, p. 121). Formally, this can be interpreted as an estimate of the increase in $s(t)$ from 1919 to 1929.

4.3.1.7 *Stock market-based estimates of* τ

As will be argued in Chapter 6, the stock market boom of 1928–1929 was largely the result of the Hoover Administration's tariff initiative aimed at securing a larger share of the domestic market for U.S. firms set against a backdrop of a widening acceleration-based output gap. By further restricting access to the U.S. market, the tariff hikes in the Smoot–Hawley Tariff Bill would provide U.S. firms with a larger share of the domestic market. Sales, earnings and profits would increase as a result, leading investors to bid up the price of shares. According to the fundamentals approach to asset pricing, the greater the anticipated increase in earnings, the greater the price increase. *Ceteris paribus*, if earnings are expected to rise, then stock prices should also increase.

In this section, estimates of τ are inferred from stock-price movements before the crash. To begin, we consider the relationship between electric unit drive-based acceleration and expected earnings/dividends. Basic theory predicts that if technological change is of the Hicks-neutral variety, then both labor and capital productivity should increase as both are more productive as should wages and dividends. However, as shown above, there are no scientific grounds for wages to increase (i.e., supervisory input), which raises an important question, namely how do investors in general, and investors in the 1920s in particular, see the relationship between technological change–in this case, electric unit drive–and real wages. For example, when estimating the earnings potential of the introduction of a new technology, do they factor in possible or probable wage increases? Or do they simply assume that wages will remain where they are?

Admittedly, this is an empirical question. For investors to factor-in anticipated wage increases, it would have to be the case that in the past, process innovations like electric unit drive-based acceleration systematically led to higher wages: otherwise, there would be no reason to believe that they would do so. On this note, the empirical evidence shows the absence of a one-to-one relationship between real wages and productivity. It would therefore not be unreasonable to assume that investors in the late 1920s played what amounted to a Nash strategy vis-à-vis wages.

This has important implications for expected dividends and, hence, for stock prices. For example, it implies that since the proportion of earnings constitutes a fraction (i.e., roughly 30 percent) of total firm income, expected dividends from electric unit drive-based acceleration would increase by more than τ percent. In fact, they would increase by a multiple of τ. Consider the following numerical example. Let a define the ratio of capital income to total firm income and suppose that $r = 0.3$. Hypothetical total firm revenue of $100 would yield factor payments to capital on the order of $30, which, capitalized at a rate of interest of 3 percent per annum, would yield a stock value of $1,000. Now, assume that τ takes on a value of 0.40. That is, electric unit drive-based acceleration increases productivity by 40 percent. For a constant nominal wage and assuming that the firm is not constrained on product markets, the resulting stock value would rise to $2,333, as the anticipated $40 rise in earnings would be factored entirely into the stock price. The rate at which the hypothetical stock price would rise is given as τ/r, which in this case is 1.33 (133 percent). Thus, a 40 percent increase in the stock price is magnified by a factor of 3.325.

This technique was used to estimate τ_s, τ_m, τ_r and τ_u, the implicit-in-stock price technology shock in the economy as a whole, manufacturing (industrials), railroads and utilities, respectively, using Standard and Poor's indexes of stock market prices from 1923 to 1929. Referring to Table 4.13, total, industrial, railroad and utilities real share prices increased 238, 231, 102 and 230 percent, respectively from 1924 to 1929. This implies that by 1929, initial hypothetical book value of $1,000 in each of these sectors would have risen to $3,380 for the market as a whole, $3,310 for manufacturing, $2,020 for railroads and $3300 for utilities. For these prices to exist in financial market equilibria, anticipated sector earnings of $101.40, $99.30, $60.60 and $99.00 are required, which, when initial earnings of $30.00 are netted out, yield values for τ_s, τ_m, τ_r and τ_u, of 71, 69, 31 and 69 percent, respectively.

The way to interpret these results is as follows. Hypothetical, fully-informed investors knowing that τ_s, τ_m, τ_r and τ_u stood at 71, 69, 31 and 69 percent, respectively, would have bid up the value of market, industrial, railroad, and utility shares by 238, 231, 102 and 230 percent, respectively. In other words, changing fundamentals would have led investors to bid share prices up by 238, 231, 102 and 230 percent, respectively. What is particularly noteworthy is the fact that the greatest gains occurred in those sectors most likely to be affected by electric power and electric unit drive, notably industry and utilities.

4.3.2 *Income and expenditure inertia-evidence*

As President Herbert Hoover and numerous others pointed out, the U.S. economy in the late 1920s found itself in a state of imbalance, by which it should be understood, a state of disequilibrium. Potential output exceeded actual output. In this section, evidence of this imbalance is presented.

Table 4.13.   Stock Market-Based Estimates of τ, 1924–1929

1924–1929				
Stock Index	1929	1923	Growth	τ
Total S&P	56.42	16.71	238	71
Industrials S&P	42.19	12.74	231	69
Industrials DJIA	352.51	95.52	269	81
Railroads S&P	91.27	45.13	102	31
Utilities S&P	117.25	35.30	230	69
1925–1929				
Stock Index	1929	1923	Growth	τ
Total S&P	51.42	17.67	191	57
Industrials S&P	42.19	13.34	216	65
Industrials DJIA	352.51	120.51	192	57
Railroads S&P	91.27	48.86	87	26
Utilities S&P	117.25	37.79	210	63
1926–1929				
Stock Index	1929	1923	Growth	τ
Total S&P	51.42	21.48	139	42
Industrials S&P	42.19	16.74	152	46
Industrials DJIA	352.51	156.66	125	37
Railroads S&P	91.27	57.63	76	23
Utilities S&P	117.25	45.05	160	48
1924–1929				
Stock Index	1929	1923	Growth	τ
Total S&P	56.42	16.71	238	71
Industrials S&P	42.19	12.74	231	69
Industrials DJIA	352.51	95.52	269	81
Railroads S&P	91.27	45.13	102	31
Utilities S&P	117.25	35.30	230	69

Source: Beaudreau (1996, p. 100).

As early as 1927, William Trufant Foster and Waddill Catchings described the problem aptly as "Business Without a Buyer":

Standards of Living Have Not Increased Proportionately. Nevertheless, in spite of all these Aladdin-like achievements in technical processes of production, and in spite of all the discoveries of new resources, the gains which we make, decade after decade, in the distribution of wealth to the people generally are not at all comparable to the gains which we make in our knowledge of the means of producing wealth (Foster and Catchings, 1927, p. 11).

A decade later, Spurgeon Bell of the Brookings Institution described the situation as follows:

In recent times, the process by which new technological developments are transmitted into higher standards of living is obviously not working smoothly. Even before the coming of the great depression, there appeared to be some doubt as to whether the system of wealth production and distribution was operating with maximum effectiveness. At a time when cumulative scientific knowledge might be expected to give us an accelerating tempo of industrial growth, the rate of advancement — for some reason or a combination of reasons — did not seem to be an increasing one. In any case, the issue in recent years has been sharply raised: can the economic system be counted upon to produce the beneficent economic results which were supposed to be the automatic accompaniment of scientific knowledge, and the increasing efficiency of production? Under modern conditions, do not technological improvements simply throw men out of work, destroy purchasing power, and retard economic advancement? (Bell, 1940, p. 669).

As pointed out above, income and expenditure inertia will, according to the model presented above, manifest itself in $h(t)$, the average number of hours worked per day, itself a measure of capacity utilization. According to Equation (4.8), an increase in $s(t)$, average economy-wide machine/process speed, will, *ceteris paribus*, create a disequilibrium between potential output, on the one hand, and actual income and expenditure, on the other, resulting in a decrease in $h(t)$. This owes to two factors, namely the fact that wages are fixed and profits (payments to capital), being a residual form of factor remuneration, remain constant. Greater machine/process speeds increase output per hour worked. However, because labor is not the source of the increase, there is no reason to believe that companies will increase — or be inclined to increase — wages. The second factor has to do with the fact that unlike labor, capital is not remunerated prior to the sale of the product/output, but rather is remunerated after. Another way of looking at this is that the owners of capital are, as University of Chicago economics professor Frank Knight pointed out in 1923, residual claimants (Knight, 1921). Together, these two factors make for income and consequently expenditure inertia in the face of greater rated capacity.

This creates a situation of income and expenditure inertia in which actual national income is less than potential output, as defined by rated capacity, making for expenditure levels that are also less than potential output. Put differently, income and expenditure are less than the level of full employment income. In such a setting, the only possible way out would consist of price (excluding wages) deflation which, in turn, would prompt an increase in real wages and an equivalent increase in real profits. As a result, the productivity gains from acceleration would be shared between the two-factor inputs. There is, however, reason to believe that companies would resist such price decreases in the short run, preferring to adjust $h(t)$, a phenomenon Thorstein Veblen referred to as "sabotage." Part of the reason owes to the fact that there was no guarantee that others would do likewise and that demand would, as a result, increase proportionately.

In other words, firms respond by decreasing $h(t)$, which will manifest itself in the form of a decrease in $h(t)$ at the firm, industry and economy-wide levels.

4.3.3   *Income and expenditure inertia: Evidence from industry data*

By the end of the 1920s, electricity and unit drive had replaced steam engines as the major source of all mechanical drive:

> By 1920 electricity had replaced steam as the major source of motive power and by 1929 — just 45 years after their first use in a factory — electric motors provided 78 percent of all mechanical drive (Devine, 1990, p. 21).

However, considerable heterogeneity continued to characterize the manufacturing sector as a whole. While most industries had, in fact, converted to electric unit drive, they differed in terms of energy use as evidenced by the fact that electric horsepower per wage earner varied considerably across industries. Referring to Table 4.14, which reports the

Table 4.14. U.S. Industry Value-Added, Wages and Electric Horsepower per Wage Earner 1914 and 1929

Industry	DVA	DWB	DELEC	DVAWB
Agricultural implements	1.27	1.20	1.61	0.07
Boots and shoes, rubber	0.15	1.32	6.03	−1.16
Boxes, fancy and paper	1.72	1.50	2.77	0.21
Bread and other bakery products	0.75	1.33	2.47	−0.58
Carpets and rugs, other than rag	1.95	1.58	2.29	0.37
Cement	1.76	1.36	2.78	0.39
Chemicals	1.72	1.35	1.94	0.36
Coke, not including gas-house	2.78	1.45	4.25	1.33
Confectionery	0.98	1.02	2.34	−0.04
Copper, tin and sheet-iron products	4.17	3.58	2.89	0.59
Cordage and twine and jute and linen goods	2.61	2.09	2.80	0.51
Dyeing and finishing	1.62	1.40	3.53	0.21
Electrical machinery, apparatus and supplies	1.63	1.36	1.17	0.26
Fertilizers	1.06	1.12	2.46	−0.06
Flour-mill and grist-mill products	1.36	1.27	3.58	0.08
Food preparations, NES	1.33	1.24	1.14	0.09
Foundry and machine shop products	2.59	2.15	3.89	0.44
Gas and Electric Fixtures and lamps reflectors	2.75	2.37	2.46	0.38
Gas, illuminating and heating	0.13	0.13	0.58	0.00
Glass	1.74	1.20	4.26	0.53
Ice, manufactured	10.56	1.23	11.07	9.32
Iron and steel works and rolling mills	1.70	1.40	3.30	0.30
Jewelry	1.43	1.30	2.38	0.12
Leather, tanned, curried and finished	1.17	1.35	2.83	−0.17
Marble and stone work	1.71	0.89	4.24	0.82
Mattresses and spring beds	1.56	1.39	2.44	0.17
Oil, cottonseed and cake	1.32	1.10	6.56	0.22
Paint and varnish	1.92	1.69	2.70	0.22
Petroleum, refining	1.63	1.29	4.92	0.34
Sewing machines, NES	0.40	0.33	0.41	0.06
Shipbuilding, including boat building	5.42	5.56	3.66	−0.14
Smelting and refining copper	0.84	1.09	4.07	−0.24
Soap	1.98	1.40	3.60	0.58
Sugar, refining	1.33	1.11	3.61	0.21
Wire	1.64	1.51	2.90	0.12

Source: U.S. Department of Commerce (1975, pp. 744–757).

increase in value-added per wage earner from 1914 to 1929 (Column 2), the increase in the wage bill per worker from 1914 to 1929 (Column 3), the increase in electric power per worker from 1914 to 1929 (Column 4) and the difference between the increase in value-added and the increase in the wage bill (Column 5) for a sample of 35 manufacturing industries (U.S. Bureau of Census, 1914, 1949), we see that the growth of electric horsepower per wage earner from 1919 to 1929 varied considerably across industries.

Conversion to electric unit drive had opened up a considerable gap between output per worker and wages. Referring to Table 4.15, which presents correlation coefficients of these four variables, we see that this gap (DVAWB) is highly correlated with DELEC ($\rho = 0.69$), which is the rate of growth of electric unit drive in the industry. Interestingly, while the rate of growth of value-added per worker is highly correlated to the rate of growth of electric power per worker ($\rho = 0.64$), the rate of growth of wages is not ($\rho = 0.07$), a fact that corroborates one of the main premises of the book.

4.3.4 *Income inertia as seen by president Hoover's committee on recent economic changes*

As it turned out, this disequilibrium and response were at the core of the *Report of the Committee on Recent Economic Changes of the President's Conference on Unemployment*, published in 1929. After having extolled the virtues of electric power, the committee focused on what it viewed as the overriding problem, namely the lack of balance, by which it should be understood, the balance between the U.S.'s ability to produce wealth and

Table 4.15.   U.S. Productivity–Wage Gap and Electrification 1914–1929

	DVA	DWB	DELEC	DVAWB
DVA	1.00	0.46	0.64	0.86
DWB		1.00	0.07	–0.03
DELEC			1.00	0.69
DVAWB				1.00

Source: U.S. Department of Commerce (1975, p. 828) (Series S-120–132).

its ability to consume it — formally, the left-hand side of Equation (4.8) being greater than the right-hand side. In short, it held that the two were increasingly out of balance, with the former exceeding the latter, contributing to growing unemployment.[24]

In its closing remarks, the signatories[25] to the Report declared:

> Informed leadership is vital to the maintenance of equilibrium. It depends upon a general knowledge of the relations of the parts to the other. Only through incessant observation and adjustment of our economy can we learn to maintain the economic balance.
>
> Underlying recent developments is an attitude of mind which seems to be characteristically American. Our nation is accustomed to rapid movement, to quick shifts in status: it is receptive to new ideas, ingenious in devices adaptable. Our economy is the embodiment of those who have made it.
>
> Our situation is fortunate, our momentum is remarkable. Yet the organic balance of our economic structure can be maintained only by hard, persistent, intelligent effort: by consideration and sympathy: by mutual confidence, and by a disposition in several human parts to work in harmony together.

4.3.5 Income inertia and unemployment: The case of the 1920s

According to Equation (4.9), an increase in $s(t)$ will, *ceteris paribus*, decrease $h(t)$, thus reducing the share of labor in each dollar of output and increasing the share of capital. This will in turn result in a reduction in overall wage income and an increase in profit or capital income as a share of overall income — that is, an increase in profits per dollar of output. As it turns out, *the Committee on Recent Economic Changes of the President's Conference on Unemployment* examined this very question — that is,

---

[24]The theoretical concept of balance is also found in the period electrical engineering literature and refers to the demand and supply of electrical power.

[25]Herbert Hoover, Walter F. Brown, Renick W. Dunlap, William Green, Julius Klein, John S. Lawrence, Max Mason, George McFadden, Adolph C. Miller, Lewis E. Pierson, John J. Raskob, Arch W. Shaw, Louis J. Taber, Daniel Willard, Clarence M. Woolley, Owen D. Young, and Edward Eyre Hunt.

Table 4.16.   Electric Unit Drive and Employment: 1923–1925

	Percent change in horsepower per establishment					
	Decrease	**Decrease**	**Increase**	**Increase**	**Increase**	**Increase**
Percent change in wage earners per establishment	20–40 percent	0–20 percent	0–20 percent	20–40 percent	40–60 percent	60–80 percent
Decrease						
20–40 percent	4	12	8	1		
0–20 percent	8	49	66	15	7	
Increase						
0–20 percent	5	12	54	25	5	7
20–40 percent		2	5	10	1	1
40–60 percent		1	2	1		1

the relationship between electric unit drive-based investment and employment in the 1920s. Specifically, in a report prepared by Willard Thorp of the *National Bureau of Economic Research*, data for 302 industries from 1923 to 1925 were used to test what at the time was the commonly held view that electric unit drive-based investment was worker decreasing — that is, the more an industry converted to the new power drive technology, the lower would be the level of employment.

Table 4.16 presents his findings. Of the 302 industries studied, employment decreased in 170 which is astonishing given that GDP growth rates throughout the 1920s varied from 4 to 5.2 percent.[26] Of these, 97 industries reported an increase in horsepower per establishment while 73 reported a decrease. Of the 132 that reported an increase in employment, the majority saw horsepower increase by considerably more than employment. For example, in 25 industries, horsepower increased by 20–40 percent while employment increased by 0–20 percent.

A number of remarks are in order. First, these results can be misleading given the nature of the new power drive technology. For example, it appears somewhat incongruous that in the 1920s, a period of robust growth, 49 industries would have reported a decrease in both horsepower

---

[26]U.S. Department of Commerce (1975, p. F31).

and employment. In fact, it may have well been the case that the conversion to electric unit drive witnessed a decrease in overall horsepower as smaller motors may have replaced larger ones (driving belts and shafts) whose rated horsepower (potential) had never been fully utilized. As Devine (1983) pointed out: "Unit drive used less energy than group drive for the same reasons that group drive used less energy than line-shaft drive" (Devine, 1983, p. 30). Another anomaly, according to LaVerne Beales of the U.S. Census Bureau was related to the conversion from steam engines to steam turbines, specifically "The lower efficiency of the steam engine and the belt system which usually accompanies it, when compared to the steam turbine used to drive an electric generator, is so considerable that the rated horsepower necessary to do the same work is greater in the first than in the second case" (p. 175). Or, it could well be the case that in some of these industries, larger more-productive electric unit drive-driven firms' market share increased at the expense of smaller firms (and even crowded them out) and that as a result overall horsepower actually decreased, but energy consumption (i.e., kwh) actually increased. Dexter Kimball, in Chapter II of the *Report on Recent Economic Changes,* pointed out:

> An important element in the increase in output has been the rapid abandonment of inefficient plants. In a recent survey of the merchant blast furnace industry, it is reported that of the 37 plants furnishing data for the prewar years 1911–1914, 15 were both hand filled and sand cast, while 34 were both mechanically filled and machine case. But in 1926, out of 49 plants furnishing data, only three were both hand filled and sand cast, while 34 were both mechanically filled and machine cast. p. 82.

4.3.5.1 *Acceleration, rationalization and profits*

As pointed out earlier, adopting electric unit drive was a profit-increasing strategy regardless of market conditions. Accelerating machine processes reduced unit variable costs per unit and thus increased profits and profitability. At the aggregate level, the conversion to electric unit drive reduced labor's share of income, and increased that of capital.

Data on the functional distribution of income in the 1920s is provided in Table 4.17 where we see that labor's share as measured by the ratio of

Table 4.17.   Value-Added and Wages: U.S. Manufacturing (Million)

Year	Value-Added	Wages	Wages/Value-Added
1914	9,386	3,782	0.4029
1919	23,842	9,664	0.4053
1921	17,253	7,451	0.4318
1923	24,570	10,149	0.4130
1925	25,668	9,980	0.3888
1927	26,325	10,100	0.3836
1929	30,591	10,885	0.3558

Source: U.S. Department of Commerce (1975, pp. 9, 10, 666).

wage income in manufacturing to value-added from 1921 to 1929 declined from 0.431 to 0.355 in 1929, a decline of 18 percent.

4.3.6 *Evidence from the popular press*

Acceleration-based increases in rated productive capacity presented and continue to present a challenge to statisticians and policymakers alike, owing in large measure to their non-material, invisible and abstract nature. Converting to electric unit drive increased a machine/tool's rated capacity. However, until the accelerated machine/tool in question actually operates at this new, higher capacity, there is no way of accurately estimating the actual increase. That being said, there is every reason to believe that the question of growing excess rated capacity would nonetheless have perco-lated into the public sphere, via news reports (radio and newspapers). In this section, anecdotal evidence of the growing presence of excess capac-ity in the public eye in the 1920s is presented in the form of keyword analysis. More specifically, keyword searches in two broad categories (excess capacity and wages) were conducted using The *New York Times* from 1901 to 1930.

4.3.6.1 *Excess capacity*

A total of eight keyword (combination of keywords) searches were con-ducted for six five-year time intervals, notably 1901–1905, 1906–1910,

1911–1915, 1916–1920, 1921–1925 and 1926–1930, using the *ProQuest Search Instrument*. The excess capacity-related keywords and keyword combinations in question were "Excess Capacity," "Over-Production," "Overinvestment," and "Mass Production, Unemployment," and "Electricity, Unemployment." The null hypothesis in this case is that the mid-to-late 1920s were no different from the 1900s, 1910s and early 1920s.

The results presented in Table 4.18 show a sharp increase in the use of the eight keywords and keyword combinations in the 1920s, especially in the period 1926–1930. For example, the use of the keyword "Over-Production" increased to 251 in 1926–1930. Similarly, the use of the keyword "Excess Capacity" went from one in the early 1900s to 36 from 1926 to 1930. While there are obvious limits to this type of analysis, the evidence appears to reject the null hypothesis in favor of the alternative, namely the presence of excess capacity. Put differently, the evidence from the popular press indicates that the U.S. economy in the late 1920s found itself increasingly in a state of generalized excess capacity. A good example is the following editorial excerpt from the November 9, 1930 edition of *The Washington Post*, titled "Cause of the Crash."

> Out of many diagnoses of the business depression economist have arrived at the conclusion that the country overproduced in the years immediately preceding the crash more goods than the public could consume with its limited buying power. The resultant surplus became a drug

Table 4.18.   The *New York Times*-Based Historical Keyword Survey Results 1900–1930

Keyword	1901–1905	1906–1910	1911–1915	1916–1920	1921–1925	1926–1930
Excess capacity	1	1	3	5	13	36
Over-production	33	21	32	35	100	251
Overinvestment	2	4	6	5	6	17
Low wage	3	9	24	13	40	76
Fair wage	13	11	22	44	45	40
Mass production, unemployment	0	0	0	0	7	108
Electricity, unemployment	0	0	11	8	32	101

on the market and it was necessary to curtail production while the slack was being taken up.

Until now, this has been mere theory. But the figures that have just been worked out by the Census Bureau sustain the theory beyond doubt. The fact that there was overproduction can no longer be questioned. But why did a surplus of goods bring hard times when thousands of people are in need of more clothes, better food, and more substantial houses, as well as the conveniences and luxuries of life?

The reason reaches far back into history. In 1849, according to the figures of the Census Bureau, the manufacturing industries of the United States produced goods valued at approximately $1,000,000,000 and $236,755,000 in wages. Since that time both wages and the value of products have increased enormously. In 1929 the output of manufacturing industries reached the highest point in history. Goods turns out by American plants were valued at $68,000,000,000. Had industries paid the same proportion of this return in wages as it did in 1849, wage earners would have received an aggregate of $16,000,000,000. Instead, they were paid $11,271,116,000.

In these figures lies the story of the industrial depression. While goods were being turned out at a pace never before equaled in history, the buying power of the public was making small gains.

4.3.7 *The Wage question*

The second keyword search focused on the question of wages, specifically on the extent to which wages were seen as being too low in the public eye given rising productivity and growing excess capacity? After all, most workers understood the notion of balance — or equilibrium — as expressed in Equation (4.8), namely that increasing productivity requires greater income and expenditure in order that balance be maintained. Given the growing perception that the "system" was out of balance, to what extent were wages and wage income seen to be the cause in the popular press? To answer this question, a second keyword search was conducted in The *New York Times* for "Low Wage" and "Fair Wage." The null hypothesis was that references to both keywords would be independent of the time interval. The results are presented in Table 4.18 where the number of references to "Low Wage" increased markedly in the 1920s, while the number of references to "Fair Wage" jumps (doubled) beginning in the late 1910s.

4.3.7.1 *Income inertia and the creation of the NBER and the Brookings Institution*

While the profession continued, for the most part, to adhere to Say's Law and hence deny the very existence of excess rated capacity, or insufficient income and expenditure, doubt continued to grow throughout the 1910s and 1920s. So much so that by the 1930s, two research organizations (a.k.a. think tanks) had been created with the explicit purpose of inquiring into the national accounts, specifically into the question of balance (see Table 4.19). The first was the National Bureau of Economic Research, founded in 1920 with the explicit mandate of examining the distribution of income.[27] More specifically, of examining the breakdown of income between what Malcolm Rorty referred to as services and property income. At the time, University of Pennsylvania economics professor Scott Nearing contended, on the basis of the available data, that the split was 50–50. Rorty, on the other hand, argued that it was 66–33. Increasing property income, it was believed, was seen as a source of macroeconomic imbalance. As it turned out, this debate would lead to the creation of the NBER.

While not explicit in the writings of both Nearing and Rorty, technological change lay at the very heart of the debate, specifically electric unit

Table 4.19. NBER and Brookings Institution: Early Publications

NBER	Brookings Institution
New Yorkers Receive One-Eight of Nation's Income (News Bulletin, August 1922)	America's Capacity to Produce 1936
Income in the United States, Vol. I	America's Capacity to Consume 1934
Income in the United States, Vol. II	Income and Economic Progress: Division of Income 1935
Distribution of Income by States in 1919	The Formation of Capital 1935
Unemployment and the Business Cycle	
Employment, Hours and Earnings in the United States, 1920–1922	
Four-Fifths of Net Value Product of Industry Goes to Employees for Services (December 1922)	

Sources: NBER, https://www.test.nber.org: Brookings Institution, Library Catalogue.

---

[27]https://www.nber.org/about-nber/history.

drive-based acceleration or the greater use of power in U.S. industry. As argued above, an increase in $s(t)$, *ceteris paribus*, resulted in a decrease in $h(t)$ and, consequently, a decrease in labor's share (Nearing's position). It should be noted that a good part of the research conducted by and for President Hoover's *Committee on Recent Economic Changes*, referred to earlier, was carried out under the auspices of the National Bureau of Economic Research, including the pathbreaking work on electric unit drive.

The Brookings Institution, like the NBER, also had its origins in the disequilibrium brought about by the introduction of a new power drive technology. Its founder and president, Robert S. Brookings, a merchant by profession, had written extensively on the widening output gap. In his 1932 book, *The Way Forward*, he focused on the source of imbalance in the post-WWI period, concluding that:

> Experience has unquestionably proved that the efficiency of the individual is stimulated by his self interest as it can be in no other way. And that no economic theory that ignores this can hope for ultimate success. On the other hand, the unequal distribution of wealth under what is known as the capitalistic system makes it clear that radical readjustment is essential, both ethically, to satisfy the just criticism of the workers, and economically, to bring about a more equitable distribution of wealth, making possible increased mass consumption and so nearly balancing out improved system of production (Brookings, 1932, p. 72).

Interestingly, this quote summarizes each of the elements of the analysis provided throughout this chapter, namely technological change, imbalance and the need to increase income and expenditure.

4.4 Clarification: The Problem Was Not with the Functional Distribution of Income, but with the Overall Level of Income

By the late 1920s, most critics held that the problem facing the nation was with the fact that the ratio of profit to overall income had increased, a fact reflected in the titles of both the NBER and Brookings Institution. However, as the analysis presented in this chapter has shown, this was not the true underlying problem, but rather the effect or consequence of the failure of overall income to increase in step with productive capacity, a condition one could refer to as under-income. For example, as shown, because wages (or income) did not increase commensurately with productivity (increased $s(t)$), this led to a decrease in $h(t)$ and an increase in profit income — at least in the short run. It is important not to confuse the two as one is the cause (income and expenditure failing to increase commensurately), while the other is the effect. The key to restoring balance, it therefore follows, lies in increasing the overall level of income, not in increasing wages as a percentage of income.

4.5 Summary and Conclusions

This chapter has examined what the *Report of the Committee on Recent Economic Changes of the President's Conference on Unemployment* referred to as the acceleration-based structural change that characterized the U.S. economy in the 1920s, both at the individual firm level and at the aggregate macroeconomic level. Specifically, a model of acceleration at the individual plant/firm level and at the macroeconomic level was developed. In keeping with the laws of kinetics, acceleration at the plant level was achieved by increasing the use of power/force per period of time. In short, machine speed and, hence, productivity increased at a rate of the square root of the growth in power usage. This result was then incorporated into a macroeconomic model, one that explicitly accounted for aggregate machine speed and one whose predictions will be used throughout the following chapters, one that describes the Roaring Twenties, the downturn, as well as the slow recovery.

Estimates of the technology shock that was the adoption of electric unit drive were provided, as well as evidence of a worsening imbalance, manifesting itself in terms of rising unemployment.

Appendix: Economic Balance as Seen by President Hoover's Committee on Recent Economic Changes

The following excerpt is taken from Section III of the Introduction to the *Report of the Committee on Recent Economic Changes of the President's Conference on Unemployment*, prepared in large part by members of the National Bureau of Economic Research.

> Many influences have been at work during the period covered by the survey, welding the people of the United States into a new solidarity of

thought and act ion. The telephone and telegraph, the automobile, the radio, and the railroads form lines of communication which have brought together East and' West, South and North.

Other and less tangible influences reaching back farther into the past, but accelerated and strengthened by the experiences of the World War, have also contributed to our solidarity. Economic reorganization, the cooperation of business leaders, economic experts, and the Government: the general spread of information: the growth of trade associations: the cooperation of labor to increase productivity: the restriction of immigration-all of these have grown in importance in peace after their stimulation by the war.

Making for solidarity has been popular education which has increased amazingly. We are spending two and one-half billions of dollars each year on public and private education-an increase of 250 percent in a decade. Expenditures for free college and university education have increased nearly 350 percent in little more than 10 years.

And there is another factor which has contributed to the welding process, and to the economic advancement of the nation: The broadening influence of America's creative minds — the minds of the leader: in Government and in education, in research, in management and in labor, in the press, and in the professions. To their influence we have come to look in large measure for the maintenance of our economic balance.

While ours has been a period of great economic activity and industrial productivity, and of a degree of economic stability which must be rated as high ·when we consider the readjustments in every department of economic life made necessary by the postwar crisis and by the transition from war economy to peace economy, and while America has a promising future, the outstanding fact which is illuminated by this survey is that we cannot maintain our economic advantage, or hope fully to realize on our economic future, unless we consciously accept the principle of equilibrium and apply it skillfully in every economic relation.

The forces that bear upon our economic relationships have always been sensitive. All parts of our economic structure from the prime processes of making and of marketing to the facilitating functions of finance, are and have been interdependent and easily affected. And therein lies the danger: That through ignorance of economic principles, or through selfish greed, or inadequate leadership, the steady balance will be disturbed, to our economic detriment.

If natural resources, especially the land, arc wastefully used: if money in quantity is taken out of production and employed for speculation: if any group develops a method of artificial price advancement which puts one commodity out of balance with other commodities: if either management or labor disregards the common interest-to this extent equilibrium will be destroyed, and destroyed for all.

To maintain the dynamic equilibrium of recent years is, indeed, a problem of leadership which more and more demands deliberate public attention and control. Research and study, the orderly classification of knowledge, joined to increasing skill,' well may make complete control of the economic system a possibility. The problems are many and difficult, but the degree of progress in recent years inspires us with high hopes.

In the marked balance of consumption and production, for example, the control of the economic organism is increasingly evident. With the development of a stream of credit to facilitate business operations, and with flexible power to energize industry and to increase the effectiveness of the workers, has come an increasing evenness in the flow of production. Once an intermittent starting and stopping of production-consumption was characteristic of the economic situation. It was jerky and unpredictable, and overproduction was followed by a pause for consumption to catch up. For the seven years under survey, a more marked balance of production-consumption is evident.

With greater knowledge of consuming habits, with more accurate records of the goods consumed, a sensitive contact has been established between the factors of production and consumption which formerly were so often out of balance.

Where pools of goods once were accumulated by the manufacturer, the wholesaler, the jobber, and the retailer: where high inventories once meant distress, shutdowns, failures, and unemployment whenever the demand subsided, there is now a more even flow from producer to consumer.

Increasing skill and scientific data have made the anticipation of demand far more accurate, and by accurate anticipation the deliberate balance between production and consumption has in a measure been maintained. By advertising and other promotional devices, by scientific fact finding, by a carefully predeveloped consumption, a measurable pull on production has been created which releases capital otherwise tied up in immobile goods and furthers the organic balance of economic forces. In many cases the rate of production-consumption seems to be fairly well under control.

To maintain this balance, and to extend it into fields which are not now in balance with the more prosperous elements of the nation, is clearly an important problem of leadership. With certain natural resources still wastefully exploited, with great industries, such as agriculture and coal mining, still below the general level of prosperity, with certain regions retarded, there remains much to do. To bring these more fully into the stream of successful economic forces is a problem of the first order.

Our complex and intricate economic machine can produce, but to keep it producing continuously it must be maintained in balance. During the past few years equilibrium has been fairly ·well maintained. We have not wasted the hours of labor by strikes or lockouts. Until recently we have not diverted savings from productive business to speculation. There has been balance between the economic forces not perfect balance, but a degree of balance which has enabled the intricate machine to produce and to serve our people.

As long as the appetite for goods and services is practically insatiable, as it appears to be, and as long as productivity can be consistently increased, it would seem that we can go on ·with increasing activity. But we can do this only if we develop a technique of balance. Toward such a technique the committee believes the skillful work of the economists, engineers, and statisticians who prepared the survey on which we have based the facts and interpretations expressed in this brief report, will contribute. Our effort has been to suggest a pattern by which their work may be appraised: to set up an orderly plan by which the facts may be articulated and against which later and better information may be more accurately judged. We recommend a study of the fact-finding survey as a whole to all who are faced with the problems of business administration and public leadership.[14]

Informed leadership is vital to the maintenance of equilibrium. It depends upon a general knowledge of the relations of the parts each to the other. Only through incessant observation and adjustment of our economy, can we learn to maintain the economic balance.[15]

Underlying recent developments is an attitude of mind which seems to be characteristically American. Our nation is accustomed to rapid movement, to quick shifts in status: it is receptive to new ideas, ingenious in devices, adaptable. Our economy is in large measure the embodiment of those who have made it.

Our situation is fortunate, our momentum is remarkable. Yet the organic balance of our economic structure can be maintained only by hard, persistent, intelligent effort: by consideration and sympathy: by mutual confidence, and by a disposition in the several human parts to work in harmony together.

Addendum

What stands out in this excerpt taken from the committee's report is the preoccupation with the question of balance or equilibrium. While not mentioned by name, the problem, according to the committee, is excess rated capacity, itself the result of technological change. The takeaway, from a policy point of view, is as diverse as it is interesting. Instead of approaching the question from a macro point of view, it focuses on the set of measures that could be deployed at the micro or industry level. In short, more information, more planning and more leadership are the keys to solving the problem of excess capacity. No mention is made of purchasing power, of wages, of the failure of wages in general to increase commensurately with productivity.

Chapter 5

The Smoot–Hawley Tariff Bill: The Republican Party Responds to Growing Excess Capacity*

The fact remains that the field of industry as a whole has made marked advances during the last decade, and the productivity per worker in most industries has been advanced markedly. Never before has the human race made such progress in solving the problem of production. If poverty and industrial distress still exist, it is because of our inability to keep our industrial machinery in operation and to distribute equitably the resulting products. It is not sufficient to be able to produce abundantly, we must also be able to distribute intelligently.

Dexter Kimball (1929, p. 82).

5.1 Introduction

As it turned out, the *Report of the Committee on Recent Economic Changes of the President's Conference on Unemployment* was not the first

---

*This chapter draws from Beaudreau, Bernard C. Electrification, Tractorization and Motorization: Revisiting the Smoot–Hawley Tariff Act, *Journal of Economic Issues*, 48(4), December 2014, 1039–1071 and Beaudreau, Bernard C. Reexamining the Origins of the Smoot–Hawley Tariff Act, *Research in Economic History*, 33, 2017, 1–18.

official reference to the relationship between rising unemployment and acceleration. Senator Reed Smoot of Utah, Chair of the *Senate Finance Committee*, attributed growing unemployment in 1927 to mass production as well as to rising imports.

> Senator Smoot insisted that the picture drawn by the Democrats on Monday, when the Senate passed the Senate resolution, was much over-drawn. He admitted that some unemployment existed, but insisted that it did not compare with that of 1920 and 1921 when the Republicans came into power after eight years of Democratic administration. As for one reason for a degree of unemployment, Senator Smoot referred to large importations of foreign merchandise that have been steadily reaching American shores in spite of the Republican protective tariff ... These imports have a tendency to supplant large quantities of American goods, despite the tariff, thus slowing down many American industries. There also was an over-supply or over-production in many lines, Senator Smoot contended, and over-production or under-consumption in the textiles industries. A slow-down of many industries helps to increase industrial unemployment, and the result is immediately felt in the lowering of the consuming power of the wage earners. This has brought about what may be called an oversupply or overproduction existing in many lines: and we might add that mass production has cut a great figure in the amount of production in the United States in special lines (*New York Times*, March 8, 1928, p. 1).

Fast forward to the 1928 Republican National Convention of June 11–13 in Kansas City, Missouri, where party officials outlined an ambitious plan to raise tariffs again. It bears noting that the 1922 Fordney–McCumber Tariff Act had literally doubled tariffs on manufac-tures. Surprisingly, however, the impetus in 1928 was not rising imports as Smoot had contended earlier in the Senate, but rather the economy-wide, acceleration-based increase in rated productive capacity identified by Hoover's 1929 Committee — what he referred to as mass production. Speaker after speaker at the convention extolled the virtues of the changes that had been brought upon U.S. industry, referring to it using a series of superlatives. Chief among these were notions such as increased efficiency and the role of the domestic market. For example, Secretary of Labor, John J. Davis, highlighted the successes and impending dangers facing U.S. industry.

Summing it all up, the protective tariff, limited immigration, exclusion of child labor, general watchfulness of women in industry, the eight-hour day, collective bargaining coupled with conciliation and arbitration of injunction, are the important things in which the American laboring man is very much interested. Industrial competition among the countries of the world has caused fundamental changes in American industry that have vastly increased output and at the same time, relatively decreased the cost of production in practically all lines of endeavor. Thus, in meeting the competition from countries where lower standards of living obtain, the mechanization of industry has been brought about a practical industrial revolution in our country. The American workers are the highest paid in the world: the American standard of living surpasses that of any country: but even with this enviable record of progress, the mechanization of industry and the development of rapid power machinery processes have displaced many veteran workers and others, necessitating their engaging in other activities. To maintain high wages, it is absolutely necessary to have a high protective tariff, a tariff that protects (*Washington Post*, June 12, 1928, p. 4).

The Party's thinking was as simple as it was convoluted: higher prohibitive tariffs would, by reducing imports, free-up room in the domestic market to accommodate the country's capacity-laden firms. Not only would this firm up a weakening labor market (i.e., declining $h(t)$), it would be beneficial to both worker and farmer by lowering costs and ultimately prices. In short, acceleration-based increases in efficiency would translate into lower product prices on the shelves, thus raising real income for all Americans.

This chapter chronicles the Republican Party's attempt at closing what was a widening output gap, an attempt that was inspired by decades of tariff bills aimed at both industrializing the nation (via import substitution) as well as financing government, and an attempt that would send ripples throughout the U.S. and world economies. The story begins in Kansas City where generalized tariffs hikes were the cornerstone of the electoral platform.

5.2 U.S. Exports and Imports in the 1920s

Table 5.1 presents U.S. manufacturing and food exports and imports from 1920 to 1930. Both exports and imports increased throughout the decade,

Table 5.1.   U.S. Exports and Imports 1920–1930

Year	Exports	Imports	Exports-Man	Imports-Man	Exports-Agr.	Imports-Agr.
1920	8,080	5,278	3,205	877	1,117	1,238
1921	4,379	2,509	1,627	620	685	368
1922	3,765	3,113	1,292	663	588	387
1923	4,091	3,792	1,478	771	583	530
1924	4,498	3,610	1,588	749	573	522
1925	4,819	4,227	1,843	796	574	433
1926	4,712	4,431	1,957	877	503	418
1927	4,759	4,185	1,982	879	463	451
1928	5,030	4,091	2,260	906	466	406
1929	5,157	4,399	2,532	994	484	424
1930	3,781	3,061	1,898	757	363	293

Source: U.S. Department of Commerce (1975), Series U190, U193.

which is consistent with the robust economic growth of the Roaring Twenties. Referring to Columns 2 and 3, we see that contrary to the official Party view, net exports were increasing from 1926 on, in general, in manufacturing and agriculture.

This raises a number of questions, notably why did Senator Reed Smoot of Utah, chair of the Senate Finance Committee, attribute growing unemployment and generalized weakness in the labor market to growing imports? After all, if anything, trade in general and net exports in particular were on the rise, strengthening not weakening employment. Was this a political strawman? The answer to these questions would come in Kansas City, where the Party would hold its National Convention in 1928.

5.3 The 1928 Kansas City National Republican Convention: The Tariff-Based Solution

By late May, early June 1928, the Republican Party had formulated its response to weakening labor markets, namely another major upward tariff revision, a mere six years after the prohibitive Fordney–McCumber Tariff Act of 1922. Tariffs on manufactures and agricultural products would once again increase.

Figure 5.1.   The Republican National Convention Kansas City, Missouri, June 11–13, 1928

The tariff platform was unveiled at the Republican National Convention, held from June 11 to 13 in Kansas City, Missouri, where the mood was upbeat, the optimism palatable (see Figure 5.1). Changes to the U.S. economy offered unlimited potential and the Republican Party was committed to seeing that it would be realized. One after the other, Party officials took to the podium to extol the virtues of protection against a backdrop of literally exploding potential (see Table 5.2). The proposed upward tariff revision would do two things, namely make more room for U.S. products in the domestic market and, second, allow firms to produce at full capacity, thus leading to lower costs and prices. Consider the following remarks by the Party's president, Republican Charles E. Hughes, in the days before the 1928 Republican Kansas City convention:

I shall not review at any length the results of the Republican tariff policy. Mr. Hoover did that in his speech at Boston. Let me recall to you what he said. Every argument urged by our opponents against the increased duties in the Republican tariff act has been refuted by actual experience. It was contended that our costs of production would increase. Their prophecy was wrong for our costs have decreased. They urged that the duties which we proposed would increase the price of manufactured goods: yet prices have steadily decreased. It was urged that, by removing the pressure of competition of foreign goods, our industry would fall in efficiency. The answer to that is found in our vastly increased production per man in every branch of industry, which indeed is the envy of our competitors (*New York Times*, October 24, 1928).

The key here is the last sentence where he invokes the "vastly increased production per man in every branch of industry." Put differently,

Table 5.2.   Kansas City Republican Party Tariff Positions

Joseph R. Grundy, President of the Pennsylvania Manufacturers Association	We therefore advocate a general revision of the tariff upward, that every section of the country with all labor in every industry and business may reap the benefit and enjoy profitable prosperity (*New York Times*, June 11, 1928, p. 1).
James J. Davis, Secretary of Labor	An utmost economic call for increased duties and that the present unemployment was due to low tariff schedules which permit cheaply made goods to come in and cripple American industry (*New York Times*, June 11, 1928, p. 1).
William M. Butler, Chairman of the Republican National Committee	"… has favored revision of the tariff for some time and while he is not impressing his personality on the platform drafters, it is believed that his views and those of others in the East will be taken into consideration. The compromise suggestion that the farm group offered for increased duties on farm-products and the decreasing of the free list has been met by the manufacturing interests with a willingness to cooperate with the farmers provided the industrial schedules are also considered favorably" (*New York Times*, June 11, 1928, p. 1).
S.D. Fess, Senator from Ohio	Even should the convention decide that there should not be a general revision of the tariff favored in the platform, any tinkering with the tariff, such as the change in the farm schedules, inevitably would lead to a general revision.
George H. Moses, Permanent Chairman of the Republican National Conference	In seeking for an economic policy for the United States, we know that our people of the Republican National Conference will not turn to the party which clings to the fetish of free trade. In seeking for a policy to make the tariff effective for every interest in the United States, we know our people will not turn to the party whose strength and weakness alike lie in its sectional character (Congressional Record, May 29, 1928, p. 10624).

Figure 5.2. Joseph R. Grundy, President of the Pennsylvania Manufacturers Association and Republican Senator

higher tariffs, by increasing domestic firms' market share, would bring down costs as firms increased output. In other words, greater domestic market share (i.e., fewer imports) would lower costs and ultimately, prices.

5.4 The Captains of Industry, Acceleration and Tariffs

Calls for higher tariffs on manufactures came in large measure from the industrialized North–East. Leading the charge was Joseph A. Grundy, President of the Pennsylvania Manufactures Association and a long-time Republican who played an instrumental role in Hoover's victory at the 1928 Republican National Convention in Kansas City (see Figure 5.2). According to historian Harold U. Faulkner: "The Smoot–Hawley Tariff was an administrative measure put through the party machine and no single person was more active than Joseph R. Grundy, president of The Pennsylvania Manufacturers Association, who became Senator in December 1929" (Faulkner, 1950, p. 342). His political agenda was limited to one item: a general upward tariff revision including manufactures.

Unfortunately, there is no known record of the rate hikes he had in mind. Were they to rise by 10 percent, 20 percent or 100 percent? What is known, however, is that when the Hawley Tariff Bill was put before the House in early 1998, Grundy was unhappy with the proposed rate revisions. The *New York Times* reported:

> The dissatisfaction in highly protected industry because the bill does not increase rates on manufactured products is apparent from a statement of Joseph R. Grundy, president of the Pennsylvania Manufacturers' Association. Mr. Grundy had an interview with President Hoover not long ago, and while he would not comment on what took place behind the doors of the President's office, the impression was created that he had yielded to Mr. Hoover's desire that he should not insist on higher duties on industrial products than the bill was then expected to provide. Today Mr. Grundy said: "The few rises that are in the bill fall short of meeting the requirements, which the past seven years of Pennsylvania's industries show, along the lines indicated in the Republican platform adopted at Kansas City" (*New York Times*, May 9, 1929).

Whether he like other Pennsylvania Republicans was satisfied with the final tariff revisions in the Hawley Tariff Bill is unknown. The record shows however that in the final stages of the Senate debate over the Smoot–Hawley Tariff Bill (i.e., in October 1929), he strongly supported the administration's tariff initiative. On October 29, 1929, with the proposed Smoot–Hawley Tariff Bill on what appeared to be its last leg, he called on the Senate to "silence the West," in reference to the Insurgent Republican senators who had broken party ranks and teamed up with the Democrats with the intention of lowering tariffs on manufactures.

Other leading tariff protagonists included Pennsylvania Governor John S. Fisher and Samuel M. Vauclain, president of the Baldwin Locomotive Works of Philadelphia. On September 5, 1929, in a meeting with President Hoover, Fisher expressed his concerns over increasing pressure to amend the tariff bill.

> Earlier in the day President Hoover heard Representative Albert Johnson of Washington vigorously oppose the Senate Tariff bill, while two others, Governor Fisher of Pennsylvania and John E. Edgerton of New York, president of the National Manufactures Association, voiced protests against administrative features of the bill. Governor Fisher said that the American valuation plan was essential to a sound tariff bill and that protection could not be given to one group alone, but must be extended

to the entire country. "During the campaign we preached protection for the East, West and all parts of the country," Governor Fisher said. "We in Pennsylvania are for a tariff that will afford protection for all of our industries. We expect agricultural protection, but we are not going to stand for recognition of any section to the disadvantage of another" (*New York Times*, September 6, 1929).

In his January 1928 address to *The Chicago Association of Credit Men*, Vauclain pointed out that high wages and high tariffs were essential for the preservation of prosperity in America.

Wages should not be governed solely by supply and demand, he asserted, but should be placed at a level which would enable workers to buy the necessities of life. It is the wage-earner who constitutes the great majority of our population, he said. These people are the spenders of the nation and upon their ability to spend freely the general business of our country depends. Foreign importations should be avoided by all, he said. We may profit individually by buying foreign goods at less than American manufacturers can produce, but the injurious consequences to general business more than offset the selfish gain, he declares. A protective tariff is necessary if we are to have full dinner pails for our boys during 1928 and the years to come, he insisted (*New York Times*, January 24, 1928).

These remarks mirrored the state of industry in Pennsylvania and throughout U.S. economy in the 1910s and 1920s: increasingly productive but constrained on product markets. The conversion to electric unit drive had radically increased potential GDP: insufficient markets (income and demand), however, prevented it from realizing this potential, a point made by Senator Smoot in the 1932 Senate campaign.

On his return to Utah in August 1932, in preparation for his final battle in political life, Smoot advised his people that it had been the common attitude in 1930 to attribute the depression to unwise governmental policies, with the Smoot–Hawley Act specified. Lest there were some obsessed with heresy, he declared, "To hold the American tariff policy, or any other policy of our government, responsible for this gigantic deflationary move is only to display one's ignorance of its sweeping universal character." He found that "The world is paying for its ruthless destruction of life and property in the World War and for its failure to adjust purchasing power to productive capacity during the industrial revolution of the decade following the war" (Merrill, 1990, p. 340).

5.5 Pennsylvania Republicans, Giant Power and Acceleration

While often disparaged in the literature as being parochial in their dealings, Joseph R. Grundy and other leading Republicans and members of the Pennsylvania Manufactures Association were anything but. Rather, the record shows that they were, in many ways, on the vanguard of the industrial revolution then under way in U.S. manufacturing, having been involved in the electrical utilities sector. Grundy, for example, had invested heavily in Pennsylvania Governor Gifford Pinchot's Giant Power project which called for the building of extremely large interconnected, steam-powered electricity-generating stations, rural electrification, trunk line railroad electrification and lower rates for all.[1] In short, Pennsylvanian manufacturers were on the vanguard of a new era, an electrified era. The only cloud on the horizon was the lack of buyers.

5.6 Obstacles on the Road to Closing the Widening Output Gap

While the leaders of the Party were steadfast in their belief that higher tariffs would solve the problem at hand and in the process lower prices, the rest of America saw things differently. The dominant view was that higher tariffs on manufactures would invariably increase prices, thus lowering the level of real income and welfare. Nowhere was this view more true than in rural America which was suffering from chronic low commodity prices. In fact, in early 1928, Senator William McMaster of South Dakota had introduced a resolution in the Senate calling for lower tariffs on manufactures as a means of increasing real farm income, the idea being that this would increase competition and lower the cost of farm inputs and manufactures, thus increasing farmers' real income. In fact, at the

---

[1] For more on Giant Power, see Hughes (1976).

Kansas City Convention, a group of disgruntled farmers had staged a protest, calling for measures that would benefit the farming community. This presented a formidable challenge to the Party's executive, namely increase tariffs on manufactures at a time when the nation's farmers, economists and journalists, not to mention the opposition Democrats, called for across-the-board decreases. Clearly, an electoral platform that called for a doubling of tariffs on manufactures could potentially spell trouble in the then upcoming November elections.

The solution: publicly announce a limited tariff bill with an emphasis on the farmer, all the while harboring the firm intention of increasing tariffs on manufactures as well. The beauty of the plan lay in the details. By not specifying which tariffs would increase, it was non-committal. As such, it was not misleading as according to the Party's new thinking on tariffs, higher tariffs on manufactures would benefit the farmer by lowering prices. The Party rallied around its new electoral platform. Midwestern Republicans, including those that had sponsored both the Haugen–McNary Bill which called for subsidies to farmers, and the McMaster Resolution, came on-board. The 1928 electoral campaign was a resounding success as the Party won the House, the Senate and the White House. As such, a new, limited tariff bill would be in the offing.

As it turned out, the 1928 election campaign was a masterful display of electoral doublespeak. The pro-tariff manufacturing wing of the party was hidden from sight. Leading figures such as Joseph R. Grundy of Pennsylvania were not heard from throughout the campaign as were other tariff zealots. In the end, voters were convinced that the proposed tariff revision would be limited to agriculture.

That farmers and their representatives swallowed the bait, hook, line and sinker, remains somewhat a mystery.[2] After all, it was well understood at the time that higher tariffs on agricultural products would do little to help farmers as the U.S. was a net exporter. In fact, it imported virtually no cereals and foodstuffs. Higher tariffs would, as such, have no effect on farmer income. Was it the fear of a repeat of 1912, when the Progressive wing of the party under Theodore Roosevelt split with the party to form the Progressive Party, which ultimately split the Republican vote, thus giving Woodrow Wilson the White House? This, however, was not the end

---

[2]Some have suggested that the Haugen–McNary proposal of bounties (subsidies) was still being considered by the leaders of the Party.

of the story as the progressive wing of the Party would come back to haunt Smoot and Grundy.

5.7 Hearings Before the Ways and Means Committee: The Cat's Out of the Bag

Encouraged by their victory at the polls, the Republican Party turned its attention to the task at hand, namely revising the tariff schedule. In January–February 1929, the House Ways and Means Committee, chaired by Oregon Representative Willis Hawley (Rep.), began hearings on the proposed tariff bill. Table 5.3 presents the schedule, complete with the various industry representatives. Lo and behold, the cat was out of the bag: the proposed tariff revision would overwhelmingly focus on industry. Of the 20 days of planned hearings, 19 would involve briefs from the manufacturing sector. While a breach of the promises made on the

Table 5.3. Hearings Before the Committee on the Ways and Means, House of Representatives — Schedule

Schedule	Industry/Sector	Dates
1	Chemicals, Oils and Paints	January 7, 8, 9
2	Earths, Earthenware and Glassware	January 10, 11
3	Metals and Manufactures of	January 14, 15, 16
4	Wood and Manufactures of	January 17, 18
5	Sugar, Molasses and Manufactures of	January 21, 22
6	Tobacco and Manufactures of	January 23
7	Agricultural Products and Provisions	January 24, 25, 28
8	Spirits, Wines and other Beverages	January 29
9	Cotton Manufactures	January 30, 31, February 1
10	Flax, Hemp, Jute and Manufactures of	February 4, 5
11	Wool and Manufactures of	February 6, 7, 8
12	Silk and Silk Goods	February 11, 12
13	Papers and Books	February 13, 14
14	Sundries	February 15, 18, 19
15	Free List	February 20, 21, 22
	Administrative and Miscellaneous	February 25

Figure 5.3.   Representative Willis Hawley and Senator Reed Smoot

campaign trail, it was consistent with those made in Kansas City: tariffs on manufactures would rise and the output gap that had plagued and continued to plague the U.S. economy would be closed as U.S. products would displace imports on the shelves of U.S. merchandisers.

A recurrent and universal theme in most of these briefs was the presence of excess capacity which was attributed to "new machinery" and to "rising imports." For example, the cement industry alleged that Belgian imports were weakening to the point of compromising East-coast producers. Interestingly, the importers of cement presented a brief in which this cast doubt on the picture painted by the industry, pointing out that from 1922 to 1928, mill shipments went from 117,701,216 barrels to 175,455,000 barrels, an increase of 57,753,784 barrels. Imports throughout this period only increased by 604,715 shipments. It concluded by pointing out that "The American manufactures of cement have enjoyed a most wonderful period of development in their industry and cannot fairly or decently claim that the importations of cement have injured them" (U.S. Congressional Record, 1929, p. 63).

The chemical industry was more forthright in their brief, pointing to a need to "ensure command of the home market."

Chemical products are ever changing. New Products take the place of old ones and the element of risk is greater in the chemical than in any other industry. We urge such a tariff on chemical products as will warrant the extension of existing plants, encourage sustained research, permit of payment of the American standard of wages, and at the same time justify the expectation of reasonable profit on the capital investment. The tariff rates must be such as to meet these conditions, thereby ensuring the permanency of this industry (U.S. Congressional Record, 1929, p. 95).

5.8 Representative Willis Hawley Introduces the Bill in the House

On May 9, the Chairman of the Ways and Means Committee and Oregon Representative, Willis Hawley, introduced the bill (H.R. 2667, An Act to provide revenue, to regulate commerce with foreign countries, to encourage the industries of the United States, to protect American labor, and for other purposes) in the House by Representatives (see Figure 5.3). After 45 hours of testimony in January and February, the committee members, dominated by East-Coast industrial interests, proceeded to revise thousands of tariff schedules upwards, much to the dismay of the minority Democrats on the Committee. In total, 900 tariffs on manufactures were revised upwards, compared with 100 on agricultural products. The reaction was swift as Democrats took every opportunity to remind their colleagues of the pledges made in Kansas City to farmers.

As mentioned earlier, the cat was out of the bag: Republicans had, from the outset (i.e., 1927 and 1928), intended to increase tariffs on manufactures in order to close the widening output gap, a gap that was weakening employment as pointed out in the previous chapter. Interestingly, while the Party had draped the tariff plank of its 1928 campaign in the welfare of the American farmer, from this point on, the focus would be on industry, all in the name of the American worker.

Democrats were quick to point this out, referring to the fact that the bill stated objectives were "to provide revenue, to regulate commerce with foreign countries, to encourage the industries of the United States, to protect American labor and for other purposes." This, they reminded the House, marked the first time that a tariff bill sought to protect American labor (i.e., increase $h(t)$).

You have made an important innovation in the bill. In the preamble you add the words "to protect American labor," which have not occurred in any bill I have been able to find in the history of the country. Did the gentleman investigate the question of the constitutionality of the innovation of putting in the words "to protect American labor"? (Congressional Record, 1929, p. 1074).

The ensuing debate revolved around the question of appropriateness, specifically of the need to raise tariffs in industries that were exporting more than they were importing. Throughout the 1920s, the U.S. merchandise trade balance was not only positive, but widening, raising the obvious question of the underlying logic, not to mention the underlying need.

The Republican response can be summarized in terms of the following quote by Senator Watson from Pennsylvania:

I want to bring before the House the fact that we are now producing by mass production, not only in America but all over the world and because of this it is particularly essential that we should now write a tariff law to curtail large importations (Congressional Record, 1929, p. 1115).

In other words, while mass production has contributed to growing unemployment in the U.S., it was likely to worsen as foreign competitors adopted these same techniques, especially given the fact that wages in foreign countries were lower than in the U.S. Hence, higher tariffs were a sort of pre-emptive defense strategy aimed at Europe and Japan, all in the name of the welfare of the U.S. worker.

On May 28, after less than a month of debate, the Bill was put to a vote (yeas and nays). The result was 264 yeas and 147 nays with voting occurring along party lines. While House Democrats had vehemently opposed the Bill, they were not in a position to overturn it. Unlike the Senate where the Republican party was divided (Progressives versus East-Coast Interests), House Republicans were, for the most part, on board.

Interestingly, House Democrats appeared to take solace in the fact that the Bill, as drafted by the Ways and Means Committee, would encounter stiff opposition from Progressive Republicans in the Senate. According to Representative Otis Wingo of Arkansas:

I am glad this farce is going to end at 3 o'clock. The bill is going to be rewritten, as this Cabinet member from Massachusetts, Secretary

Adams, boasted last night. Instead of being written by this House, as the Constitution provides, it will be written in fact in the Senate and in conference, and the time to learn what you are getting will be next fall when the conference report comes in and you will have to vote it up or vote it down, and do not squeal then. You missed your opportunity to have any consideration of this bill in the House when you voted for the gag rule which will bring you to — a vote at 3 o'clock under the leadership of the distinguished gentleman who sits in the chair [Mr. SNELL], of whom the gentleman from Massachusetts who made this speech in Boston last night, evidently, had never heard. He thought only of the distinguished gentle-man who regularly presides over us, the gentleman from Ohio [Mr. LONGWORTH]. I congratulate the gentleman from Ohio, our distinguished Speaker, that the administration recognizes the fact that they have at least got to deal with him, that under his leadership the Speakership once more is clothed with and exercises power. This was the only gratifying thing that I read in this speech of the gentleman from Massachusetts who is a member of the Cabinet (Congressional Record, 1929, p. 2092).

Coincidentally, on the very same day, the House turned its attention to the unemployment problem. Specifically, Representative Pittenger (Rep.) from Minnesota raised the problem of growing unemployment.

Mr. Speaker, I believe that the unemployment problem is a proper subject of legislative inquiry and I feel certain that legislative action will be required to meet it. While agricultural relief and tariff changes may help the situation, such legislation cannot wholly solve the question .... In speaking of the unemployment problem, I refer to a condition brought about in recent years, resulting from the rapid changes in our economic, industrial, and business life .... In the early days, in the development of America, the circle of opportunity was an expanding one. There was the undeveloped West, with free land and fertile prairies for men seeking opportunity. Overcrowded industry, such as it existed in those days, could always find an outlet. Today, there is no such room for freedom, for expansion, for the building of new railroads, and the development of new enterprises and the founding of new cities.

He went on to describe the source of this imbalance/disequilibrium.

Then within a period of time, so brief that we hardly realize it has taken place, the consolidation and concentration of industrial and business establishments, everywhere and in every line, has completely changes our economic structure ..... Hand in hand with the changes that have given us a new structure of society is the displacement of labor in industry by labor-saving machinery and improved methods ..... In 1913, a factory worker would make 500 razor blades. He now turns out 32,000 razor blades in the same length of time. In the bottle-making industry one man who turned out 77 bottles now turns out in the same given time 3,000 bottles (Congressional Record, 1929, p. 2112).

Lastly, he cited an article by Richard T. Jones, district director of the United States Employment Service, at Minneapolis, Minn.

Unemployment is a major problem before the country at this time. It persists in spite of the great social progress made in the last quarter century. The country is showing increasing concern over the displacement of labor by machines. Perhaps the amount of this displacement is exaggerated because the fear has been with us since the first power spinning and weaving were inaugurated. Each of the new major inventions has thrown many men out of work, but has also created an immense amount of new labor. The automobile, for instance, has displaced some 9,000,000 horses and mules, but it has also called forth the enormous petroleum industry, automobile service stations, oil stations, bard roads, etc. New machinery takes the place of glass workers, but new demands for glass bring the total of those employed in the industry close to what it was under manual operation. But there is great temporary displacement from this source as, for instance, just now the theater musicians are widely displaced by the talking pictures-perhaps we are now in a period where there may be some permanent displacements, and I would like to call attention to the possibility that drawing more of the resources for our factories from our own territory might be an important solution for this displacement problem. Increasing the amount of such raw material as could be drawn from our farms would greatly increase the amount of employment available. As we get close to such raw material, machinery becomes of less importance relatively and labor more (Congressional Record, 1929, p. 2112).

5.9 Senator Smoot Introduces the Bill in the Senate

Democrat rumblings in the Ways and Means Committee, echoed in the House, made it clear that the Bill would face an uphill battle in the Senate, where Progressive Republicans were more numerous. The task before Senator Reed Smoot, the chair of the Finance committee, would be to navigate what was a divided Republican party. Clearly, his only hope would be to convince a significant number of Mid-West progressive senators to widen their support to the U.S. worker, who as Smoot had mentioned in 1927, was the victim of mass production.

House Record 2667 was received in the Senate on May 28, 1929 and immediately referred to the Committee of Finance, presided by Smoot. Like the House Ways and Means Committee, the Senate Finance Committee was dominated by North–East industrial interests. The deliberations lasted roughly three months, over which period the Committee heard testimony from various interest groups and witnesses. The Committee wrapped up the hearings and sent the bill to the Senate on September 4.

5.10 The Party Formally Splits: 13 Insurgent Republicans Cross the Floor and Vow to Lower Tariffs on Manufactures

No sooner had it arrived in the Senate that the party solidarity begin to crumble as Republican senators from the Mid-West and the South — essentially, from rural America — announced their opposition to the rates on manufactures, arguing that U.S. industry was in an enviable position in 1928, having broken many records in so far as sales and profits were concerned. In little time, the debate degenerated as a number of Insurgent Republicans and Democrats pushed Senate leaders to provide data on corporate profits by industry with the intent of showing beyond all doubt that industry was not in any need of more protection.

The coalition of Insurgent Republicans and Democrats alleged that the rates on manufactures would benefit mass producers, who in their view were in no need of any assistance. Republicans with Reed Smoot leading the charge countered with the allegation that they had done so with the small, struggling manufactures in mind. Estimates of the cost to the American people of the various tariff hikes abounded throughout this period.

The Republican Senate leadership (Senators Smoot, Reed and Watson) insisted the rates on manufactures were aimed at protecting labor, something the opposition Insurgents and Democrats rejected arguing that U.S. labor costs were not higher than abroad, especially given the technological change noted by President Hoover's Committee on Recent Economic Changes.

With the benefit of hindsight, the Republican leadership was unable to diffuse the simmering discontent within the party. As pointed out earlier, the main objective of H.R. 2667 was to close the output gaps that had been opened by electric unit drive and the resulting mass production. Tariff hikes on all manufactures were the chosen instrument, despite the fact that U.S. manufacturing firms controlled 95 percent of the domestic market. Nonetheless, the leadership pressed on, hoping to diffuse the growing discontent. Clearly, higher tariffs would not solve the problem: however, it was, to put it candidly, all they had, policy-wise, to deal with the growing problem of technological unemployment.

This turn of events begs an interesting question, namely how had the Party leadership contained the Insurgents when it was clear from the start (i.e. from the Kansas City convention on June 11–13, 1928) that a generalized tariff review was in the cards? And why did things seem to fall apart in September? We believe that the answer to this question lies in the question of farm relief. As it turned out, the question of farm relief, from the Republican point of view, rested on two policy instruments, namely the Haugen–McNary concept of debentures and tariff revision. Throughout the first half of 1929, the question of farm relief was vigorously debated in the Senate, which passed a farm relief bill which included debentures (export subsidies). Unfortunately, when the bill was returned to the House, it was defeated.

Thus, by the fall, the only hope, in so far as farm relief was concerned, was tariff hikes on farm products and tariff reductions on manufactures — essentially, the McMaster Resolution of January 1928. Put differently, had the debenture plan been approved, it would have allayed some, if not all, of the Mid-West angst.

Thus, from September on, the Mid-West Insurgents made their intentions clear: they would vote with the Democrats to lower, not increase rates on manufactures. In short, they would take control of the tariff bill.

The electoral ruse that had brought Mid-Western Representatives and Senators on board during the convention and the ensuing electoral campaign had been outed. The electoral promise of a limited tariff bill with emphasis on the farmer had been dispelled, starting in the Ways and Means Committee hearings as well as in the House and the Senate. The Bill in front of the Senate had all the ear-markings of the promises made in Kansas City: tariffs on all manufactures would rise, in many cases doubling.

5.11 Summary and Conclusions

History has not been especially kind to the Smoot–Hawley Tariff Act. Repudiated, rejected and ridiculed, its architects have been disparaged and dismissed. In this chapter, we have revisited this controversial piece of legislation, paying particular attention to mitigating factors. According to the "standard" Smoot–Hawley narrative, what began as an attempt on the part of the Republican Party to win votes in farm states in the 1928 presidential election was transformed via the log-rolling and pork-barreling into the most injurious tariff bill of all times. E.E. Schattschneider and Frank Taussig both viewed the resulting tariff bill as an example of the U.S. political process gone amok. Senators, motivated by their constituent interests, traded favors on the Senate floor with the result that what was intended as a limited tariff bill, metamorphosed into an omnibus bill, covering all industries and all products.

In this chapter, an alternative — and complementary — view according to which a technology shock in the form of the introduction of electric unit drive and the resulting mass production lay at the root of both the demand for additional protection, on the part of farmers as well as on the part of manufacturers, was presented. Facing growing excess capacity (both in agriculture and manufacturing), the Republican Party under the forceful guidance of Senator Reed Smoot and Joseph Grundy resorted to its economic policy workhorse, namely, upward tariff revision. The resulting view should be seen as both an extension and refinement of the "party platform" view found in the literature, and consistent with the predictions of the "log-rolling hypothesis," that is, across-the-board tariff hikes. While tariff policy had, until then, been used primarily as a tool of industrial strategy (i.e., import substitution) and government revenue, now it would be used as a tool of macroeconomic stabilization.

Anecdotal and statistical evidence was brought to bear on the subject. In addition to providing primary source excerpts from the various senators, governors and businessmen, data on the extent of the excess capacity were provided. Lastly, historical survey data using the *New York Times* as the source were used to test the associated sub-hypotheses. Taken as a whole, the evidence points to an altogether different view of the Smoot–Hawley Tariff Act, one that is more in keeping with its stated goals, and one that is set against the underlying economic conditions in the 1920s. It was neither an electoral strategy aimed at farmers in the North–West, nor the result of extensive log-rolling, but rather the best possible response on the part of the Republican Party to the problem of growing excess capacity. The Smoot–Hawley Tariff Bill offered the hope of greater sales, profits and earnings, not to mention higher employment and overall growth.

It innovated by providing an integrated, synthetic view of the 1920s and 1930s, based on the massive energy shock that was electric power. The latter increased industrial productive capacity. By making fossil fuel-powered prime movers affordable (automobiles, trucks and tractors), it reduced the demand for hay and oats significantly, the effects of which were catastrophic for farmers. U.S. legislators were confronted for the first time with a problem, the likes of which only one other country, Great Britain, had experienced in the early 19th century. Not surprisingly, it struggled to come to terms with the problem of over-capacity. Whereas the British made free-trade the cornerstone of their response, the U.S. reacted in the exact opposite way, namely by attempting to close its domestic market in the hope of providing its firms with greater market share.

Analytically, we provided an additional rationale for tariff protection, namely acceleration-based excess capacity. At the disaggregated level, insufficient demand in the face of rising capacity leads firms to covet a larger share of the domestic market at the expense of foreign exporters. Seen in this light, the Smoot–Hawley Tariff Bill was a response on the behalf of manufacturers and farmers to electrification, tractorization, motorization-induced excess capacity. From 1928 to October 1929, the tariff bill sought to close this gap. However, from November 1929 on, new macroeconomic developments transformed the debate, notably falling investment and employment — the fallout from the Stock Market Crash. In fact, it could be argued that final passage in June 1930 owed in large measure to these factors, making for a situation in which both structural and cyclical factors were at play.

Appendix: The Petition Against the Smoot–Hawley Tariff Bill: What 1,028 Economists Overlooked[3]

On May 30, 1930, Swarthmore College economics professor Clair Wilcox presented President Herbert Hoover with a petition, signed by 1,028 prominent U.S. economists denounced the proposed Smoot–Hawley Tariff Bill. Citing a panoply of reasons, they strongly urged him to veto the Bill. Hoover ignored their plea, signing the bill into law on June 17, 1930. In Beaudreau (2016), it was argued that the originators and signatories had overlooked both the underlying rationale for the proposed tariff revision and the proposed solution. In short, the profession viewed it like all others, while the Republicans viewed it as a stop-gap measure aimed at dealing with the growing problem of acceleration-based excess capacity that ironically found itself at the core of Paul Douglas's and other signatories' thinking and writings at the time.

The petition read:

"We are convinced that increased restrictive duties would be mistake. They would operate, in general, to increase the prices which domestic consumers would have to pay. By raising prices, they would encourage concerns with higher costs to undertake production, thus compelling the consumer to subsidize waste and inefficiency in industry. At the same time they would force his to pay higher rates of profit to established firms which enjoyed lower production costs. A higher level of duties, such as is contemplated by the Smoot–Hawley bill, would therefore raise the cost of living and injure the great majority of our citizens.

Few people could hope to gain from such a change. Miners, construction, transportation and public utility workers, professional people and those employed in banks, hotels, newspaper offices, in the wholesale and retail trades and scores of other occupations would clearly lose, since they produce no products which could be specially favored by tariff barriers. The vast majority of farmers would also lose. Their cotton, pork, lard and wheat are export crops and are sold in the world market. They cannot benefit, therefore, from any tariff which is imposed upon basic commodities which they produce.

---

[3]Beaudreau, Bernard C. The Petition Against Smoot–Hawley: What 1,028 Economists Overlooked, *Real World Economics Review*, 74, 2016, 124–138.

They would lose through the increased duties on manufactured goods, however, and in a double fashion. First, as consumers, they would have to pay still higher prices for the products, made of textiles, chemicals, iron and steel, which they buy. Second, as producers their ability to sell their products would be further restricted by the barriers placed in the way of foreigners who wished to sell manufactured goods to us.

Our export trade, in general, would suffer. Countries cannot permanently buy from us unless they are permitted to sell to us, and the more we restrict the importation of goods from them by means ever higher tariffs, the more we reduce the possibility of our exporting to them. This applies to such exporting industries as copper, automobiles, agricultural machinery, typewriters and the like fully as much as it does to farming. The difficulties of these industries are likely to be increased still further if we pass a higher tariff.

There are already many evidences that such action would inevitably provoke other countries to pay us back in kind by levying retaliatory duties against our goods. There are few more ironical spectacles than that of the American government as it seeks, on the one hand, to promote exports through the activity of the Bureau of Foreign and Domestic Commerce, while on the other hand, by increasing tariffs it makes exportation ever more difficult.

We do not believe that American manufacturers in general need higher tariffs. The report of the President's Committee on Recent Economic Changes has shown that industrial efficiency as increased, that costs have fallen, that profits have grown with amazing rapidity since the end of the World War. Already our factories supply our people with over 96 percent of the manufactured goods which they consume, and our producers look to foreign markets to absorb the increasing output of their machines. Further, barriers to trade will serve them not well, but ill.

Many of our citizens have invested their money in foreign enterprises. The Department of Commerce has estimated that such investments entirely aside from war debts amounted to between 12,555,000,000 and 14,555,000,000 on January 1, 1929. These investors, too, would suffer if restrictive duties were to be increased since such action would make it still more difficult for their foreign debtors to pay them the interest due them.

America is now facing the problem of unemployment. The proponents of higher tariffs claim that an increase in rates will give work to the idle. This is not true. We cannot increase employment by restricting trade. American industry in the present crisis might well be spared the burden of adjusting itself to higher schedules of duties. Finally, we would urge our government to consider the bitterness which a policy of higher tariffs would inevitably inject into our international relations. The United States was ably represented at the world economic conference which was held under the auspices of the League of Nations in 1927. This conference adopted a resolution announcing that the time has come to put an end to the increase in tariffs and move in the opposite direction.

The higher duties proposed in our pending legislation violate the spirit of this agreement and plainly invite other nations to compete with us in raising further barriers to trade. A tariff war does not furnish good soil for the growth of world peace.

Originators and First Signatories:

Paul H. Douglas, Professor of Industrial Relations, University of Chicago. Irving Fisher, Professor of Economics, Yale University. Frank D. Graham, Professor of Economics, Princeton University. (Trade theorist) Ernest M. Patterson, Professor of Economics, University of Pennsylvania. Henry R. Seager, Professor of Economics, Columbia University. (Student of Patten, UPenn) Frank W. Taussig, Professor of Economics, Harvard University (Trade theorist) Clair Wilcox, Associate Professor of Economics, Swarthmore College.

The Economics Profession and the Tariff Bill: A Glaring Disconnect

Ironically, many of the signatories and originators, while opposing the tariff bill, unknowingly shared its basic underlying premise, namely the presence of growing generalized excess capacity. For example, the main author of the bill, University of Chicago professor Paul Douglas, maintained throughout this period that the U.S. economy was increasingly characterized by significant excess capacity. In fact, his pathbreaking work on production functions with mathematician Charles Cobb was intended to serve as a basis for his long-standing view that wages would need to rise. For example, in a paper titled "The Modern Technique of

Table 5.4. Indexes of Production in Manufacturing as Reported by Douglas (1927) 1919–1926 (1919–100)

Year	Federal Reserve Board	Day–Thomas	Harvard
1919	100	100	100
1920	102		106
1921	79	80	82
1922	103		110
1923	120	122	130
1924	112		120
1925	125		133
1926	129		

Mass Production and Its Relation to Wages," published in 1927, he referred to the 29 percent increase in the volume of physical production from 1919 to 1926 (see Table 5.4).

Similar concerns were voiced by Columbia University economics professor Rexford G. Tugwell who would go on to draft the signature piece of legislation of President Franklin Roosevelt's New Deal, the National Industrial Recovery Act. In his view, potential output had increased faster than income and expenditure, leading to the downturn. This owed principally to electrification.

> The electrification of industry has now progressed to the extent of between 55 and 60 percent completion. So widespread an adoption of this new flexible means of moving things cannot have taken place without numerous secondary results in lowered costs, improvements in quality, and a heightened morale among workers. For the new power is not only cheaper to use: it is also cleaner, more silent and handier. On the whole, the electrification of industry must be set down as the greatest single cause of the new industrial revolution (Tugwell, 1927, p. 182).

Irving Fisher and electrification

Irving Fisher, like Paul Douglas and Rexford Tugwell, felt that changes in technique had served to vastly increase America's capacity to produce,

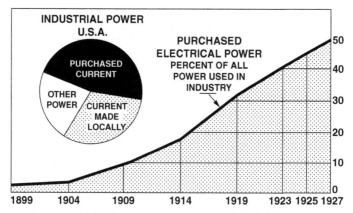

CHART 15 – Total primary factory power applied through electric
motors increased, 1919–1927, from 55 per cent to 78 per cent.
Inset: 50 per cent purchased, 28 per cent made locally.

Figure 5.4.   Purchased Electrical Power in the U.S.
Source: Fisher (1930, p. 132).

echoing the views of the leading members of the Republican Party (see
Figure 5.4). On the day after the crash (October 24, 1929), he declared:

> The stock market rose after the war above the pre-war level by 50–100
> percent because of war inflation and that since, it has doubled because
> of increasing prosperity from less unstable money, new mergers, new
> scientific management and the new policy of waste saving.

In *The Stock Market Crash and After*, published in 1930, he was more
explicit:

> But after 1919, something happened. The implications of which are not
> yet sufficiently gauged. It was of enough significance to cause President
> Hoover's Committee on Recent Economic Changes to remark that
> "acceleration rather than structural change is the key to an understanding
> of our recent economic developments." The committee added: "But the
> breadth and the tempo of recent developments gives them new impor-
> tance." What happened was indicated by the fact that in the United
> States, 8.3 million workers produced in 1925 one quarter more than

9 million workers turned out in 1919. The new indexes of the Federal Reserve Board measuring production record this gratifying advance which reflects an increase in the American standard of living .... The general volume of production had increased between 1919 and 1927 by 46.5 percent: primary power by 22 percent, and primary power per wage earner by 30.9 percent (between 1919 and 1925), and productivity per wage worker by 53.5 percent between 1919 and 1927 (Fisher, 1930, p. 120).

However, unlike Tugwell and Douglas, he stopped short of invoking this manifold increase in productivity as the cause of the structural weakness in the 1927–1928 period.

How Did They Miss It

Our findings raise an important question, namely how and why did 1,028 leading U.S. economists misunderstand and misinterpret the well-known and well-publicized intentions of the Republican Party in its proposed tariff bill? As we have shown, many of its guiding principles can be found in the writings of the petition's instigators and signatories. We submit two reasons, namely incomplete information and the state of flux in which economics as a whole found itself in the 1920s. By incomplete information, it should be understood the failure of the instigators to fully comprehend and appreciate the economic reasoning/logic behind the Bill. For example, if Paul Douglas had followed the electoral and legislative debate over the proposed tariff bill, from late 1927 on, he would have discovered a set of objectives that were largely consistent with his own writings at the time. Ibid for Rexford G. Tugwell.

Second, the idea/theory that the U.S. economy was "operating" significantly below capacity in the 1920s was a new one. Most subscribed to Say's Law, according to which supply creates its own demand. Hence, the many references to unused capacity and mass production-based unemployment were orthogonal to the dominant ideology at the time. Combined with what was an incomplete knowledge and appreciation of the Bill's stated goals, it comes as little surprise that 1,028 leading U.S. economists misunderstood and misinterpreted the intentions of the Republican Party in its quest to raise tariffs in 1928.

A More Appropriate Petition

With the benefit of hindsight, it is clear that the 1,028 instigators and signatories to the petition had failed to appreciate the subtleties of the act, making for a situation in which its bases were orthogonal to those of the actual petition. This then raises the following counterfactual, namely had this not been the case (i.e., had they been aware of the intentions and underlying principles), what would their petition have resembled? Consider the following:

Owing to the genius of its entrepreneurs, engineers and scientists, the U.S. has benefited from a manifold increase in its ability to generate wealth and so increase the standard of living. Unfortunately, for reasons that are not fully understood at the present moment, markets (income and expenditure) have not followed suit, resulting in a situation of generalized excess capacity, especially in manufacturing and agriculture.

The Republican Party is currently proposing yet another upward tariff revision in the hope of securing a greater share of the domestic market for U.S. firms, arguing that higher utilization rates will decrease prices and hence benefit consumers. Unfortunately, such a policy, while appealing to the layman, is based on faulty logic and cannot bring long-run prosperity to the U.S. Its basic flaw is to assume that our trading partners will not react. While Europe did not react to Fordney–McCumber Tariff Act of 1922, owing no doubt to the goodwill from our involvement in the Great War, we believe that it will react, closing markets to U.S. exports. U.S. firms will be no further ahead, as imports and exports contract.

Beggar-thy-neighbor policies have failed and will continue to fail in the long run, and the proposed Smoot–Hawley Tariff Bill is an example of such a policy. We believe that the Republican Party should examine other options to stimulate markets, thus allowing the country to exploit its newly-found potential.

Chapter 6

Wall Street Responds Favorably to the Proposed Tariff Bill*

> The stock market rose after the war above the pre-war level by 50–100 percent because of war inflation and that since, it has doubled because of increasing prosperity from less unstable money, new mergers, new scientific management and the new policy of waste saving.
>
> Irving Fisher (1930)

6.1 Introduction

Yale University economics professor Irving Fisher was adamant throughout the late 1920s and 1930s: the stock market boom was not a bubble, but rather owed to vastly improved fundamentals, a view he would hold for the rest of his life. In *The Stock Market Crash and After* published in 1930, he pointed to a number of causes including electrification. In Chapter 3, he provided details, pointing to the rise of large electrical utilities, interconnection and low-cost electricity. Figure 6.1 is taken from Fisher (1930) and shows the percentage of all electrical power purchased

---

*This chapter draws from Beaudreau, Bernard C. Discriminating Between Tariff Bill-Based Theories of the Stock Market Crash of 1929, *Essays in Economic and Business History*, 32(1), 2014, 80–99 and Beaudreau, Bernard C. Electrification, the Smoot–Hawley Tariff Act and the Stock Market Boom and Crash: Evidence from Longitudinal Data, *Journal of Economics and Finance*, 42(4), 2018, 631–650.

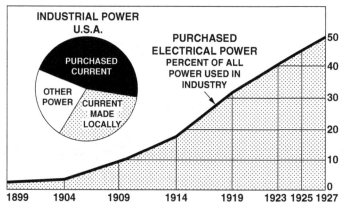

CHART 15 – Total primary factory power applied through electric
motors increased, 1919–1927, from 55 percent to 78 percent.
Inset: 50 percent purchased, 28 percent made locally.

Figure 6.1.   Purchased Electric Power (Irving Fisher)
Source: Fisher (1930, p. 132).

from public utilities, which can be seen as a proxy for the extent of the
spread of electric unit drive.

Just why Fisher would put electrical power at the core of his argument
is not entirely clear given the state of production theory at the time. After
all, in 1930, GDP and production were defined solely as increasing functions of capital and labor. Why then should purchased electricity as
opposed to generated on-site electricity matter? Unfortunately, he was
unable to make a convincing argument. While he was unable to articulate
the underlying rationale, the analysis provided in Chapters 3 and 4 shows
that purchased power was a proxy for the adoption of electric unit drive,
which in turn was a proxy for acceleration.

This raises the question, why then is it that Fisher who wrote extensively on the boom and crash, both at the time and afterward, stands
today as somewhat of a forgotten, if not disparaged, figure in the debate
over the stock market crash? The answer, we maintain, lies not in his
account of the boom, but in that of the crash, which he was unable to
explain — at least, convincingly. After all, the fundamentals that he so
eloquently and convincingly invoked had not suddenly vanished in

October 1929. Like Ellen McGrattan and Edward Prescott who recently also argued that the boom in prices was not a bubble, he was unable to account for the crash, which unfortunately undermined the bulk of his argument.

This chapter fills in the missing pieces by providing an alternative account of the stock market boom and crash as resulting from the legislative trials and tribulations (i.e., ups and downs) of the proposed Smoot–Hawley Tariff Bill, set against a backdrop of vastly improved fundamentals.[1] Like Fisher, the latter are attributed to the adoption of electric unit drive and the resulting acceleration of production processes, which, as shown in the previous chapters, increased the rated capacity of U.S. industry. Heralded by the Republicans as a solution to the problem of excess rated capacity, the proposed tariff legislation was passed by the House on May 23, 1929, and introduced in the Senate where the Republicans held a majority. Investors responded positively to the proposed higher tariffs, increased market share, increased profits and increased earnings.

This near-perfect scenario, however, came to a screeching halt in July 1929 when 13 Republican Senators broke ranks with the party and joined forces with the Democrats to not only defeat the proposed hikes, but to actually lower tariffs on manufactures — a nightmarish scenario if ever there was one for the Party executive. Senator Smoot responded by suspending deliberations on the Bill, hoping to find a way to accommodate their demand. After months of often acrimonious debate, the Insurgent Republican–Democrat coalition shifted into high gear. On October 21, they defeated the Thomas Amendment, an attempt on the part of the Party executive to limit the damage by refocusing the Bill on agriculture and agriculture alone.

The Coalition was steadfast: rates on manufactures would not only not rise, they would fall. The next day, they began their assault on manufacturing tariffs, voting to lower the tariff on medicinal tannic acid. The next day, the stock market crashed for the first time. Less than a week later, when leading Republicans announced that the bill before the Senate

---

[1]Most writers on the stock market boom, including most recently Eugene White (1990), pointed to or point to improving fundamentals as one of the key underlying causes without specifying the underlying mechanics — that is, the changes that prompted the price increases. This book is the first to provide a comprehensive account of the fundamentals in question and how they contributed to both the boom and the crash.

was as good as dead, it crashed for a second time, wiping out the tariff bill-inspired gains (from June 1928).

6.2   What Fisher (1930) and McGrattan and Prescott (2004) Overlooked

Fisher (1930) and McGrattan and Prescott (2004) maintained that the stock market boom was not a bubble, but rather based on improved fundamentals. McGrattan and Prescott (2004) pointed to innovation and technological advances without however specifying them. Neither of the two, however, was able to account for the crash. After all, fundamentals are just that, fundamental or structural. In recent work, Beaudreau (1996, 2005, 2014, 2017c), however, showed why they were both right and wrong. Specifically, he argued that while fundamentals had indeed improved, the stock market boom was largely fueled by the promises made in Kansas City, and the crash, by a legislative putsch by 13 Insurgent Republican senators. Put differently, the boom was based on investors' expectations that the fundamentals Fisher, Grattan and Prescott referred to would translate into greater revenue, profits and dividends, while the crash resulted from the implosion of the tariff bill in the Senate. This chapter provides a detailed account of the legislative events leading to the crash. Specifically, it shows that movements in the stock market were intimately tied to the proposed tariff bill from its beginnings in the Ways and Means Committee to the crash itself.

6.3   The Tariff Bill Hits a Wall: 13 Republican Senators Break with the Party and Vow to Lower Tariffs

From the Kansas City Republican National Convention to May 1929, the proposed tariff revision went from an election promise, to hearings by the Ways and Means Committee, to a bill introduced and passed in the House of Representatives in May 1929. Tariffs on manufactures and agricultural products would increase significantly, thus providing the impetus for an increase in U.S. firms' share of the domestic market. It bears reminding that what was sought was not protection from low-cost imports as had been the case for most of the 18th and 19th centuries, but rather more

Table 6.1. The Thirteen Insurgent Republican Senators

Senator	State
John J. Blaine	Wisconsin
William E. Borah	Idaho
Smith W. Brookhart	Iowa
Bronson M. Cutting	New Mexico
Lynn J. Frazier	North Dakota
Robert B. Howell	Nebraska
Robert M. La Follette	Wisconsin
William H. McMaster	South Dakota
George W. Norris	Nebraska
Gerald P. Nye	North Dakota
Thomas D. Schall	Minnesota
Hiram W. Johnson	California
Peter Norbeck	South Dakota

room or space in the domestic market. Not surprisingly, these developments were well received on Wall Street as investors anticipated higher sales, revenues and, ultimately, profits.

Much to the surprise of the Party leaders, this almost blissful scenario came to a grinding halt in July of 1929 when 13 senators from the Mid-West (see Table 6.1), unhappy with the generalized nature of the tariff bill, broke with the Party and vowed to vote with the Democrats to decrease, not increase, tariffs on manufactures. Known as the Insurgent Republicans, they maintained that the Party had reneged on its promise of a limited tariff bill with emphasis on the farmer.

What would follow would be an epic legislative struggle between Senators Reed Smoot of Utah and David Reed on the one hand, and the 13 Insurgents on the other. On July 31, Smoot suspended Committee hearings, promising to rewrite portions of the tariff bill with the Insurgents in mind. From then on, a struggle would ensue, a struggle over the breadth of the tariff bill, a struggle between fellow Republicans, and a struggle that would ultimately lead to the collapse of stock prices.

Table 6.2 provides a sample of good and bad tariff bill news coming out of Washington as reported by The *New York Times*. Perhaps the most

Table 6.2.   Selected Examples of Tariff Good and Bad News Headlines from the *New York Times*

Tariff Good News	Tariff Bad News
Demand revision of the entire tariff: manufacturers of three western states adopt resolution in Chicago meeting (April 6, 1929)	Tariff bill causes concern in Europe: high duties and increases in our exports disquieting to economists at league meeting (May 8, 1929)
Summary of features of new tariff bill: new rates on sodium compounds, laminated, rolled and plate glass, provisions on some metal products (May 8, 1929)	Rising tariff bill revolt stirs republican chiefs (May 9, 1929)
Hawley defends tariff measure: says public interest justifies revision proposal (May 8, 1929)	Geneva concerned about our tariff rise (May 12, 1929)
Republican chiefs hint of concessions on tariff to check party protests (May 10, 1929)	Borah hits tariff bill: says farmers rather than manufacturers need protection (August 16, 1929)
Hoover will press for tariff action (August 26, 1929)	Borah asks for defeat of tariff bill (August 23, 1929)
Republicans call Caucus today to act on tariff threats (September 19, 1929)	Tariff filibuster charged in Senate: Smoot says Simmons' plan to get corporate data is aimed to kill bill (September 10, 1929)
Form lines to win control of Senate: administration leaders plan or 1930 campaign when 33 seats are to be filled. Hoover wants majority (September 22, 1929)	Tariff cuts forced in chemical rates: Senate coalition wins test vote 45 to 33 on first schedules taken up (October 22, 1929)

damning of tariff bad news occurred on October 20, 1929, when the Insurgent Republican–Democrat coalition defeated the Thomas Amendment which called for a limited tariff bill — one limited to agricultural products alone. Sensing the impending defeat of the H.R. 2667 and the Insurgent Republican–Democrat's stated intent of lowering tariffs on manufactures, Senator Thomas of Kentucky proposed to limit the bill to agriculture. The Amendment, however, was defeated, keeping open the door to the possibility of lowering tariffs on manufactures.

TARIFF CUTS FORCED IN CHEMICAL RATES

Senate Coalition Wins Test Vote, 45 to 33, on First Schedules Taken Up.

LA FOLLETTE LEADS ATTACK

Charging Favoring of du Pont and Other Companies, He Warns of Farm Revolt on Bill.

Special to The New York Times.

WASHINGTON, Oct. 22.—Aided by four Old Guard Republicans, the Democratic-Progressive coalition won the first test vote on the rates of the Smoot-Hawley tariff bill when the chemical schedule was taken up in the Senate today. The item on which the vote was taken was incidental, but the result served to show that the coalition was nearly intact in its initial drive and also that it still held control in the Senate.

The roll-call was taken toward the end of a session of nearly ten hours, marked by a sharp address by Senator La Follette of Wisconsin, in which he warned of a Republican party split.

He told the regulars that if they proposed to "betray" 1928 campaign pledges to the farmers they had better look back to 1908, when tariff revision broke the Republican party.

Mr. La Follette attacked the chemical industry, which, he said, was reaping exorbitant profits. Naming the "big three" of the chemical field as E. I. du Pont de Nemours & Co. Inc.; the Allied Chemical and Dye Corporation and the Union Carbide and Carbon Corporation, he asserted that their combined net earnings were $122,000,000 in 1928, "and the rates of profits on their annual investment were extraordinary and excessive."

Figure 6.2. *New York Times* Headlines October 23, 1929

Table 6.3.   The Proverbial Nails in the Coffin of the Smoot–Hawley Tariff Bill

Date	Nail	Effect
October 20, 1929	Defeat of the Thomas Amendment	Insurgent Republican–Democrat coalition intent on lowering tariffs on manufactures
October 22, 1929	Vote to lower tariff on medicinal tannic acid passes	Beginning of the Coalition's assault on tariffs on manufactures
October 27, 1929	Senator David Reed of Pennsylvania, in an address in Philadelphia, pronounces the de facto death of the tariff legislation	Ends all hope of the promised increases in tariffs on manufactures

Another equally damning piece of tariff bad news occurred on the following day when the Coalition fired the opening salvo in its stated purpose of lowering tariffs on manufactures. In short, a proposition was introduced to reduce the tariff on medicinal tannic acid (see Figure 6.2). The vote was 54–42 in favor of the proposal to lower the tariff on medicinal tannic acid. Thus began what would in all likelihood become the Insurgent Republican–Democrat rewrite of the Smoot–Hawley Tariff Bill.

Needless to say, the fallout from these two votes would be colossal as they signaled the end of what had been over a year of expectations, expectations that the nation's manufacturers would produce at their higher-rated capacity, expectations that sales, revenues and profits would increase. And, the stock market reacted accordingly, losing one-third of its value.

The days following the defeat of the Thomas Amendment and the Coalition-sponsored reduction in the tariff on tannic acid were filled with doom and gloom. The Republican Party, with a history of splintering, had imploded and with it, the proposed fix for the nation's manufacturers. While senior Party officials, notably senator Reed Smoot, felt they could steer the bill back on course, others were overcome with a sense of certain defeat. One such senator was David Reed of Pennsylvania, who in a speech in Philadelphia on Sunday, October 27, claimed that the Tariff Bill was dead (see Figure 6.3). The Dow Jones Industrial Average crashed for a second time on Monday, October 28, and again on Tuesday, October 29 (see Table 6.3).

LEADERS INSIST TARIFF WILL PASS

Smoot and Borah Contradict Reed, Who Told Philadelphians Bill Was Dead.

LONG DELAY ADMITTED

Pennsylvania Senator Asserted Farm Bloc Was Killing the Measure.

Special to The New York Times.

WASHINGTON, Oct. 27.—While the fate of the tariff bill admittedly is in doubt in the minds of many of the Senators now trying to agree on a measure that can be passed and meet the approval of the President, a statement made by Senator Reed of Pennsylvania in a Philadelphia address last night that the bill would die in the present session came as a great surprise to the Rpublican and Democratic leaders here.

Senator Smoot, Republican, of Utah, chairman of the Senate Finance Committee, took direct issue with Senator Reed and, although agreeing that chances of the bill passing in the special session were dim, predicted that it would be acted on in the regular session opening in December.

"If that is Senator Reed's opinion," said Mr. Smoot, "I suppose he has a right to express it. But it isn't the view of the Finance Committee. If they take as much time debating it as they have been taking, it will not pass this session, but it will go on in the next session."

Figure 6.3. GOP Response to Senator David Reed's Philadelphia Address

6.4 The Tariff Bill and the Stock Market Boom and Crash: Empirical Evidence

In previous work, Beaudreau (2014) showed how tariff news (good and bad) out of Washington moved the market, from the introduction of the bill in the House, to the signing of the bill in June 1930. Specifically, tariff bill-related news was scored on a scale of –4 to +4, and analysis of variance and regression analysis were used to test for a statistically significant relationship between stock prices and tariff-related news. Table 6.4, which presents the results, shows a statistically significant positive relationship between tariff news scores and stock prices, which confirms the obvious, namely that investors were very much on board with the Republicans' plan to close the ever-widening output gaps using tariffs. Accordingly, the DJIA appreciated on tariff good news, and depreciated on tariff bad news — or tariff setbacks.

In later work, he replicated the analysis using stock price data for the 15 Dow Jones Industrial Average stocks (Column 1 of Table 6.5). Specifically, using an augmented Fama–French model, he was able to show the existence of a similar relationship between tariff news (Column 6 in Table 6.5) and individual stock price movements (see Table 6.5). Moreover, the magnitude of the estimated coefficient (i.e., strength of the relationship) was found to be increasing in the extent of electric unit drive conversion in the associated industry. In other words, the greater the extent of conversion to electric unit drive in the industry, the greater the impact of tariff news on the firm's stock price. Last, he was able to show that tariff good news in 1928 and 1929 was able to account for roughly 73 percent of the boom in stock prices in this period.

This resulting view of the stock market boom as being fueled by rising tariff policy-based optimism (of greater market share, sales, revenue and profits) against a backdrop of acceleration-based increases in

Table 6.4. Event Study Regression Results

Independent Variable	Coefficient	*t*-statistic
Constant	–0.2045	–0.634
NEWS-I	1.9798	7.574

Note: Complete Sample (236 DJIA Trading Days); Dependent Variable: ΔDJIA; R^2: 0.1968; $F(1,234)$: 57.36.
Source: Beaudreau (2014).

Table 6.5.   Tariff News-Augmented Fama–French Model-Estimates 1928–1929

Company	Constant	RI	SMB	HML	Tariff News	R^2	F(4,286)
Mack truck	−0.00057	0.00962	0.00198	−0.00142	0.00547	0.52617	161.0179
	(−0.9602)*	(21.1884)	(2.2242)	(−1.1545)	(7.5117)		
American smelting	−0.00070	0.00912	0.00293	0.00117	0.00511	0.16500	28.65420
#	(−0.5565)	(9.4329)	(1.5435)	(0.4436)	(3.2914)		
Atlantic refining	−0.00006	0.01347	0.00072	0.00465	0.00516	0.22692	42.56150
	(−0.4048)	(11.8222)	(0.3255)	(1.4995)	(2.8269)		
Bethlehem steel	0.00043	0.01032	−0.00458	0.00526	0.00620	0.53011	163.5827
	(0.6719)	(21.0596)	(−4.7539)	(3.9411)	(7.8834)		
Chrysler	−0.00033	0.01306	0.00660	−0.00136	0.00668	0.48198	134.9155
	(−0.3910)	(20.0788)	(5.1631)	(−0.7677)	(6.3986)		
Standard oil	0.00068	0.01063	−0.00179	0.0021	0.00642	0.58768	206.6745
	(1.1668)	(23.9845)	(−2.0552)	(1.7438)	(9.0273)		
General motors	−0.00177	0.01081	−0.00581	−0.00479	0.00546	0.31621	67.05531
	(−1.4754)	(11.8236)	(−3.2360)	(−1.9219)	(3.7242)		
American sugar	0.00003	0.01587	−0.00232	0.00398	0.00910	0.25032	48.41718
	(0.0204)	(11.7891)	(−0.8765)	(1.0841)	(4.2126)		
Intl. harvester	−0.02045	0.02479	0.00328	0.01011	−0.00737	0.02972	4.44201
	(−2.4305)	(3.8781)	(0.2617)	(0.5802)	(−0.7190)		
Texas corporation	−0.00005	0.00718	0.00074	0.00493	0.00473	0.48080	134.2770
	(−0.1162)	(20.9778)	(1.1080)	(5.2813)	(8.6194)		
American tobacco	−0.00006	0.00789	−0.00365	0.00087	0.00390	0.58017	200.3840
	(−0.1439)	(22.5183)	(−5.2974)	(0.9157)	(6.9468)		

Note: *t*-statistic.
Source: Beaudreau (2018, p. 646).

productivity and rated capacity is not only consistent with Fisher (1930) and McGrattan and Prescott (2004), it completes their analysis by (i) showing why and how prices increased and decreased and (ii) when and why the market crashed. Specifically, stock prices moved upward not in response to the new technology *per se*, but rather in response to tariff bill-based hope on the part of investors that the technology would bear fruit, so to speak. That is, higher tariffs would secure a larger share of the domestic market for U.S. firms, allowing them to ramp up production and operate at the new greater capacity.

6.5   The Tariff Bill and the Stock Market Crash: Evidence from Newspaper Headlines

The extent to which the fate of the tariff bill before the Senate weighed heavily in the minds of investors and Americans in general can be seen from the headlines in the nation's newspapers. Specifically, in both the first stock market crash (October 23 and 24) as well as the second (October 28 and 29), the headlines in most of the nation's newspapers included developments on the tariff-bill front as well as of the stock market crash. Table 6.6 provides a sample of the headlines in 15 newspapers. Interestingly, in each of these cases, bad tariff news and bad stock market news appear to go hand-in-hand. The former include lobbying activity on the part of the President of the Pennsylvania Manufacturers Association and leading Republican Joseph R. Grundy, as well as the decision on the part of Connecticut Republican Senator Hiram Bingham III, member of the influential Senate Finance Committee, to hire a member of the Connecticut Manufacturers Association as a consultant. Clearly, the fate of the tariff bill was very much on the minds of Americans–and investors. Interestingly, headlines from foreign newspapers (not reported) focused uniquely on the crashes, with no mention of the tariff bill.

6.6   The Aftermath

Where did this leave the nation's manufacturers? Throughout this period, many had pinned their hopes on the Republican promise of greater market share and increased revenues and profits. Further, many who had, until

Table 6.6. The Tariff Bill and the Stock Market Crash: Evidence from Newspaper Headlines

Newspaper and Date	Stock Market Crash Headline	Tariff Bill Headline
Brooklyn Daily Eagle October 24	Wall Street in Panic as Stocks Crash	High Duty Group Gave $700,000 to Coolidge Drive
New York Times October 23	Stocks Collapse in 16,410,030 Share Day	
Santa Ana Register October 23	Billions Lost as Stocks Crash	Senate "Farm Bloc" Starts Battle for Higher Tariffs
The Milwaukee Leader October 28	Billions Lost in New Stock Crash	May Punish Senator for Aiding Tariff Lobbyists
Decatur Evening Herald October 29	Wall Street in New Panic	West Not Concerned with Tariff Fight, Says Grundy
New York Times October 25	Worst Stock Crash Stemmed by Banks	Grundy Says Lobby Is Needed to Uphold Party Tariff Vows
The Pittsburgh Press October 23	Selling Panic Wrecks Stock Exchange: New York Frenzied	Grundy Defends Lobbying: Regards Work as Fulfilling Party Pledge
Harrisburg Telegraph October 29	Market Losses Reach New Level	Grundy Startles Western Senators on Witness Stand
The Klameth News October 29	Stocks Lose 10 Billion in Day	Senator Faces Censure by Body for Hiring Man
Wilkes-Barre Record October 29	Prices Again Collapse On Stock Market	Bingham Hits Back at Senate Accusers
The Minneapolis Morning October 29	Bankers Act on Stock Crash	Norris to Ask Censure Vote for Bingham
Binghamton Press October 29	Bankers Stop Stock Crash	Bingham Faces Loss of Senate Financial Post
Green Bay Press-Gazette October 30	Wall St. Business Better	Grundy Doesn't Worry How He is Classified

(Continued)

Table 6.6.   (*Continued*)

Newspaper and Date	Stock Market Crash Headline	Tariff Bill Headline
The Detroit Free Press October 30	Eleventh-Hour Rally Checks Stock Crisis: Huge Losses	Insurgents Seek Truce With G.O.P.: Wish to Regain Loss in Conflict Over Tariff Bill
Wilkes-Barre Record	Frantic Stampede on Market Checked	Grundy Hands Lobby Probers a Few Jolts
The St-Louis Star October 30	Stock Market to Close Friday and Saturday	Grundy Airs Skeletons in G.O.P. Closet
The Springfield Leader October 30	Stock Market Declares Recess	Grundy Denies Boise Penrose Chose Harding
Great Falls Tribune October 30	Stock Market in Severe Collapse	Senate Lobby Probers Get Big Surprise: Members Hear Grundy Tell Them That He Would Bar Some States From Vote

then, resisted converting to electric unit drive, did so. Table 6.7, which reports census data for the electrical machinery industry, shows that value-added increased by roughly $350,000,000 in 1928 and 1929, with its share of manufacturing value-added and employment increasing from 4 percent to 4.5 percent.

Figure 6.4 plots employment indexes for manufacturing as a whole and the electrical equipment industry. We see that from roughly June 1928 to October 1929, employment in the electrical equipment industry outpaced that in manufacturing as a whole, which can be seen as evidence of an acceleration in the conversion to electric unit drive in response to Republican promises on the tariff.

The Smoot–Grundy initiative, aimed at closing the ever-widening gap, had ended in failure. In fact, by November, the Senate Insurgent Republican–Democrat coalition, emboldened by its victories, set about the task of lowering tariffs on manufactures, which in the eyes of investors would make matters worse. With no solution in sight and growing excess rated capacity, the U.S. economy faced an uncertain future. What would follow would be the complete collapse of investment expenditure, followed by the complete collapse of the U.S. economy. We now turn to the fall in investment and the ensuing contraction.

Table 6.7.   Census Data for the Electrical Machinery Industry 1899–1939

Year	Value-added ($000,000), (% of Man.)	All Employees (% of Man., of Tot. Empl.)	Value of Products ($000,000)	Number of Estab.
1899	44 (0.9)	48,491 (1.0,na)	94.7	592
1904	80 (1.3)	75,019 (1.3,0.2)	151	798
1909	121 (1.5)	111,067 (1.6,0.3)	233	1,027
1914	201 (2.1)	155,699 (2.1,0.4)	362.3	1,048
1919	672 (2.8)	305,222 (3.1,0.7)	1,156.5	1,570
1921	547 (3.2)	239,944 (3.2,0.6)	932.2	1,487
1923	806 (3.3)	331,505 (3.5,0.8)	1,400.3	1,782
1925	940 (3.7)	308,592 (3.4,0.7)	1,601.1	1,807
1927	1,049 (4.0)	322,397 (3.6,0.7)	1,743.6	1,837
1929	1,389 (4.5)	421,283 (4.4,0.9)	2,397.8	1,861
1931	763 (4.1)	—	—	1,596
1933	404 (2.9)	202,129 (3.1,0.5)	—	1,365
1935	686 (3.7)	275,343 (3.8,0.7)	—	1,589
1937	1,102 (4.4)	374,290 (3.8,0.8)	—	1,597
1939	941 (3.8)	—	1,727.4	1,979

Source: Backman (1962, p. 46, 77, 204).

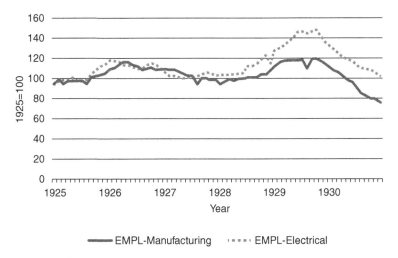

Figure 6.4.   Employment in Manufacturing and Electrical Equipment

Source: NBER Macrodata series M-08213a and M-08224.

6.7 Summary and Conclusions

In this chapter, it was argued that the nation's investors were (i) well aware of the growing acceleration-based output gap and (ii) understood the underlying objective of the Republican's proposed solution, namely higher tariff-induced market shares, complete with greater revenues, profits and earnings. As such, they responded favorably to positive or good tariff news, and unfavorably to negative or bad tariff news. Were it (i.e., the Hawley Tariff Bill) to have cleared the Senate without amendments in the summer/fall of 1929, there is every reason to believe that the stock market would not have crashed — at least not when it did.[2] In short, in the eyes of investors, tariffs were the proverbial key to higher revenues, profits and earnings.

This, however, was not to be. The Insurgent Republican–Democrat coalition decided otherwise, first by defeating the Thomas Amendment and second, by lowering the rate on tannic acid. The writing was on the wall: tariffs on manufactures would not only not rise, they would in all likelihood fall.

Underlying this schism was an ideological difference on tariffs and prices. The Republicans felt that higher tariffs, by securing greater market share, would allow U.S. manufacturers to exploit the acceleration-based economies of scales, thus providing the wherewithal to lower prices. The Insurgent Republican–Democrat coalition, on the other hand, adopted the more traditional approach of tariffs increasing prices, one that resonated throughout not only the public, but the economics profession at the time (and today).

Appendix: The Insurgent Republican–Democrat Coalition Responds to Accusations That It Caused the Stock Market Crash

In the days, if not hours, following the stock market crash, allegations were being leveled at the Insurgent Republican–Democrat coalition that

---

[2]There is every reason to believe that the crash would have been delayed, conceivably until such time as the U.S.'s trading partners raised tariffs on U.S. goods, thus wiping out all possible gains in sales, revenues and profits. In short, as import substitution is a zero-sum game, it was only a matter of time that the Republican Party attempt at closing the growing output gap would have failed.

its stance on tariffs (i.e., defeating the Thomas Recommittal Plan and announcing its intention to reduce tariffs on manufactures) had caused the crash. Newspaper editorials, Wall Street analysts and numerous others held that failure to deliver on the Kansas City tariff-for-all promises was what provoked the crash. Not surprisingly, the Insurgent Republican–Democrat coalition responded vigorously, denying any responsibility, all the while placing the blame on excessive speculation, the Federal Reserve, and a number of Wall Street bankers, notably the National City Bank and its president, Charles E. Mitchell.

This appendix presents an integral account of two such debates, one provoked by a *Washington Post* editorial on November 21, 1929, in which it was alleged that the Coalition was responsible for the crash, while the second is taken from a Hearing of the Senate sub-committee on the Judiciary, in which Fred I. Kent, an influential Wall Street banker and financial analyst, defended his view (quoted by Irving Fisher) that the stock market crash was caused by the Insurgent Republican–Democrat coalition. In both cases, what is noteworthy is the vigor with which the Coalition senators deny any and all responsibility, a vigor that bordered on outright bullying.

Excerpt from the Senate Congressional Record November 21, 1929

Immediately following that fine service the senior Senator from Kentucky [Mr. SACKETT], a member of the Finance Committee, a member of the sub-committee which drafted many of the rates in the bill on cotton and flax and wool, got recognition from the Chair and asked unanimous consent to have inserted in the CONGRESSIONAL RECORD, for distribution throughout the country, with governmental sanction and approval, an editorial, the most malicious, the most unwarranted, the most mendacious toward the Senate that I have read in a long time.

Mr. SACKETT. Mr. President

The VICE PRESIDENT. Does the Senator from Mississippi yield to the Senator from Kentucky?

Mr. SACKETT. Will the Senator yield?

Mr. HARRISON. I yield to the Senator.

Mr. SACKETT. When I rose to offer that editorial, I rose because the matter had been exploited upon the floor on yesterday in connection with an article from Mr. Babson. I offered to put the editorial into the

RECORD in order that the country should see the abuse that was being heaped on the Senate. I had to ask the privilege of the Senator from South Carolina, which he offered to me if there was to be no comment. I wanted that editorial as a text, in order that I might say later what my thought is upon the methods by which the Senate is excoriated by reputable journals in this country.

Mr. HARRISON. Well, I

Mr. SACKETT. One moment more.

Mr. HARRISON. If the Senator wants to make a speech in my time

Mr. SACKETT. Before the Senator proceeds, I want to place myself before the country in the proper light. Every group in the Senate is excoriated in that editorial.

Mr. HARRISON. Mr. President, I refuse to yield for a speech.

The VICE PRESIDENT. The Senator declines to yield.

Mr. HARRISON. I refuse to yield for a speech, because I want to make a speech myself.

Mr. SACKETT. I will return to the speech: I think the Senator misunderstands my purpose.

Mr. HARRISON. The Senator will have ample opportunity, and I hope he can get recognition to reply to me.

When the Senator offered that editorial the only fair construction to put ol his action was that he indorsed the editorial, that the many accusations and charges that are made in that editorial, untrue and unwarranted, received the approbation of the Senator from Kentucky. That the slush and dirt prepared by the editorial writer of that paper was to be applied by the Senator from Kentucky

Mr. SACKETT. Mr. President, will the Senator yield?

The VICE PRESIDENT. First let the Chair suggest that there has been a good deal of debate which he thinks is tending toward a violation of Rule XIX, and he would like to have section 2 of that rule read, so that Senators may keep themselves within the rule.

The Chief Clerk read as follows:

No Senator in debate shall, directly or indirectly, by any form of words impute to another Senator or to other Senators any conduct or motive unworthy or unbecoming a Senator.

Mr. HARRISON. Mr. President, I am thoroughly familiar with that rule, and I do not think I have said anything to impute any motive to anyone.

The VICE PRESIDENT. The Chair did not intend to indicate that the Senator had, but the Senator must admit that

lately on the floor of the Senate this rule has been in fact violated several times, and the present occupant of the Chair does not want to have it violated. He has simply had it read as a warning.

Mr. HARRISON. I am not going to violate it myself. I never violate the rules of the Senate if I call help it.

Mr. GLENN. Mr. President, the Senator from Mississippi has just stated that he believed, from what the Senator from Kentucky did in reference to this editorial, that the editorial met with his approval. I presume the speech of the Senator from Mississippi is proceeding upon that theory. The Senator from Kentucky has explained, or endeavored to explain, that it did not meet with his approval, but met with his disapproval.

Mr. HARRISON. I did not understand the Senator from Kentucky to say that it met with his disapproval. I can not understand how anyone in the wildest flight of imagination who disapproves of It should want it placed in the CONGRESSIONAL RECORD.

Mr. SACKETT. Mr. President, will the Senator yield?

The VICE PRESIDENT. Does the Senator from Mississippi yield to the Senator from Kentucky?

Mr. HARRISON. I yield.

Mr. SACKETT. The Senator from Kentucky endeavored to state that he disapproved of the editorial. He offered to put it in the RECORD in order that he might comment on it later and show the reason for it.

Mr. HARRISON. I will accept the Senator's statement and I will pass up the Senator. I apologize to him if, as he says, he disapproves of the editorial. I am glad indeed to hear that I misinterpreted the Senator's position.

Mr. NORRIS. Mr. President

The VICE PRESIDENT. Does the Senator from Mississippi yield to the Senator from Nebraska?

Mr. NORRIS. No, Mr. President: I thought the Senator from Mississippi had finished.

Mr. HARRISON. No: I have not finished. I want to say something about the editorial, and I hope when I shall have finished that the Senator from Kentucky can say that he indorses my remarks.

Mr. JOHNSON. Mr. President, will the Senator permit me to interrupt him?

The VICE PRESIDENT. Does the Senator from Mississippi yield to the Senator from California?

Mr. HARRISON. I yield.

Mr. JOHNSON. If I have acted under a misapprehension as to the attitude of the Senator from Kentucky, I want to make that plain. But here is the record. May I read it?

Mr. HARRISON. I yield for that purpose.

Mr. JOHNSON. The record is as follows:

Mr. SMITH obtained the floor.

Mr. SACKETT. Mr. President

The VICE PRESIDENT. Does the Senator from South Carolina yield to the Senator from Kentucky?

Mr. SMITH. I yield.

Mr. SACKETT. Without commenting thereon, but asking that it may receive the thoughtful consideration of the people of the country, I send to the desk and ask that the clerk may read an editorial appearing in the Washington Post this morning.

The VICE PRESIDENT. Is there objection?

Mr. HARRISON. Mr. President, a parliamentary inquiry.

Mr. SMITH. Mr. President, if the request of the Senator from Kentucky Is going to bring about a discussion I shall not yield to It.

Mr. SACKETT. Without comment, I have asked that the editorial may be read.

Mr. HARRISON. Is the Senator asking to have inserted in the RECORD the editorial appearing In the Washington Post this morning?

Mr. SACKETT. I am.

Mr. HARRISON. I desire to say that while I have no objection to having it put into the RECORD, I wish to have something to say about it If that shall be done.

Mr. JOHNSON. Mr. President-'

The VICE PRESIDENT. Does the Senator from Kentucky yield to the Senator from California?

Mr. SACKETT. Certainly.

Mr. JOHNSON. I glanced very hurriedly at the editorial in question. May I inquire whether the editorial which the Senator from Kentucky has asked to have read is the one that is bitterly and abusively critical of the Senate?

Mr. SACKETT'. It is.

Mr. JOHNSON. Very well.

Mr. SACKETT. That is the reason I have asked to have it read.

Mr. JOHNSON. I see.

Mr. SMITH. May I suggest to the Senator from Kentucky that when I get through-1 do not think It will take very long for me to do so, he can then ask that the editorial may be inserted in the RECORD?

The VICE PRESIDENT. The Senator from South Carolina declines to yield further.

Mr. SMOOT. Mr. President

The VICE PRESIDENT. Does the Senator from South Carolina yield to the Senator from Utah?

Mr. Smith. I yield.

Mr. SMOOT. In order to save any further discussion of the matter, I object to the request which has been made by the Senator from Kentucky. There is the incident in full, fresh from the official reporters' notes.

Mr. HARRISON. Mr. President, I do not believe that the Senate has ever in all its history held the confidence of the people in higher esteem than today. There was a time when this body reacted immediately and favorably by a very large majority to the wishes and desires of certain special interests. There was a time when the Senate was called the " Plutocrats' Club." There was a time when it might have been in disfavor among the great masses of the American people. There was a time when special privilege entered this Chamber, assured that it would be protected. But today the Senate is more responsive to the will of the American people than ever before. It is responsive at this particular time because a group of forward looking and progressive men on the other side of the Chamber, inspired by a purpose to serve the whole country and to give equality of treatment to every class and industry in the country, are willing to join with us over here and force the legislation through. Of course, there are still some on the other side of the aisle who have been repudiated day after day in this body, who would still listen to the voice of those who sit in the big offices and try to exact greater privileges from the Government.

That is what is the matter with the Washington Post, Mr. President. It is not often that its editorial columns contain favorable expressions about the Senate of the United States, and especially has it been true during this extraordinary session of the Senate that it has condemned our action. It was against us in our farm-relief policy. It has been against us in our fight to equalize the duties so that every industry and every class of our people might be treated fairly by the Government. The Post has said that this group of progressive Republicans and the Democrats have betrayed the farmers: that they have not met their promises to the agricultural elements of the country.

Mr. President, the Washington Post will never make the farmers of the country believe that. Higher rates are carried in the bill for the agricultural interests of the country than in any prior bill, and to clinch that proposition we have given them the debenture plan in order to make the rates at least in part effective. If the fight we have waged for farm relief in connection with the farm relief bill had been successful, and if we had been able to force the adoption of the debenture plan at that time, the wheat farmers and the cotton farmers and other agricultural interests of the country would to-day be getting greater consideration with better results than they are now at the hands of the board which is now operating.

There is to-day a subtle plan chartered, upon the part of certain people who dislike what has been done during this extraordinary session of Congress, to belittle the Senate of the United States, to make light of its achievements, to put it in unfavorable light before the country. It is a plan to throw up a smoke screen in order to cover up what others in high places have done or have failed to do in this great crisis. That is a part of the plan of this newspaper in the city of Washington. We know propaganda when we see it. Those of us who have been in politics for more than a year can see it when it is written by the special newspaper correspondents who dine at the White House and who take fishing trips down into Virginia with the President, and then with their subtle pens write this propaganda, hoping that they might create an impression in the country unfavorable to the Senate and favorable to some one else in high places. I could mention by name some of the special writers, and the time may come In the Senate when we will mention them by name, who are creating such propaganda. They are as well organized as were the propagandists under the leadership of Grundy in his fight against the tariff bill. This editorial is a part of that plan to try to put the President of the United States in a favorable light before the farmers of the country and the business interests of the country, and in order to do so they think they must tear down the work of this body. The Senate of the United States has always been a great body. It is the forum that guarantees at this time the rights of the great masses of the American people. Congressional Record (1929, p. 5869).

The debate continued for hours, with Republican senators vigorously defending either the tariff bill as passed by the House, or in the case of the Coalition, their intent on reducing all tariffs on manufactures, preferring to put the blame on Wall Street, specifically on Charles E. Mitchell of National City Bank.

Excerpt from the Hearings Before a Sub-Committee of the Committee of the Judiciary Regarding Wall Street Banker Fred I. Kent's View that the Tariff Fight Caused the Crash
As it turned out, the next day, November 22, a Senate Judiciary sub-committee held a hearing on the stock market crash in which the chief witness was New York banker Fred I. Kent who had since the crash developed a following for having alleged that the crash was the result of the tariff, specifically of the Insurgent Republican–Democrat coalition's attempt to cut tariffs on manufactures.

FRIDAY, NOVEMBER 22, 1929

UNITED STATES SENATE,
SUB-COMMITTEE OF THE COMMITTEE ON THE JUDICIARY,
Washington, D. C.

The sub-committee met, pursuant to adjournment, at 10 o'clock a.m., in room 212, Senate Office Building, Senator Thaddeus H. Caraway, chairman, presiding.

Present: Senators Caraway (chairman), Borah, Robinson of Indiana, Blaine, and Walsh of Montana.

Present also: Senator Carter Glass, of Virginia: John G. Holland, Esq., counsel to the committee.

TESTIMONY OF FRED I. KENT

(The witness was duly sworn by Senator Caraway.)

Senator CARAWAY. Will you give your name and residence and occupation to the stenographer, please, sir.

Mr. KENT. My name is Fred I. Kent: my residence is Scarsdale, N. Y.: my occupation has always been a banker. I am director of the Bankers' Trust Co. now, but two years ago I asked to be relieved from executive duty, so that I am not acting as an executive at the moment.

Senator WALSH of Montana. Your presence here, Mr. Kent, is due to some extent at least to the proceedings in the Senate appearing in the record as follows:

Mr. HAWES. Mr. President, I wish to recall the statement made by Mr. Fred I. Kent, director of the Bankers' Trust Co. of New York, in which he asserts that the second reason why we had a great crash in the stock market-two of the greatest financial panics this country has ever had-was the situation in the United States Senate, due to an alleged coalition in the Senate and due to the manner in which we have been discussing the tariff. It seems to me, Mr. President, that this is propaganda, because no sensible man for a moment would assume the truth of the statement. I desire to ask the chairman of the lobby investigating committee whether, in his opinion, Mr. Kent could not be brought before his committee and asked to explain why he has reached such a conclusion.

Mr. CARAWAY. Mr. President, I have no doubt but that Mr. Kent's alleged propaganda falls directly within the purview of the committee, but I do think that before we start investigating Mr. Kent. we ought at least to wait until at least we reach the joke column, because anybody who would put forth a statement like that, and expect anybody to believe it, of course, is suffering from arrested mental development. Since there is a demand for it. however, I think we can let him waste an hour spinning a tale that nobody believes, including himself.

Mr. HAWES. I should like publicly to request the chairman of the lobby committee to summon Mr. Kent.

Mr. CARAWAY. It will be done, sir. Do you recall the speech to which reference is made in this extract from the record which I have read you?

Mr. KENT. I have heard about it, but I hadn't read it.

Senator WALSH of Montana. No: I mean -

Mr. KENT. You mean the speech I made?

Senator WALSH of Montana. Yes.

A gracious witness in the circumstances, Kent explained his reasoning in the following terms:

The direct and particular forces which caused the tremendous crash in prices were, first, capital-gain taxes, which prevented readjustment of investments as prices reached a point where men would otherwise have sold certain of their stocks and naturally would have invested the proceeds in bonds. This resulted in the security market going forward too fast and causing stagnation in the bond market.

Second, fear engendered in the mind of the business public by the action of the coalition bloc in Congress in connection with the tariff bill. The activities of this bloc and their methods aroused a feeling of uncertainty on the part of industry, and uncertainty is the most difficult thing for business to face. There was the fear that if this bloc succeeded in rewriting the tariff bill in its own way that it might come to believe that it had the power to reduce existing tariffs. The real fear was not due so much to the questions involved in possible forward changes over the present tariff as in such changes as might reduce the present tariff in such manner as to injure industry and result in unemployment. As soon as dealers in securities, who are constantly on the watch for indications as to business changes, realized that this feeling of uneasiness was spreading throughout industry, they began selling stocks.

As the days went on and the power of the coalition bloc seemed to be growing, more and more selling entered into the market. While this was going on new securities issues were being offered, which could not be satisfactorily distributed.

The result was that the market became so top heavy that the first adjustment selling carried values down in such proportion that a vast public which had been purchasing securities both outright and on margin began to sell at once.

Such action, together with the uneasiness caused by the coalition bloc in connection with the tariff, changed the psychology of millions of potential investors who, instead of being willing to buy on the prospects of growing business, determined to hold off until prices had reached what might be called current business values.

With a tremendous public trying to sell and the potential buying public not caring to act, it became necessary for financial and business men to step in and buy stocks which they did not want in order first to try and create an orderly market while prices were going down to the point where investment buyers would come to the support of the market on a strictly present investment basis and then to supplement such investment buying to the extent that proved to be necessary.

It is interesting, important, and valuable to note what happened in connection with the great market break of Tuesday, October 29. On the one hand, we had the business interests of the country, who in their desire to protect the people from loss and catastrophe and to enable the continuation of production on a basis necessary and valuable to every citizen, be he rich or poor, went into the market and bought stocks before they had reached what could be called a current business market investing level with the certain feeling that for the moment they must meet with loss. On the other hand, what of the politicians? An announcement appeared in the paper Tuesday morning, October 29, that the Governor of the State of New York had said that the next investigation would be a public utility investigation. Was there anything helpful about that in an unfortunate emergency situation? A Senator from Iowa was quoted as calling attention to the fact that the situation that was developing might result in bankruptcy of the banks. Was there anything helpful about that to the American people?

Another Senator, a leader of one of. the great parties, followed the break by trying to capitalize it for his party, and all kinds of investigations have been threatened.

It would seem well for the people to ponder these things. There is no doubt whatsoever but that in every great human activity there are those who may use bad judgment, and, what is more unfortunate, those who may carry on in ways which are not ethical. But a situation such as that which developed in the recent panic sale of securities in the United States is one where the good of the people requires the application of sound judgment in weighing the experience, and knowledge through research of what has happened by those competent to carry it out without prejudice, political bias, or unfortunate publicity, and not the breaking of men for the purpose of adding to political power.

Summarizing, we find that sound business growth was at the bottom of the normal rise in the price of securities, that politics as exercised in the capital-gain tax prevented sales of securities which would have acted to hold the price within bounds, that uncertainties caused by political blocs in Congress changed a forward-looking national psychology into one of uncertainty, that new securities were created and issued more rapidly than the public could absorb and that their inclusion in brokers' loans and other security loans was not intelligently understood, that certain of these forces worked to create high prices for securities and others to undermine such prices after they had been attained.

The great question of the moment is what can be done to add further safety to our security dealings while maintaining a great open market that will enable industry to expand as it should and continue the employment of labor and allow those who desire to buy and sell stock to do so on the soundest possible basis.

Interestingly, Senator William Borah, the *de facto* leader of the Insurgent Republicans–Democrat coalition and member of the sub-committee appeared to be engaging in a form of historical revisionism, arguing that the Coalition had no intention to lower tariffs on manufactures.

> Senator BORAH. Now as a matter of fact, the position of the so-called coalition from the beginning was not to touch industrial schedules at all, and we undertook to put through a resolution to leave them untouched and came within one of passing it. So the sole program was to increase the agricultural duties, so as to give reasonable protection to agriculture, and to leave the act of 1922, which gives industry 97 percent of the home market, untouched. That was the position of the coalition announced time and time again.
>
> Mr. KENT. Well, it was not announced in a way.
>
> Senator BORAH. Yes: it was announced.
>
> Mr. KENT. It was not announced in a way that impressed people that way. I know that there was fear among industrialists as to how that tariff was going to develop. I do not think they paid so much attention to it the first few months, because they realized it would take time to get it in order, but I do feel that the last two months they were very much

exercised about it. I think it had an effect in changing the psychology of the people.

Senator BORAH. Now another thing: Do you know of any industrial rate which the coalition has undertaken to reduce?

Mr. KENT. I have not paid any attention to the details of the tariff bill, because I am not a tariff expert.

Senator BORAH. Have you seen anywhere in any newspaper any account of any industrial rate assailed by the coalition?

Mr. KENT. No. I only know that there was a feeling that that was the point of view. Maybe that feeling was wrong, but that was the feeling on the part of many. Maybe they were wrong.

Senator BORAH. Have you made any study of the rates as they have been passed upon by the Senate thus far?

Mr. KENT. No. I have made no study of that. I was studying the psychology of the people, based on the development.

Senator BORAH. You have no detailed information then, that is to say. no fact which you can give to the committee based upon any act of the Senate which would justify the criticism that you have made?

Chapter 7

The Stock Market Crash and the Decline in Investment: The Depression Sets In*

7.1 Introduction

The previous chapter presented a blow-by-blow account of the October stock market crash, of the failure on the part of the Republicans to deliver on their electoral promise. The proposed higher tariffs would have, by reducing imports, made more room in the domestic market for U.S. products. Investors were on board, so to speak. The promises made in Kansas City would be kept. Sales, revenues and profits would rise. Electric unit drive-based acceleration would, given the expanded domestic market, ramp up profits. The future looked bright. The roar of the twenties would be even louder, perhaps even deafening.

However as shown, two Senate votes on amendments would seal the fate of the Bill, or so it was thought. The promise, the hope, the dream would not come true. Tariffs, the workhorse of U.S. economic policy from the very birth of the nation, would falter.

This brings us to the fallout. Strapped with growing excess rated capacity as conversion to electric unit drive continued throughout the late 1920s, companies canceled planned investment ($\pi^v(t)$ in Equation (4.8)). After all, why invest in new plant and equipment when existing capacity

---

*This chapter draws from Beaudreau, Bernard C. Electrification, the Smoot–Hawley Tariff Act and the Decline in Investment Expenditure in 1931–1932: Testing the Excess-Capacity Hypothesis, *International Advances in Economic Research*, 2017, 1–14.

(increasing) is not fully utilized? Add to this the threatened retaliation on the part of the U.S.'s trading partners to the eventual passage of the tariff bill in June 1930 which would see U.S. exports plummet and what followed was a severe economic downturn, one whose breadth was unequaled since.

In this chapter, evidence is presented which shows that the decrease in the level of investment was intimately tied to the fallout of the tariff bill, specifically the growing excess rated capacity. Put differently, by October 1929, companies were swimming in excess rated capacity. To this end, it will be shown that the decrease in investment at the industry level in the post-crash period was increasing in the industry's experience with electric unit drive. In other words, the more firms in an industry had converted to the new power drive technology, the greater the decrease in investment expenditure.

7.2 Acceleration and Autonomous Expenditure-Based Disequilibrium: A Numerical Example

This section presents a numerical example of a decline in autonomous expenditure ($\pi^y(t)$ or $\varphi(t)$) investment expenditure or net exports set against a background of electric unit drive-based acceleration. Specifically, acceleration is assumed to occur at $t = 1$, and the decrease in autonomous expenditure at $t = 2$.

In this simulation (see Table 7.1), acceleration increases $s(t)$ from 5 per hour to 7 per hour, a 40 percent increase at $t = 1$. Initial GDP is 1,200, with wage income of 840 and profit income of 360. In the first iteration, output rises to 1,680 which is not sustainable given income and expenditure, thus forcing firms to readjust, decreasing $h(t)$ in the second iteration to 17.14, which brings the level of output back down to 1,200. At $t = 2$, the wage bill decreases to 600 which in combination with a decrease in autonomous expenditure of 50 percent (from 360 to 180) results in an overall decrease in expenditure to 780. The downward spiral continues for eight periods until $t = 10$ at which time equilibrium is reestablished at $h(10) = 5.18$.

This example illustrates the combined effect of an acceleration-based increase in output per hour and a decrease in autonomous expenditure. Comparing the results with those of Table 4.5 in Chapter 4 (base case), both output, wage income and profits are substantially lower. In the following sections, this example will be used to illustrate the effect of the

Table 7.1. Acceleration and Autonomous Expenditure-Based Disequilibrium: A Numerical Example

t	*h(t)*	*p(t)s(t)h(t)k(t)*	*w(t)h(t)k(t)*	*π(t)+φ(t)*	*π(t)*
0	24	1,200	840	360	0
1	24	1,680	840	360	0
2	17.14	1,200	600	180	240
3	11.14	780	390	180	30
4	8.14	570	285	180	−75
5	6.64	465	232	180	−127
6	5.89	412	206	180	−154
7	5.51	386	193	180	−167
8	5.33	373	186	180	−173
9	5.23	366	183	180	−177
10	5.18	363	181	180	−178

Note: $p(t) = 1$, $s(t) = 5$, $k(t) = 10$, $w(t) = 3.5$, $\pi(t) = 360$.

ongoing conversion to electric unit drive that occurred throughout the 1930s, the important decrease in investment expenditure that followed the stock market crash as well as the decrease in net exports that resulted from the tariff war prompted by the final passage of the Smoot–Hawley Tariff Act in June 1930.

7.3 Electric Unit Drive: Profitable in the Upturn and Downturn

Conversion to electric unit drive has the unique property of being highly profitable both in the upturn and in the downturn. In the former, it provides companies with a means to meet growing demand without necessarily investing in new greenfield capacity–that is, adding new plant and equipment and hiring new workers. Moreover, the cost consists of replacing belting and shafting with electric unit drive — in short, of fitting each tool/machine/work station with an AC or DC electric motor, powered by purchased utility-generated electricity. Factories would be reorganized, paving the way for mass production.

As it turned out, the conversion to electric unit drive was also highly profitable in the downturn. In the face of weakening demand, companies could cut labor costs by accelerating existing processes. For example, a company faced with a decrease in sales of 20 percent could accelerate production by 33 percent, thereby decreasing $h(t)$ by 40 percent, all the while meeting demand. Given that labor costs represent roughly 65 percent of total costs per dollar output, doing so would decrease total labor costs by 40 percent.

While this is a dominant strategy at the company level, it does two things at the macroeconomic level. First, it serves to exacerbate the problem of excess rated capacity and, second, it reduces the overall wage bill — in short, it reduces purchasing power, thus widening the imbalance in two distinct ways. This, it should be pointed out, highlights the difference between the model presented here and the standard Keynesian model where falling income (wage bill) is the sole factor that widens the imbalance.

7.4 Investment Expenditure Declines

With the stock market crash came what could best be described as a rude awakening. The country found itself with growing excess rated capacity and no solution in sight. The decade-long conversion to electric unit drive had increased and continued to increase rated capacity throughout the economy, making new investment in plant and equipment increasingly redundant. Not surprisingly, investment expenditure fell precipitously in the aftermath of the crash.

Given the role of electric unit drive in increasing rated capacity, it would stand to reason that the decline in investment expenditure at the firm level would be an increasing function of the company's investment in the new drive technology throughout the 1910s and 1920s. Companies and industries that had invested heavily would be more inclined to curtail planned investment in light of the failed tariff bill. In previous work, Beaudreau (2017c) tested this hypothesis using industry data. Specifically, using Bernstein's (1987) data on equipment and plant investment by industry from 1925 to 1940 and Census of Manufactures data on investment in electric motors, he examined the relationship between industry investment in plant and equipment in the downturn and the growth of electric unit drive.

Industry data on both installed horsepower and workers from the U.S. Bureau of the Census' Survey of Manufactures for 1909 and

Table 7.2. Electric Power Use Growth 1909–1929

Industry	HPE/WE1909	HPE/WE1929	Growth
Textile Mill Products	0.622	3.784	6.077
Men's Clothing	0.095	0.221	2.323
Women's Clothing	0.104	0.186	1.781
Lumber	0.188	2.110	11.223
Paper and Allied Products	1.712	15.646	9.135
Printing and Publishing	0.887	1.905	2.147
Chemicals	6.604	10.404	1.575
Stone, Clay and Glass	0.819	7.330	8.947
Petroleum	0.632	7.493	11.850
Rubber	0.710	6.143	8.644
Fabricated Metals	2.984	15.071	5.049
Transportation Eq.	0.552	6.483	11.737

1929 were used to generate growth rates for horsepower per worker at the industry level, presented in Table 7.2. We see that conversion to electric unit drive from 1909 to 1929 was greatest in the Petroleum and Transportation industries and slowest in the Clothing industries (Men's and Women's).

Analysis of variance was performed on six specific sub-periods, namely 1927–1928, 1929–1927, 1929–1930, 1931–1929, 1932–1929 and 1933–1929. Referring to Table 7.3, we see that while investment in equipment (DEQ) and plant (DPL) was positively correlated with the measure of conversion to electric unit drive (EUD2909) in 1928, it turned negative afterward as evidenced by the negative correlation coefficients for the subsequent years. Put differently, from 1929 on, investment in plant and equipment was decreasing to the extent to which companies in the industry had converted to electric unit drive, the latter being a proxy for $s(t)$, industry machine speed and thus of the extent to which the industry was characterized by excess rated capacity.

It is important to bear in mind that despite the negative levels of investment reported in the 1930s by Bernstein (1987), investment in electric unit drive (i.e., electrical equipment) continued throughout the 1930s, increasing firms' rated capacity. Laggard firms in industries that had

Table 7.3. Correlation Coefficients–Equipment
and Plant Investment and Electric Unit Drive

Variable	Estimated Correlation Coefficient EUD2909
DEQ2827	0.524
DEQ2927	-0.199
DEQ3029	-0.337
DEQ3129	-0.478
DEQ3229	-0.383
DEQ3329	-0.277
DPL2827	0.506
DPL2927	-0.221
DPL3029	-0.118
DPL3129	-0.397
DPL3229	-0.234
DPL3329	-0.244

Source: Beaudreau (2017c).

experienced above average growth in electric power usage, as well as firms in other industries, converted to the new technology throughout the 1930s. As argued earlier, this owed to the fact that acceleration, even in the face of declining sales, was a profit-increasing strategy. Consider the following article that appeared in The *New York Times* on December 1, 1935, under the headline "Faster Machines Sought: Manufacturers Demanding Speed Attachments for Equipment" which reports: "Demands made upon machine tool builders for special attachments to increase productive speed and accuracy are becoming an increasing problem to producers, it was pointed out here yesterday (*New York Times*, December 1, 1935)."

7.5 The Smoot–Hawley Tariff Act, The Tariff War and the Collapse of World Trade

By signaling the end of the Republican promises made at the Kansas City national convention in June 1928, the stock market crash of October 1929 led firms to revise downwards their investment expenditure, thus marking the beginning of the downturn. The latter, in turn, led Reed Smoot to reintroduce the original bill in the spring of 1930, which, given rapidly deteriorating economic conditions (employment and output), won approval in the Senate. As it turned out, a number of Insurgent Republican senators had a change of heart in light of growing concerns that the U.S. economy was sliding into a recession. The original Bill (H.R. 2667) was signed into law by President Hoover on June 17, 1930.

In little time, trading partner after trading partner raised tariffs on U.S. goods, touching off a global tariff war, which in the end saw world trade decrease by 50 percent. U.S. exports fell drastically, which added to the decrease in investment in plant and equipment spelled disaster for the economy. Against a backdrop of continuing conversion to electric unit drive, aggregate expenditure decreased throughout the early 1930s, thus widening the already important output gap. Formally, what was a structural output gap was now both a structural and contractionary (i.e., conjectural) output gap.

With the benefit of hindsight, the Republican Party's attempt at closing the growing output gap in the late 1920s had gone horribly wrong, prompting a stock market boom and crash, a subsequent decrease in investment as companies found themselves with excess rated capacity, and last, a global tariff war that reduced world trade by 50 percent, impacting U.S. industry and agriculture alike. By 1933, U.S. GDP had fallen by 45 percent, and unemployment had increased to 35 percent.

Hope had been lost, giving way to an overall sense of gloom and doom. Ironically, what at the time was the most advanced and productive wealth-producing nation of all time found itself in a state of despair, having prompted a worldwide downturn of epic proportions. In the words of the *Report of the Committee on Recent Economic Changes of the President's Conference on Unemployment*, the U.S. economy was more out of "balance" in the early 1930s than it had ever been before.

7.6 Summary and Conclusions

The results of the 1932 general elections brought to an end a highly controversial, a highly eventful and a highly misunderstood period in U.S. history, one that witnessed the decline into a downward spiral of the greatest wealth-producing machine man has ever created. It also marked the end of the Hoover Administration's naïve, poorly thought-out and highly divisive attempt to close the ever-widening output gap using an unlikely instrument, namely tariff policy. A combination of tradition, opportunism and ignorance, the Smoot–Hawley Tariff Act was the Republican Party's best response to a problem that scholars had, for the most part, not begun to grapple with, namely acceleration-based increases in potential GDP.

In all fairness, however, it would be a travesty to associate Hoover's name to the tariff bill, for he was, in large measure, opposed to the use of tariffs as a means of dealing with the imbalance. Like his fellow engineers, he was well aware of the growing imbalance in the U.S. economy and had, over the course of his tenure as Secretary of Commerce in the Coolidge Administration, advocated a form of business–government cooperation aimed at correcting the situation, known as the Associative State. As it turned out, the task of closing the gap and removing the imbalance would from 1933 fall upon the shoulders of the newly-elected Roosevelt Administration. Unlike senators Reed Smoot and Joseph R. Grundy, President Franklin D Roosevelt and senator Robert F. Wagner would draw heavily from a non-mainstream school of thought that advocated generalized wage increases as a means of closing the gap. These included the writings of Columbia University economics professor Rexford G. Tugwell, University of Chicago economics professor Paul Douglas, and a number of corporate liberals, including Henry Ford and Edward A. Filene, the renowned Boston merchant. In the next chapter, the flagship piece of legislation of the Roosevelt Administration (and cornerstone of the New Deal), the National Industrial Recovery Act of 1933, will be presented and examined critically.

Appendix: Hoover and the Associative State

It is well known that President Herbert Hoover, despite signing the Smoot–Hawley Tariff Act into law, was opposed to it, almost from the start. An engineer by training, he like his fellow engineers believed that the imbalance could be better addressed by a series of measures intended to increase income and expenditure. In his tenure as Secretary of Commerce in the Coolidge Administration, his thinking coalesced in what is known as the concept of the Associative State. In this appendix, President Herbert Hoover's response to the growing output gap, known as the Associative State, is presented. As it turned out, despite winning the nomination in Kansas City in June 1928, he was, in general, not in favor of the Party's chosen solution to the problem at hand, namely the growing output gap and weakening labor markets. Rather, his approach to the problem was a New Deal of sorts, one between government and industry, one based on better information, productivity growth and rising wages. He referred to this as the Associative State.

According to history professor Ellis W. Hawley:

Hoover in 1921 saw himself as the protagonist of a new and superior synthesis between the old industrialism and the new, a way whereby America could benefit from scientific rationalization and social engineering without sacrificing the energy and creativity inherent in individual effort, "grassroots" involvement, and private enterprise. Such a synthesis, he argued, would make the "American system" superior to any other, particularly in its ability to raise living standards, humanize industrial relationships, and integrate conflicting social elements into a harmonious community of interests (Hawley, 1974, p. 116).

Chapter 8

The National Industrial Recovery Act: FDR'S Bold Attempt at Closing the Gap*

A glance at the situation today only too clearly indicates that equality of opportunity as we have known it no longer exists. Our industrial plant is built: the problem just now is whether under existing conditions it is not overbuilt. Our last frontier has long since been reached, and there is practically no more free land. More than half of our people do not live on the farms or on lands and cannot derive a living by cultivating their own property. There is no safety valve in the form of a Western prairie to which those thrown out of work by the Eastern economic machines can go for a new start. We are not able to invite the immigration from Europe to share our endless plenty. We are now providing a drab living for our own people.

As I see it, the task of Government in its relation to business is to assist the development of an economic declaration of rights, an economic constitutional order. This is the common task of statesmen and businessmen. It is the minimum requirement of a more permanently safe order of things. Happily, the times indicate that to create such an order not only is the proper policy of Government, but it is the only line of safety for our economic structures as well. We know, now, that these

---

*This chapter is based on Beaudreau, Bernard C. Why Did the National Industrial Recovery Act Fail? *European Review of Economic History*, 2016, 79–101.

economic units cannot exist unless prosperity is uniform, that is, unless purchasing power is well distributed throughout every group in the Nation.

Franklin D. Roosevelt, Commonwealth Club Address
(September 23, 1932)

8.1 Introduction

As shown in Chapter 4, the widening, acceleration-based output gap — aka the imbalance — had been on the minds of many prior to the crash and during the subsequent downturn, including businessmen, academics and government officials. From early on, Henry Ford, founder and president of the Ford Motor Company, a company that had invested heavily in electric unit drive-based acceleration, advocated higher wages — and lower prices — as the solution, as the way out.[1] He was joined by other prominent businessmen including Boston merchant Edward A. Filene. Academics of the likes of Thorstein Veblen had denounced the failure of businessmen in general to lower prices in response to electric unit drive, alleging that to refuse to do so consisted of a form of sabotage, in short sabotaging the transition to the new equilibrium growth path. Others such as Columbia University economics professor Rexford G. Tugwell advocated higher wages, as did MIT-trained economist Stuart Chase, Brookings Institution founder and president, Robert E. Brookings, and numerous others.

Another less-known advocate of the high-wage doctrine (i.e., in order to close the gap) was professional engineer, Secretary of Commerce in the Coolidge Administration and former president Herbert Hoover. As a trained engineer, he like most in his profession was well aware of the changes and challenges prompted by the new power drive technology. Throughout his tenure as Secretary of Commerce in the Coolidge Administration, he advocated a concept known as the Associative State, the cornerstone of which was higher wages. The Associative State was a view of the government as a partner with business, providing information

---

[1] In fact, mass production *à la* Ford consisted of accelerating via the application of electric unit drive of the production lines-chains of the time. Many industries, including meat packing, had organized production along the line or chain principle, the only difference being that the line or chain was not power driven.

that would give them the wherewithal to increase output, wages and employment. He felt that with sufficient information, business leaders would, of their own volition, do the right thing and increase purchasing power in the face of acceleration, thus restoring balance to the system. To this end, he revamped the Department of Commerce, starting with information. The Survey of Current Business and other such publications are examples.

Unfortunately, Hoover was at the wrong place at the wrong time. Those who nominated him at the Kansas City 1928 GOP convention had an altogether different view of how to close the output gap, namely higher tariffs — which it bears noting he openly and repeatedly opposed. His belief in the high-wage doctrine came through in the 1930–1932 downturn during which, in keeping with his earlier beliefs, he pleaded with the business community to resist cutting wages.

While he, like Ford, favored higher wages, he stopped short of advocating third-party coercion on the part of the government. Ford believed in persuasion while Hoover believed in spontaneous cooperation. Unfortunately, in both cases, the result was the same: wages in general failed to rise. While higher wages appeared to be viable in new, booming sectors like automobiles, it was less obvious in mature industries that had adopted electric unit drive. In short, they were more likely to have made sense if sales and revenues had increased, or were increasing. Furthermore, it is important to note that not all sectors and not all firms within each sector adopted the new power drive technology. With the benefit of hindsight, the idea of somehow steering the U.S. economy on to its new growth path via a form of government coercion was not at all obvious.

Enter New York governor Democrat Franklin D. Roosevelt who, on the advice of senator Robert F. Wagner and Columbia University economics professor Rexford G. Tugwell, called for a New Deal with the American people, one that would see wages and purchasing power increase. This would be achieved by (i) wage and price legislation (ii) government expenditure and (iii) strengthening the labor movement. To their way of thinking, the Great Depression was the result of a structural problem, namely of purchasing power failing to keep pace with the capacity of the U.S. economy to create wealth — in other words, macroeconomic imbalance. Like Hoover, they rejected calls for the Federal Government to run deficits in order to stimulate the economy as they felt that the problem was structural in nature, and would require structural, not short-term,

Seventy-third Congress of the United States of America;

At the First Session,

Begun and held at the City of Washington on Thursday, the ninth
day of March, one thousand nine hundred and thirty-three.

AN ACT

To encourage national industrial recovery, to foster fair competition, and to provide for the construction of certain useful public
works, and for other purposes.

---

*Be it enacted by the Senate and House of Representatives of the
United States of America in Congress assembled,*

TITLE I—INDUSTRIAL RECOVERY

DECLARATION OF POLICY

SECTION 1. A national emergency productive of widespread unemployment and disorganization of industry, which burdens interstate
and foreign commerce, affects the public welfare, and undermines
the standards of living of the American people, is hereby declared
to exist. It is hereby declared to be the policy of Congress to remove
obstructions to the free flow of interstate and foreign commerce
which tend to diminish the amount thereof; and to provide for the
general welfare by promoting the organization of industry for the
purpose of cooperative action among trade groups, to induce and
maintain united action of labor and management under adequate
governmental sanctions and supervision, to eliminate unfair competitive practices, to promote the fullest possible utilization of the
present productive capacity of industries, to avoid undue restriction
of production (except as may be temporarily required), to increase
the consumption of industrial and agricultural products by increasing purchasing power, to reduce and relieve unemployment, to
improve standards of labor, and otherwise to rehabilitate industry
and to conserve natural resources.

ADMINISTRATIVE AGENCIES

SEC. 2. (a) To effectuate the policy of this title, the President is
hereby authorized to establish such agencies, to accept and utilize
such voluntary and uncompensated services, to appoint, without
regard to the provisions of the civil service laws, such officers and
employees, and to utilize such Federal officers and employees, and,
with the consent of the State, such State and local officers and employees, as he may find necessary, to prescribe their authorities,
duties, responsibilities, and tenure, and, without regard to the Classi-

Figure 8.1.   The National Industrial Recovery Act 1933

solutions. Put differently, in their eyes, government expenditure would not fix the underlying structural problem.

This chapter chronicles what was and perhaps what is the greatest economic policy experiment in all of history, namely the National Industrial Recovery Act of 1933 (see Figure 8.1).[2] Inspired by the same WIB that had advocated large-scale public electrical utilities and mass production in the closing years of World War I, it proposed a top-down approach to closing the widening output gap via greater income and expenditure — in short, Hoover's Associative State augmented by state-sponsored coercion. Put differently, firms would not be asked to raise wages: they would be told to.

8.2 U.S. Structural, Contractionary and Overall Output Gaps: Definitions

A structural output gap is, by definition, a gap between potential and actual U.S. GDP that results from technological change. A contractionary output gap, by definition, is a gap between potential and actual output that results from conjectural factors. The structural output gap, in so far as we are concerned, is that which existed in October 1929 (i.e., that is, before the downturn), while the contractionary output gap is that which existed between the beginning of the downturn (i.e., 1929) and January 1933 when Roosevelt assumed power. Assuming an output gap (conservative) of 30 percent, potential U.S. GDP in 1929 would have stood at $103.1 \times (1.3)$ or $133.9 billion ($264.68 billion in 1958$), which implies a structural output gap of $33.6 billion ($61.8 billion in 1958$). As actual GDP had fallen to $55.6 billion ($141 billion in 1958$) by the end of 1932, the contractionary output gap would have been $48 billion ($62.1 billion in 1958$). The overall output gap would have been the sum of the two, or $78.3 billion ($123.18 billion in 1958$). In short, the task before the Roosevelt Administration was colossal as not only would it need to close the contractionary output gap, it would also have to close the structural output gap alleged to have been the root cause of the downturn. Success would require an overall increase in real U.S. GDP of $78.3 billion, or roughly 88 percent of 1933 GDP.

---

[2] That is, within the context of a market economy.

8.3 Policy Options

As President Franklin D. Roosevelt and members of the Brains Trust, especially Columbia University economics professor Rexford G. Tugwell, felt that the structural output gap was the root cause of the downturn, they focused first and foremost on getting the underlying fundamentals right, so to speak. As pointed out in Chapter 4, there are a number of ways of closing an acceleration-based structural output gap (Equation (4.8)). These include lower prices, higher wages, government expenditure and an increase in net exports. However, each of these is problematic in its own right. As shown in Chapter 4, acceleration-based productivity gains had nothing to do with the physical contribution of labor. As pointed out, workers simply were called upon to supervise what were faster material processes. Thus, there is every reason to believe that employers would have resisted — or not acquiesced to — wage increases on what were technological grounds. Put simply, the increase in output/productivity owed to the application of more power, leading to greater machine speeds and more output, not to labor.

Increased government expenditure was also problematic for a number of reasons. First, it would need to be substantial given the overall output gap of $88 billion. Second, it would be distortionary owing to the fact that it would affect all sectors equally despite the fact that the gap varied across industries. Third, it would need to be recurrent given the underlying structural problem (insufficient income — wages). Fourth, it would need to be financed by printing money as taxation would not increase overall income and expenditure.

This brings us to generalized price deflation. As pointed out in Chapter 4, price deflation could restore balance by increasing the real wage (at the industry level) — ideally in proportion to the rate of productivity growth. This, however, was also problematic as it would require that companies hold nominal wages constant. Add to this the fact that cutting prices would not necessarily increase market share and one gets resistance on the part of CEOs to cut prices along the lines suggested by Henry Ford.

For price cutting to be an optimal strategy, two conditions would have to hold, namely that a decrease in price will have to lead to a non-negligible increase in demand, and second, that all other firms do likewise. For example, if a 40 percent increase in productivity results in a 40 percent decrease in price, then the firm's real revenues and profits would not have increased. However, if all firms cut prices by 40 percent, then real profits would increase by 40 percent.

The Problem of Assigning Property Rights to the Energy-Based Increase in Wealth

With the benefit of hindsight, the problem both before and after the downturn was one of assigning ownership of what were energy rents — in this case, electric power rents. As shown in Chapter 4, the increased productivity owed to more electric power, more speed — in short, to acceleration. As the value of the additional output was significantly greater than the monetary costs (price of kWh), rents were created (Beaudreau 1998). The relevant question was then: who was entitled to these rents? Labor? Capital? Theoretically, the answer is neither as neither was the source/cause.

It's important to point out that these rents were virtual in nature — that is, not monetized. As the conventional way to monetize (or incomize) output is via wage-based purchasing power, this presented a conundrum. How to monetize (or incomize) the increased productivity, given that labor was not the cause?[3]

8.4 The Roosevelt Administration Opts for Government-Imposed Wage Increases and Government Expenditure

In this section, the Roosevelt Administration's proposed solution, namely the National Industrial Recovery Act (NIRA) of 1933, is presented. The NIRA acted on a number of fronts, namely increasing aggregate demand via wage increases, increased unionization and government expenditure aimed primarily at creating short-run make-work programs. As it turned out, the instrumentalization of the underlying principles (i.e., higher wages and purchasing power) would prove to be as controversial as it was nightmarish in its execution. First, as mentioned, there was no underlying scientific basis for higher wages given the nature of the technology shock. Companies saw no legitimate reason to increase wages, especially in the depths of the downturn. Second, electric unit drive-based acceleration was not universal. In other words, not all firms and industries were affected. In fact, many such as the important service sector were unaffected.

---

[3] The Technocrats (Scott, 1933) were aware of this problem and suggested an overhaul of income distribution based on a guaranteed income, a new currency based on energy, and a new class of civil servants known as the Technate.

Further, not all firms within the affected sectors had converted to the new drive technology. Ideally, the wage increases would be tailored to the firm and industry's experience with electric unit drive. For example, wage increases could be tied to — and thus proportional to — increases in electric power use per worker or increases in $s(t)$, average machine speed, ideally at the firm level, but also at the industry level. Anything more would only exacerbate the underlying problem. In other words, imposing wage increases in the absence of greater productivity would invariably reduce, not increase, employment.

8.5 Wage Developments in the 1920s and 1930s

Referring to Table 8.1, the average hourly wage rate stood at 0.55 in 1920 and 0.56 in 1929 (real terms). Clearly, if the Roosevelt Administration was to close the 30 percent output gap, then it would need to increase the average real wage by an equivalent amount, namely 30 percent, *ceteris paribus*. This could be accomplished either by increasing the average nominal wage by 30 percent holding prices constant, by decreasing prices by 30 percent, holding wages constant, or by some combination of these two policies.

By 1933, the average nominal wage had fallen to 0.44 per hour. As prices had fallen by roughly 20 percent (49.3 to 39.3 Implicit GDP deflator), the real wage in 1933 was roughly equal to that in 1929. It therefore follows that in order to close the structural output gap, the average real wage in the U.S. economy would have had to rise by 30 percent. This could be accomplished by either holding prices constant and raising nominal wages by 30 percent, by decreasing prices by 30 percent, or by some combination thereof.

8.6 The Plan

Upon taking office, President Roosevelt assembled a group of scholars known as the Brains Trust with the specific purpose of outlining a course of action. Among these were Columbia University economics professor Rexford G. Tugwell, Columbia University law professor Adolf A. Berle Jr, Raymond Motley and numerous others.[4] Within 100 days, they came

---

[4]The complete list includes: Noël Segarajasinghe, Harry Hopkins, Adolf Berle, Benjamin V. Cohen, Thomas Gardiner Corcoran, Felix Frankfurter, Louis Howe, Raymond Moley,

Table 8.1. U.S. Manufacturing Wage and Price Data 1923–1945

Year	Nominal Wage	CPI*	Real Wage**
1923	0.52	51.30	1.01
1924	0.54	51.20	1.05
1925	0.54	51.90	1.04
1926	0.54	51.10	1.05
1927	0.54	50.00	1.08
1928	0.56	50.80	1.10
1929	0.56	50.60	1.10
1930	0.55	49.3	1.11
1931	0.51	44.8	1.13
1932	0.44	40.2	1.09
1933	0.44	39.3	1.11
1934	0.53	42.2	1.25
1935	0.54	42.6	1.26
1936	0.55	42.7	1.28
1937	0.62	44.5	1.39
1938	0.62	43.9	1.41
1939	0.63	43.2	1.45
1940	0.66	43.9	1.50
1941	0.73	47.2	1.54
1942	0.85	53.0	1.60
1943	0.96	56.8	1.69
1944	1.01	58.2	1.73
1945	1.02	59.7	1.70

Note: *1958 = 100; **Constant 1958 $.
Source: U.S. Department of Commerce (1975), Series D802, F5.

up with a plan in the form of a bill, known as the National Industrial Recovery Bill. In short, it contained provisions to raise wages, freeze prices, provide workers with improved collective bargaining rights and increase government expenditure. The thinking was straightforward: close

---

Basil O'Connor, George Peek, Charles William Taussig, Rexford Tugwell, Hugh S. Johnson, Frances Perkins, Samuel Rosenman, Bernard Baruch.

the structural output gap and, in doing so, the contractionary output gap would also be closed.

8.6.1　*The NIRA in the House and Senate*

H.R. 5755 was introduced in the House on May 17 and passed on May 26. It was then introduced in the Senate and passed on June 9, being signed into law by the President on June 17, 1933. Unlike H.R. 2667, the Smoot–Hawley Tariff Bill which had been the subject of extensive deliberations, debate over the proposed "New Deal" was limited by House Resolution 160 to six hours. However, what is clear from the little deliberation there was, is the extent to which the objectives of the proposed legislation were misunderstood. While the Brains Trust had focused on the imbalance raised by, among others, the members of the *Committee on Recent Economic Changes of the President's Conference on Unemployment*, the House and Senate appeared to focus on the decrease in purchasing power since the downturn. Among their other preoccupations were the question of presidential power, the wisdom of suspending the antitrust laws, and the financial burden on the taxpayer of the $3,300,000,00 of planned government expenditure contained in the Bill.

8.6.2　*The thinking behind the NIRA*

Contrary to the often-held view, the NIRA was not a policy heuristic born of a desire on the part of naïve, zealous New Dealers to restore full employment, but rather was based largely on a body of literature from the early 20th century which focused on technological change and its impact on the U.S. economy. Among its main contributors were Edward Bellamy, Thorstein Veblen, Simon Patten and his student Rexford G. Tugwell.

The core underlying principles of The National Industrial Recovery Act were based for the most part on the writings of Tugwell and Harold G. Moulton of the Institute of Economics (Brookings Institution).[5] In

---

[5] In 1933, the Brookings Institution launched an exhaustive study of the problem of overcapacity/underincome/underconsumption titled "The Distribution of Wealth and Income in Relation to Economic Progress," of which there were four divisions, namely "America's Capacity to Produce," "America's Capacity to Consume," "The Formation of Capital" and

1927, Tugwell had examined the ramifications of electrification of U.S. industry in the 1910s and 1920s. America, he argued, was in the throes of a new industrial revolution. In *Industry's Coming of Age* (1927), he described the "revolution underway in U.S. industry." Foremost among the "technical causes" of increased productivity, he argued, was "the bringing into use of new and better power resources more suited to our technique, more flexible and less wasteful: and continued progress in the technique of generating and applying power" (Tugwell, 1927, p. 180) — in short, the electrification of U.S. industry.

> The electrification of industry has now progressed to the extent of between 55 and 60 percent completion. So widespread an adoption of this new flexible means of moving things cannot have taken place without numerous secondary results in lowered costs, improvements in quality, and a heightened morale among workers. For the new power is not only cheaper to use: it is also cleaner, more silent and handier. On the whole, the electrification of industry must be set down as the greatest single cause of the new industrial revolution (Tugwell, 1927, p. 182).

His work was part of a growing literature on the electrification and the ensuing problems, notably the relationship between wages and productivity growth, and the ensuing insufficient income and expenditure. Among the other notable contributions were the writings of Harold Moulton, as well as the populist writings of Henry Ford and Edward A. Filene (Ford, 1922, 1926a, 1926b; Filene, 1931). Like Ford who advocated (and

---

"Income and Economic Progress." Its findings corroborated the underlying premises of the NIRA and NRA, ex-post.

According to Romasco, the NIRA and NRA were created in the image and likeness of Roosevelt — in a word, eclectic. Describing Roosevelt's forays into policymaking, he explains:

> Ideologically Roosevelt and the New Deal were a no-man's land. Roosevelt's leadership and the New Deal had nothing to do with logic and consistency. Instead, he used his position of power to carry out what was essentially an exercise in political eclecticism: he drew freely from a wide and contradictory variety of ideological programs, both home grown and imported, and more often than not, he used them simultaneously (Romasco, 1983, p. 5).

introduced) higher wages, Tugwell felt that wages had not kept pace with productivity, depressing consumption and output in general.[6]

> But high wages are so necessary a condition of social progress that one, even, who is not a wage-earner might well argue for the strengthening of the workers' cause. For wages, more than any other income, are spent for staple goods, goods which, in the best sense, strengthen the race by their use. These too are the goods which can be made in the most efficient ways. But quite as important, income which is distributed as wages becomes immediate purchasing power for consumers goods, and so completes that productive circuit of which we have spoken. A nation of well-paid workers, consuming most of the goods its produces, will be as near Utopia as we humans are ever likely to get. It is necessary to this result that not too much income shall go to profits: for if it does, this will either be spent for wasteful luxuries which have to be made in extravagant ways, or will, if it is not spent, be distributed by bankers to enterprises who will over expand their productive facilities, forgetting that the worker's buying power is not sufficient to create a demand for them (Tugwell, 1933, p. 183).

Harold G. Moulton of the Brookings Institution was of a similar view. The failure of wage income to rise commensurately with productivity acted as a brake on economic growth.

> This diagnosis of the economic mechanism may then be summarized as follows. Our study of the productive process led us to a negative conclusion-no limiting factor or serious impediment to a full utilization of our productive capacity could be discovered. Our investigation of the distribution of income, on the other hand, revealed a maladjustment of basic significance. Our capacity to produce consumer goods has been chronically in excess of the amount which consumers are able, or willing, to take off the markets: and this situation is attributable to the increasing proportion of the total income which is diverted to the

---

[6]Besides the wage problem, Tugwell (1933) focused on a number of issues, including the challenges of vertical integration — especially, the coordination problem — the role of skill in the serialization of production, and the role of competition, notably the theory of competition, in an era of rising concentration. The Industrial Discipline and the Governmental Arts published in 1933 should be seen as an ode to the second industrial revolution and its many challenges, organizational as well as macroeconomic.

savings channels. The result is a chronic inability-despite such devices as high-pressure salesmanship, installment credits, and loans to facilitate foreign purchases-to find market outlets adequate to absorb our full productive capacity (Moulton, 1935, p. 46).

Tugwell offered a solution: government-imposed wage increases. In *The Industrial Discipline and the Governmental Arts* (1933), Tugwell made the case for government control of wages and prices. In his view, wages and purchasing power had failed to keep up with productivity, a result he attributed to the changing face of the labor input as well as to the nature of the labor market, namely of being competitive. In short, technological change had lessened labor's bargaining power.

> Yet men have never been content with disorder. They have sought to plan and control. Often their institutions, to be sure, which were planned for one purpose, have prevented the achievement of another. Our Constitution is an illustration of this. It preserves certain rights, but it makes the preserving of others impossible. Then there is the inevitable lag of institutions behind changes in specific techniques.
>   A social structure built slowly and piecemeal to provide for activities of one kind prevents, if the structure fails to change, activities of other kinds, and our institutions are so built into our regard that we award them the loyalty they have not deserved (Tugwell, 1933, p. 84).

Throughout *Industry Comes of Age* and *The Industrial Discipline and The Governmental Arts*, Tugwell referred repeatedly to the gap between what he referred to as "our possibilities and our performances." For example, in Chapter VIII titled "Government and Industry," he remarked: "Evidently, what we have done is not enough. There has never been a more conspicuous disparity between our possibilities and our performances. The question whether we do not need something more than an enforcement of competition and a defining of its standards is being insistently raised. Do we need some kind of compulsion to efficiency, to adhere to common purpose (Tugwell, 1933, p. 200)." Henry Ford and Edward A. Filene shared this view/premise, but differed over the appropriate "course of action." While they too felt that wages had to rise, they pleaded with their fellow businessmen to raise wages spontaneously (i.e., without third-party intervention), arguing that business success based on mass production "will be impossible except as it makes for both high wages and low prices. Low

Table 8.2. The Underlying Principles of The National Industrial Recovery Act

The presence of a paradigm technology shock in the form of electrification
The failure of wages and purchasing power to keep pace with productivity[a]
The resulting imbalance and the ensuing downturn
The need to address the structural imbalance

Note: [a]This principle is analogous to the current "compensation–productivity gap" according to which growth in inflation — adjusted hourly compensation has lagged behind real productivity growth, resulting in a declining share of labor income.

wages and high prices manifestly cut down the widespread and sustained buying power of the masses without which mass production sooner or later defeats itself. In other words, the business of the future must produce prosperous customers as well as saleable goods (Filene, 1931, p. 201)."

Their argument can be recast in terms of basic growth theory (e.g., the Solow–Swan growth model), namely of the presence of a paradigm technology shock (e.g., electrification), but of the inability of a private, for-profit economy to move to the new higher equilibrium growth path owing to the failure of wages to keep pace with productivity. By 1932, this view had entered popular culture with the writings of Thorstein Veblen, Henry Ford, Edward A. Filene, Howard Scott, Stuart Chase and numerous others.[7] It can be reduced to a series of principles, summarized in Table 8.2.

That these were the structural issues underlying the NIRA and PRA was well understood among scholars. For example, Charles Beard, reviewing the book *The American Political Science Review*, wrote:

> If Professor Tugwell's volume fairly represents the thought of the New Deal, we have gone a long way beyond the New Freedom. Under President Wilson, the enterprise of the small producer was to be liberated from the control of the "big interests — by government intervention in economic affairs, by the restoration of competition to its normal basis, whatever that may mean. Under President Franklin D. Roosevelt, all enterprises, large and small, are to be regimented, ordered, and controlled with respect to stability, security and a fair standard of living all around. The "natural" distribution of wealth, so dear to many economists, is to be altered by the Power of the State.
>
> Professor Tugwell writes the philosophy of the New Deal. He seeks to reduce the technical trends in industrial society to simple patter for

---

[7]It was also an integral part of the writings of Edward Bellamy's Progressive Movement, the Institutionalist Movement, and the Technocracy Movement.

understanding, to discover ways in which social arrangements may further these trends, and to shape the whole process toward more desirable results" (Beard, 1933, p. 833).

Morris Cohen, writing in the *Columbia Law Review*, left little doubt that the NIRA and National Recovery Administration (NRA) were based on the principles outlined in Tugwell's "Industrial Discipline and the Governmental Arts":

> Professor Tugwell's general view of economic history leaves him with no doubt that our competitive system has broken down, that it cannot achieve sufficient stability to assure anyone in it continuous employment. We need a radical transformation ...... How is this to be attained? Not, we are assured, by the present methods pursued by labor. "Simple bargaining for higher wages and shorter hours achieves immediate relief: but at best it gains relief only." .... we need drastic reconstruction ...... Professor Tugwell does not give much attention to the difficulties in the way of realizing his general program. Such a program clearly involves regulating prices as well as wages and production, and this means limiting profits (Cohen, 1933, p. 1275).

William S. Hopkins of Stanford University echoed this view:

> Although he invests Government with extensive control over industry, a large part of this function seems to be to assure the continuity of profit. The machinery for this control is suggested by factors of the present environment, as follows.
>
> Industry's ability to produce has already been adequately demonstrated by experience. Scientific organization and development conducted within industries or concerns, have borne abundant fruit. But between different industries or concerns, there is almost anarchy, with the result that some are underdeveloped, while others are over-developed. The gains made in technical progress within one industry are offset by the competitive practices of another. And periodically, due chiefly to our economic anarchy, the business cycle reduces much of our vaunted progress to dust.
>
> But such ability as industry has demonstrated is to be made use of, according to Dr. Tugwell's suggestion, by a system of democratic coordination. He proposes that all of the concerns within an industry be formed into an "association." These cartelised industries, then, are to be largely self-governing, but subjected to specific control by some powerful agency, or Board.

That Dr. Tugwell's plan is in close harmony with President Roosevelt's policy is evident by a consideration of the Industrial Control (National Recovery) Act, which became law in the United States on June 16, 1933 (Hopkins, 1933, p. 502).

8.7 The Devil Was in the Details

The discussion at the time implicitly assumed that all companies had adopted the new drive technology and had experienced comparable increases in productivity and the rated capacity of their plant and equipment. Clearly, this was not the case. In fact, complete sectors were unaffected, notably the service sector. And many companies within the affected sectors were unaffected, raising the problem of firm/industry heterogeneity. In short, electrification affected some companies within any given sector, and some sectors entirely, but left others unchanged. Referring to Table 8.3 taken from the National Bureau of Economic

Table 8.3.   NBER Recent Economic Changes in the United States: Changes in Technical Production Factors for 12 Industries 1914–1925

	Productivity Per Man-Hour	Primary Power Per Man-Hour
Industries in the First Class		
Automobiles	210	52
Rubber Tires	211	n/a
Petroleum Refining	58	37
Cement Manufacturing	58	54
Blast Furnaces	54	23
Steel Works and Rolling Mills	69	46
Industries in the Second Class:		
Flour Milling	39	16
Slaughtering and Meat Packing	27	61
Leather Tanning	28	46
Cane Sugar Refining	27	42
Paper and Wood Pulp	26	28
Boots and Shoes	17	54

Source: National Bureau of Economic Research (1929, p. 147).

Research's "Recent Economic Changes in the United States," published in 1929, we see that industries differed markedly in terms of productivity gains from 1914 to 1925. Specifically, industries such as automobiles and rubber tires saw their productivity soar, while boots and shoes were largely unaffected. This raises the question of optimal policy design. A blanket, one size fits all wage policy would be counterproductive for the reasons mentioned above. Only a policy tailored to each firm's experience with electric unit drive and mass production would be successful.

8.8 Brains Trust Challenges

Acutely aware of the complexity of the problem at hand, the Brains Trust came up with what it felt was a solution, namely industry-specific Codes of Fair Competition that would be negotiated by cartel-like industry associations. In short, industry CEOs would convene and voluntarily agree on a set of wages, hours and prices for their industry, wages, hours and prices that would be in line with overriding goals of the NIRA. It is important to remember that such discussions/negotiations occurred against a backdrop of falling wages and prices, not to mention falling sales.

There were, however, glaring problems with this solution, including the heterogeneous nature of firms within any given industry, and the very definition of an industry. By the 1930s, many U.S. firms were vertically and horizontally integrated multi-product and multi-service entities, making it hard if not impossible to assign firms to a specific industry. Second, there was the question of possible strategic behavior. Dominant firms could conceivably impose substantial wage increases on fringe firms, or in industries with many small firms, the latter could block or veto the proposed wage increases. Last, Codes of Fair Competition-based wage increases would only be successful if all industry associations (i.e., cartels) increased wages in concert. If not, then the wage increases would serve to increase a firm's costs without increasing its revenues, thus imposing losses on firms. Clearly, the logistics of the raising wages were overwhelmingly complex, raising the very real specter of failure.

The first sign of impending failure came in the summer of 1933 when the Administration, seeing the little progress in the drafting of codes, took extraordinary measures to increase wages and wage income by enacting the President's Reemployment Agreement, which was an executive order imposing minimum wages on all of the nation's workers of $15 per week.[8] For the reasons outlined above, progress on the Code front was slow, as only one of over 500 Codes had been drafted. To kick start, or accelerate the process, a minimum wage of $15 per week would be imposed until a Code of Fair Competition had been approved by the National Recovery Administration. The wisdom of such a policy is unclear as it imposed higher labor costs on all firms in all industries, regardless of whether they could afford them — in short, whether they had the wherewithal to pay them.

In an all-out effort to force firms and industries to comply with the provisions of the NIRA, the administration devised the Blue Eagle Program, which consisted of a national advertising campaign aimed at convincing consumers to purchase goods and services from firms that complied. Such firms could display a blue eagle on their products as a testimony of their compliance. Non-complying firms would, accordingly, lose market share, thus inciting them to conform.

As pointed out, success would require a swift response on the part of firms and industries. The high-wage policy would only close the structural output gap if wages in the affected firms and industries increased at roughly the same time. The longer the code-writing process would last, the lower would be the chances of success.

8.9   Failure on the Code and Expenditure Fronts

As pointed out, success would require that the NIRA close an overall output gap (structural and contractionary) of roughly $78.3 billion. This would be achieved by higher wages and purchasing power as well as

---

[8] Here are the specifics: Not to pay any of the classes of employees mentioned in paragraph (2) less than $15 per week in any city of over 500,000 population, or in the immediate trade area of such city: or less than $14.50 per week in any city of between 250,000 and 500,000 population, or in the immediate trade area of such city: or less than $14 per week in any city of between 2,500 and 250,000 population, or in the immediate trade area of such city: and in towns of less than 2,500 population to increase all wages by not less than 20 percent, provided that this shall not require wages in excess of $12 per week. (6) Not to pay any employee of the classes mentioned in paragraph (3) less than 40 cents per hour unless the hourly rate for the same class of work on July 15, 1929, was less than 40 cents per hour, in which latter case not to pay less than the hourly rate on July 15, 1919, and in no event less than 30 cents per hour. It is agreed that this paragraph establishes a guaranteed minimum rate of pay regardless of whether the employee is compensated on the basis of a time rate or on a piecework performance.

greater government expenditure. The various expenditure provisions in the Act amounted to roughly $3.3 billion. What was obvious is that by 1934, things were not moving in the right direction. The code-writing process was not going as planned and the expenditure provisions were inconsequential to say the least. Clearly, the NIRA, as a policy experiment, was failing, despite what were legitimate intentions. As the old adage goes, it looked good on paper, but was far from looking good in practice. With the benefit of hindsight, the Roosevelt Administration was attempting the impossible: closing a structural and contractionary output gap with literally no information and without a constitutional leg to stand on. Nowhere in the U.S. Constitution was it written that the federal government could set wages, hours and prices.

8.10 The NIRA Found to be Unconstitutional

Reeling from the lack of support on the part of firms and industries (i.e., the compliance crisis) as well as the slow Code writing process, the NIRA suffered its greatest challenge when a New York city meat company, the Schechter Poultry Company, which, after having been fined under the legislation, launched a legal-constitutional challenge to the Act, alleging that the federal government did not have the power to set wages, hours and prices. The case wound its way up to the Supreme Court where a decidedly Republican majority, led by Chief Justice Charles Hughes (who as President of the Republican National Conference had emphatically endorsed the Smoot–Hawley Tariff Act in Kansas City in June 1928), ruled it to be unconstitutional and, thus, struck it down, bringing an end to the second policy attempt to deal with the acceleration-based imbalance. By then, the country was five years into the worse industrial downturn in history, with no hope in sight. Moreover, the structural issues that had been front and center in the late 1920s were giving way to the contractionary issues of the day. In the next section, an in-depth analysis of firm behavior throughout this tumultuous period is provided.

8.11 Firms React to the PRA and NIRA: The Evidence

With the striking down of the NIRA came the end of what was the most ambitious attempt ever on the part of a government to steer an advanced industrial economy onto a higher growth path in response to technological change. Never before and never since has a Western government been as ambitious. This raises the question, how did the U.S. economy fare before, during and after the NIRA? In other words, how did firms and industries respond to the idea of the NIRA in the months prior to it being enacted? Did wages rise? Did prices stabilize? Did employment increase? How did they respond to the PRA? And how did they respond to its repeal? This section presents evidence taken from earlier work on the NIRA (Beaudreau, 2016a). Using a sample of 12 industries, it examines wage, price, employment and output responses to the NIRA and PRA. More specifically, it examines firms' responses to the run-up to the Act (December 1932–June 1933), the Presidents Reemployment Act (July 1933–December 1933), and the NIRA itself (January 1934–June 1935). It is assumed that these would have been conditioned by the presence of electric unit drive-based acceleration and the resulting higher productivity and excess rated capacity. In other words, firms and industries that had "electrified" the most — and thus found themselves with excess capacity — are assumed to have reacted differently to the various measures, than those that had not.[9]

8.11.1 *Electrification: Sector and industry heterogeneity*

The breakdown of 1929 U.S. GDP by sector is shown in Table 8.3, where we see that manufacturing dominated, followed by Trade, Finance, Agriculture and Services. Output per worker in each sector is reported for 1909 and 1929. We see for example that GDP per worker in 1909 stood at $730.19, which had more than doubled by 1929 to $1,584.92 (current dollars). The increase in constant 1909 dollars was 22.68 percent. Broken down by sector, we see that output per worker growth varied from a low of –35 percent in Trade, to 52 percent in Mining, and 48 percent in Manufacturing. Labor productivity in agriculture remained relatively constant. Clearly, electric unit drive was not universal in scope. Referring to Table 8.5 which reports the use of electric energy per sector, we see that, of the sectors listed in Table 8.4, only the manufacturing and mining

---

[9]Here, nominal wages are assumed to be upwardly rigid. As it turns out, much of the labor market disequilibrium literature focused and focuses on downward — not upward — rigidity, nominal/real wage rigidity. The recent compensation–productivity gap literature focuses on structural factors such as unionization, offshoring and developments in labor supply.

Table 8.4. U.S. Output and Employment by Sector 1909–1929

Total	Total	Agriculture	Mining	Construction	Manufacturing	Transportation	Trade	Finance	Services	Government
GDP 1909	25,400	19.4	3.4	4.1	18.3	10.9	16.4	13	9.1	5.4
EMPL 1909	34,785	30.4	3.1	5	22.1	8.8	11.8	1.6	12.5	4.7
GDP 1929	75460	11.5	3	4.2	22.2	11.2	14.5	14.3	10.4	8.7
EMPL 1929	47611	21.2	2.2	5	22.2	8.6	16.9	3.3	13.9	6.7
GDPEMPL 1909	730.19	465.98	800.86	598.76	604.64	904.45	1,014.85	5,932.87	531.58	838.95
GDPEMPL 1929	1,584.92	859.74	2,161.26	1,331.33	1,584.92	2,064.09	1,359.84	6,868.02	1,185.84	2,058.04
1929–1909										
Current $	2.1705	1.8450	2.6986	2.2234	2.6212	2.2821	1.3399	1.1576	2.2307	2.4531
Constant $	1.2268	1.0428	1.5253	1.2567	1.4815	1.2899	0.7573	0.6543	1.2608	1.3865

Source: U.S. Department of Commerce (1975, p. 239). (Series F226-237). Sectorial entries are expressed in percentage terms.

Table 8.5.   U.S. Electric Power Consumption by Sector 1912–1929

Year	Total	Residential	Commercial	Manufacturing	Extracting	Miscellaneous
1912	25,000	910	4,076	9,250	2,000	6,000
1929	103,682	11,747	11,589	45,561	5,797	16,524
Ratio	3.1472	11.9087	1.8432	4.0336	1.8985	1.7540

Source: U.S. Department of Commerce (1975, p. 828) (Series S-120-132).

sectors were affected by what Brain Truster Rexford G. Tugwell referred to as "the greatest single cause of the new industrial revolution." This implies that based on the employment data presented in Table 8.3, at least 58.7 percent of the labor force would have been largely unaffected — or hardly affected — by electric unit drive-based acceleration and, thus, by the "new industrial revolution."

8.11.2   *Firm heterogeneity and the Wage, hour and employment provisions of the NIRA*

How did firms react to the provisions of the NIRA? In Beaudreau (2016a), it was argued that firms in industries that converted the most to electric unit drive would have reacted differently from those in industries that converted the least. For example, the latter would have responded to the introduction of a higher wage by varying hours and employment more than those in the former industries. One way to look at this is that firms in industries that converted the most had more of a margin to work with. From an optimal policy design point of view, it would stand to reason that the wage, hour and employment provisions of the NIRA ought to have been designed in such a way so as to target such firms — say, by tying wage increases in electric power consumption per worker.[10]

---

[10]The U.S. Committee of Industrial Analysis (1937) made a similar point: "Along with these effects went the lack of adequate information to furnish a basis for policy and for reviewing proposals of interested groups. It appears also that there was not available, and could not be brought into existence in times, a large enough personnel with the exacting combination of qualities, background and training required for NRA administration (U.S. Committee of Industrial Analysis, 1937, p. 228).

8.12 The NIRA and PRA

In Beaudreau (2016a), wage, price, employment, hours and payroll developments in 12 manufacturing industries (NBER Macrohistory) were examined.[11] Wage, price, employment, hours and payroll data were obtained for January 1929, January 1933, July 1933, June 1935 and December 1935. This allowed for the analysis of wage, price, employment and hours developments in five periods, namely the first three years of the Depression (January 1929–January 1933), the run-up to the NIRA (January 1933–July 1933), the early PRA period (August 1933–December 1933), the entire PRA/NIRA era (August 1933–June 1935), and lastly the six months after the NIRA (July 1933–December 1933). In keeping with Rexford Tugwell's writings on the role of electrification on productivity and productivity growth in the early 20th century, U.S. Census of Manufactures industry data on total horsepower and electric motor horsepower were used, as well as the number of wage earners by industry for 1909 and 1929, to generate two indexes of electrification. The first is electric horsepower per wage earner growth from 1909 to 1929 (ELECGROWTH), measured as the ratio of the latter to the former, and the second is the rate of growth of electric power as a percentage of overall power (ELECPERCENT) in the same period.[12]

Referring to the first two columns of Table 8.6, electric-power per wage earner growth (ELECGROWTH) and electric power as a percentage of overall power (ELECPERCENT) varied considerably across the

---

[11] The sample industries were chosen on the basis of wage and price data availability as reported in the NBER Macrohistory database. The price series used were, m4095, m4097, m4166, m4093, m4165, m4180, m4130, m4077, m4154, m4087b, m4096a, m4100, m4133a: the wage series were m8206a, m8204a, m8202a, m8235a, m8207a, m8203a, m8219a, m820a, m8230, m8214, m8143, m8205: the employment series m08109a, m08102, m08087, m08104, m08144, m08220a, m08236b, m08232, m08216a, m08098, m08103: the hours series, m08200a, m08198a, m08196a, m08234a, m08201a, m08208a, m08230a, m08215a, m08197a, m08199a: the payroll series were m08133aa, m08126, m08111, m8072a, m8072a, m08145, m08221a, m08073, m08233, m08217a, m08122, m08127a. Data on Total horsepower and Electric Motor horsepower were obtained from the Abstract of the Census of Manufactures for 1909 and 1919, Tables 206 and 216 (1909), Table 222 (1919).

[12] These two variables were constructed using total horsepower and electric motor horsepower data for the 12 industries taken from the Abstract of the U.S. Census of Manufactures for 1909 and 1929 U.S. Bureau of the Census (1914, 1949).

Table 8.6.   Pre-NIRA Industry Data 1929–1932

Industry	ELECGROWTH	ELECPERCENT	Price 1/29–1/33	Wage 1/29–1/33	Empl 1/29–1/33	Hours 1/29–1/33	RPW 1/29–1/33	Payroll 1/29–1/33
Furniture	6.640	0.662	-0.223	-0.272	-0.533	-0.248	-0.049	0.812
Leather	6.452	0.567	-0.392	-0.193	-0.217	-0.152	0.199	0.086
Meat	3.468	0.332	-0.538	-0.220	-0.013	-0.066	0.318	0.222
Newsprint	9.135	0.574	-0.274	-0.204	-0.240	-0.248	0.070	0.296
Paper products	9.135	0.574	-0.163	-0.204	-0.236	-0.248	-0.040	0.296
Passenger cars	11.737	0.399	-0.151	-0.177	-0.507	-0.079	-0.025	0.915
Rubber	8.644	0.896	-0.843	-0.171	-0.404	-0.361	0.672	0.080
Steel sheet	5.049	0.498	-0.453	-0.254	-0.435	-0.517	0.199	0.368
Wool	16.838	0.595	-0.578	-0.144	-0.267	-0.144	0.433	0.174
Chemicals	1.575	0.006	-0.252	-0.220	-0.478	-0.192	0.031	0.683
Cotton	6.153	0.535	-0.767	-0.273	-0.269	-0.171	0.494	-0.140
Total shoe	3.490	0.499	-0.096	-0.224	-0.156	-0.155	-0.128	-0.045
Average	7.360	0.511	-0.394	-0.213	-0.313	-0.215	0.181	-0.551

sample industries. The former was greatest in Wool (1,583 percent), Passenger Car (1,073 percent), and lowest in Meat (246 percent). Industries that saw their use of electric horsepower as a percentage of overall horsepower usage increase the most, include Meat (33 percent) and Chemicals (6 percent).

8.13 The Downturn

Columns 3–8 present the variation in wage, price, employment, hours, real-product wage (RPW) and payroll from January 1, 1929 to January 1, 1933, the pre-Roosevelt years (percent). The real product wage is defined as the nominal wage index divided by the industry price index. We see that wages and prices fell across all industries as did employment, hours and payroll. The real-product wage (nominal wage divided by the product price) increased on average (0.18), as prices fell by more than wages. Payroll decreased by 55 percent, on average. Table 8.7, which presents the correlation coefficients between these variables, shows that variations in wages across the 12 industries were positively correlated with ELECGROWTH and ELECPERCENT, suggesting that firms in industries that converted the most to electric unit drive were less likely to cut wages in the downturn. Further, they were also more likely to cut price and employment. Consequently, the real-product wage was increasing in both variables.[13] Put differently, industries that had adopted electric unit drive the most were less likely to cut wages, but more likely to cut prices, thus raising the real product wage.[14]

8.14 The Run-Up to the NIRA and PRA

It could be argued that rational forward-looking firms would have, beginning in late 1932, anticipated the NIRA and PRA (Friedman and

---

[13]This is consistent with the conventional view that large firms cut employment by less early in the downturn, whether by choice or in response to President Hoover's request to do so. We also see that larger firms were more likely to cut hours, which could be their response to his request to implement a form of job sharing.

[14]One could argue that the market was de facto moving the economy to the new equilibrium growth path via price deflation. Firms in industries that had electrified were more likely to cut prices, owing to a greater wage–productivity gap.

Table 8.7.   Pre-NIRA Correlation Coefficient Matrix

	ELECGROWTH	ELECPERCENT	Wage 1/29–1/33	Price 1/29–1/33	Empl 1/29–1/33	Hours 1/29–1/33	RPW 1/29–1/33	Payroll 1/29–1/33
ELECGROWTH	1.000							
ELECPERCENT		1.000						
Wage 1/29–1/33	0.660	0.167	1.000					
Price1/29–1/33	–0.142	–0.395	–0.075	1.000				
Empl 1/29–1/33	–0.108	0.007	0.124	–0.127	1.000			
Hours 1/29–1/33	0.109	–0.363	0.258	0.207	0.403	1.000		
RPW 1/29–1/33	0.243	0.412	0.231	–0.987	0.144	–0.161	1.000	
Payroll 1/29–1/33	–0.142	–0.333	0.153	0.223	0.761	0.518	–0.114	1.00

Schwartz, 1963; Taylor and Neumann, 2014) and acted accordingly. Throughout the 1932 general election campaign, Democratic Presidential candidate Franklin D. Roosevelt had promised decisive action to end the downturn. The question then is to what extent did firms act on these promises, making the resulting expectations self-fulfilling? For example, anticipated higher sales and/or higher labor costs, firms would have stopped laying workers off, and started hiring, which in turn would have increased purchasing power and aggregate demand.

The question then is: to what extent did firms in the 12 sample industries react differently according to their experience with electric unit drive — that is, according to ELECGROWTH and ELECPERCENT? To answer this question, consider wage, price, employment, hours and payroll growth from January 1933 to July 1933 in Table 8.8. First, in most industries wages stopped falling and began rising (0.015), as did prices (0.31). Employment and hours increased on average throughout the 12 industries, as did payroll. The real-product wage, however, decreased on average by 29 percent. Referring to Table 8.9 which reports the corresponding correlation coefficients, we see that variations in wage and price were increasing in ELECGROWTH, indicating that firms in industries that had converted to electric unit drive the most were less likely to cut wages/more likely to increase wages, and more likely to increase price/less likely to cut price. However, employment and hours growth were both lower in these industries, which is consistent with Equation (4.9). Overall payroll growth, however, was higher.

These changes can be viewed as largely anticipatory in nature, as firms increased output in order to either (i) avoid higher NIRA labor costs, and/or (ii) meet the anticipated higher demand for goods and services. Milton Friedman and Anna Schwartz made a similar argument, attributing the spurt in activity in 1933 to anticipations. More specifically:

> The revival was initially erratic and uneven. Reopening of the banks was followed by a rapid spurt in personal income and industrial production. The spurt was intensified by production in anticipation of the codes to be established under the National Industrial Recovery Act (passed June 16, 1933), which were expected to raise wages and prices and did (Friedman and Schwartz, 1963, p. 49).

Table 8.8.   The Run-Up to the NIRA/PRA January 1933–July 1933

Industry	ELECGROWTH	ELECPERCENT	Price 1/33–7/33	Wage 1/33–7/33	Empl 1/33–7/33	Hours 1/33–7/33	RPW 1/33–7/33	Payroll 1/33–7/33
Furniture	6.640	0.662	0.026	-0.114	0.205	0.142	-0.140	0.153
Leather	6.452	0.567	0.252	-0.016	0.219	0.243	-0.269	0.412
Meat	3.468	0.332	0.055	-0.015	0.097	0.048	-0.071	0.112
Newsprint	9.135	0.574	-0.111	-0.043	0.130	0.194	0.067	0.012
Paper products	9.135	0.574	0.083	-0.043	0.080	0.194	-0.126	0.012
Passenger cars	11.737	0.399	-0.018	0.041	0.163	-0.049	0.059	0.266
Rubber	8.644	0.896	1.580	0.052	0.289	0.342	-1.527	0.821
Steel sheet	5.049	0.498	-0.823	0.01	0.328	0.570	0.833	0.730
Wool	16.838	0.595	0.581	0.159	0.358	0.189	-0.421	0.609
Chemicals	1.575	0.006	0.016	0.048	0.717	0.023	0.031	-0.018
Cotton	6.153	0.535	2.136	0.040	0.352	0.132	-2.095	0.535
Total shoe	3.490	0.499	-0.026	0.070	0.162	0.284	0.097	0.491
Average	7.360	0.511	0.312	0.015	0.258	0.193	-0.296	0.344

Table 8.9. The Run-Up to the NIRA/PRA January 1933–July 1933 Correlation Coefficient Matrix

Blank	ELECGROWTH	ELECPERCENT	Wage 1/33–7/33	Price 1/33–7/33	Empl 1/33–7/33	Hours 1/33–7/33	RPW 1/33–7/33	Payroll 1/33–7/33
ELECGROWTH	1							
ELECPERCENT	0.471	1						
Wage 1/33–7/33	0.358	-0.101	1					
Price 1/33–7/33	0.172	0.387	0.305	1				
Empl 1/33-7/33	-0.231	-0.493	0.419	0.158	1			
Hours 1/33-7/33	-0.069	0.487	0.030	-0.142	-0.048	1		
RPW 1/33-7/33	-0.144	-0.406	-0.223	-0.996	-0.124	0.148	1	
Payroll 1/33-7/33	0.222	0.540	0.384	0.538	0.106	0.651	-0.345	1

8.15   The President's Reemployment Agreement (PRA)

As mentioned, the code writing and approval process proved to be more challenging than had been anticipated and in the summer of 1933 (August 1, 1933), the Roosevelt Administration, using Section 4(a) of the NIRA, proceeded to adopt a temporary solution in the form of the President's Reemployment Agreement which consisted of a "blanket code" designed to raise hourly wage rates and reduce the average workweek.[15] Accordingly, firms were to shorten the workweek to no more than 35 hours (40 hours for clerical and sales workers), agree to raise the minimum hourly wage to 40 cents per hour (and raise wages in high-wage industries), and recognize the rights of workers to bargain collectively.[16] The resulting wages and prices would be in effect until such time as an industry's "Code of Fair Competition" was approved of by the NRA."[17] To further encourage/incite compliance, the National Recovery Administration introduced a disciplining device/forcing rule in the form of the Blue-Eagle Program, designed to reward compliant firms and punish non-compliers. Compliant firms were allowed to display a Blue Eagle on their products, advertisements and store windows. A nation-wide publicity campaign was launched, the intention of which was to encourage consumers to patronize complying firms.

Underlying the PRA was the view (Brains Trust) that U.S. firms had benefited from the new power drive technology and could as such afford to pay higher wages, but had not done so. Lacking, however, were data on the extent and severity of the problem. Beyond the rhetoric (i.e., productivity had risen), the Administration had little information on the alleged aggregate productivity–wage gap, let alone the gap by sector, industry, or

---

[15]One could argue that strategically speaking, there was no first-mover advantage to agreeing to — and signing — a code, but instead there was a "last mover" advantage. If all other industries raised their wage, then overall purchasing power would increase, thus raising sales and revenues in advance of higher labor costs.

[16]It is important to point out that the emphasis on job sharing in the PRA was a new feature of the NIRA, having no basis in the original act. In fact, it was discouraged as it would fail to raise purchasing power.

[17]Industries where the average wage was above 40 cents were encouraged to nonetheless raise wages in keeping with the spirit of the Agreement.

firm as mentioned, blanket agreements are recipes for disaster in the presence of heterogeneity. Non-affected firms (whether in non-affected or affected industries) would find themselves facing unjustified and unjustifiable (by productivity) higher labor costs. Further, not complying could be potentially disastrous given the threat of a Blue-Eagle-based consumer boycott.[18]

How did firms in the 12 sample industries respond to the PRA? Consider Tables 8.10 and 8.11 which present the wage, price, employment, hours, real product wage (RPW) and payroll variation data as well as the corresponding correlation coefficients for the period July 1933–December 1933. Wage growth varied considerably across industries, but was mostly positive. Prices increased, but were more or less stable. Employment growth was weak, and in four cases negative. Hours growth which had been positive in the run-up to the NIRA turned negative in this period, a direct result of the job-sharing provisions in the PRA. The correlation coefficients in Table 8.11 show that wages and prices were decreasing in ELECGROWTH. That is, firms in high ELECGROWTH industries were less likely to raise wages and prices, owing no doubt to the fact that wages were already high (above the new minimums established by the PRA). Firms in industries that had electrified less, it follows, would have raised wages and prices in response to the PRA. Employment growth was increasing in both, while hours were decreasing.[19] In other words, firms that had converted to electric unit drive the most (the larger concerns), raised wages by more, and cut prices and hours by more. Both the real product wage and payroll were increasing in both ELECGROWTH and ELECPERCENT, largely the result of the fact that firms in high ELECGROWTH and ELECPERCENT industries were more likely to raise wages by more and less likely to raise prices, making for higher real product wages and given that hours were increasing in both variables, for higher payrolls.

---

[18] This was true from an ex-ante point of view. In time, as it became obvious that the NRA could not effectively punish non-complying firms, the program literally broke down. For more on this, see Taylor and Klein (2008).

[19] This result is consistent with the findings of Taylor (2011), and Taylor, Neumann and Fishback (2013).

Table 8.10.   The PRA July 1933–December 1933

Industry	Elec Growth 1919	Growth Elec	Price 7/33-12/33	Wage 7/33-12/33	Empl 7/33-12/33	Hours 7/33-12/33	RPW 7/33-12/33	Payroll 7/33-12/33
Furniture	6.640	0.662	0.082	0.281	0.071	-0.16	0.198	0.416
Leather	6.452	0.567	0.033	0.233	0.052	-0.212	0.200	0.046
Meat	3.468	0.332	-0.107	0.324	0.029	-0.188	0.432	0.244
Newsprint	9.135	0.574	0	0.2	0.126	-0.238	0.2	0.145
Paper products	9.135	0.574	0.045	0.2	0.058	-0.238	0.154	0.145
Passenger cars	11.737	0.399	0.009	0.140	0.002	-0.238	0.131	-0.057
Rubber	8.644	0.896	0.1	0.142	0.039	-0.202	0.042	-0.051
Steel sheet	5.049	0.498	5.416	0.194	0.073	-0.214	-5.222	0.057
Wool	16.838	0.595	0.221	-0.303	-0.062	-0.303	-0.525	-0.131
Chemicals	1.575	0.006	0.004	-0.091	-0.159	0.143	-0.095	0.469
Cotton	6.153	0.535	-0.463	0.371	-0.055	-0.279	0.834	0.038
Total shoe	3.490	0.499	0.063	0.352	-0.150	-0.366	0.288	-0.221
Average	7.360	0.511	0.450	0.170	0.002	-0.208	-0.280	0.092

Table 8.11.   The PRA July 1933–December 1933 Correlation Coefficient Matrix

	ELECGROWTH	ELECPERCENT	Wage 7/33-12/33	Price 7/33-12/33	Empl 7/33-12/33	Hours 7/33-12/33	RPW 7/33-12/33	Payroll 7/33-12/33
ELECGROWTH	1.000	0.471	−0.542	−0.133	0.239	−0.455	0.066	−0.463
ELECPERCENT		1.000	0.187	0.001	0.523	−0.627	0.021	−0.454
Wage 7/33-12/33			1.000	−0.020	0.286	−0.314	0.141	−0.064
Price7/33-12/33				1.000	0.253	−0.014	−0.992	0.155
Empl 7/33-12/33					1.000	−0.199	−0.216	0.146
Hours 7/33-12/33						1.000	−0.024	0.803
RPW 7/33-12/33							1.000	0.066
Payroll 7/33-12/33								1.000

8.16   The NIRA/PRA Period July 1933–June 1935

From August 1933 on, firms would be governed by either the PRA or an approved industry "Code of Fair Competition." By February 1934, most industries had agreed on a code, thus superseding the PRA.[20] In this section, firm behavior over the course of the ensuing months and years is examined. As such, the sample period extends from August 1933 to June 1935. Figure 8.2 presents a sample of Codes of Fair Competition — specifically, Codes 245–286. Referring to the list, it becomes immediately obvious that most of these industries would not have benefited from electrification (at least not in terms of their material processes), yet were called upon to raise wages (i.e., via the PRA). For example, it is highly unlikely that the Laundry Trade, the Railway Car Building, the Steam Heating Equipment industries would have been affected by electric unit drive. The same would have been true of the service sector. Waiters, building staff, theater agents, laundry workers saw their wages rise despite being unaffected by the new technology. Clearly, higher wages in these sectors could not be justified and undoubtedly contributed to decreasing employment. Not surprising, the most frequent complaints leveled at the PRA came from small firms, notably those in the service sector.[21]

The corresponding growth rates and correlation coefficients are presented in Tables 8.12 and 8.13. Wages in general increased substantially in this period while prices increased only marginally. In the 12 sample industries, employment increased, while hours decreased in keeping with the work-sharing objectives of the NIRA/PRA. Firms in industries that had converted to electric unit drive the most were more likely to increase wages, less likely to increase prices: less likely to increase employment, and less likely to increase hours. As was the case in the PRA period, firms in high ELECGROWTH AND ELECPERCENT industries were less likely to increase prices throughout the NIRA period. Specifically, firms in these industries were more productive (i.e., higher $s(t)$) and thus were

---

[20] Altogether, 557 Codes of Fair Competition and 189 supplemental Codes were approved. The median date of code passage was November 17, 1933. For dates of passage by industry, see Taylor (2011).

[21] A *Wall Street Journal* article titled "Ten Months of the New Deal" reported: "Steel, automobile and other large industries have found satisfaction in the NRA system, but floods of complaints appeared from small, essentially non-monopolistic industries, notably those in the service field." December 22, 1933.

CONTENTS

Code No.	Industry	Date Approved, 1934	Page
	CODES OF FAIR COMPETITION		
245	Corrugated and Solid Fiber Shipping Container	Feb. 1	1
246	Paper Disc Milk Bottle Cap	Feb. 1	15
247	Food Dish and Pulp and Paper Place	Feb. 1	29
248	Glazed and Fancy Paper	Feb. 1	41
249	Tag	Feb. 1	53
250	Wire, Rod, and Tube Die	Feb. 1	65
251	Witch Hazel	Feb. 1	75
252	Cylindrical Liquid Tight Paper Container	Feb. 1	83
253	Animal Soft Hair	Feb. 2	97
254	Athletic Goods Manufacturing	Feb. 2	107
255	Table Oil Cloth	Feb. 2	125
256	Schiffli, the Hand Machine Embroidery, and the Embroidery Thread and Scallop Cutting	Feb. 2	133
257	Printing Equipment Industry and Trade	Feb. 2	151
258	Cast Iron Boiler and Cast Iron Radiator	Feb. 3	173
259	Hat Manufacturing	Feb. 5	187
260	Ornamental Moulding, Carving and Turning	Feb. 5	205
261	Foundry Supply	Feb. 5	219
262	Shoulder Pad Manufacturing	Feb. 5	231
263	Machine Knife and Allied Steel Products Manufacturing	Feb. 6	243
264	Foundry Equipment	Feb. 6	255
265	Coffee	Feb. 6	267
266	Inland Water Carrier Trade in the Eastern Division of the United States Operating Via the New York Canal System	Feb. 6	281
267	Used Textile Bag	Feb. 8	295
268	Secondary Aluminum	Feb. 8	305
269	Carbon Black Manufacturing	Feb. 8	319
270	Wood Heel	Feb. 9	329
271	Nonferrous and Steel Convector Manufacturing (Concealed Radiator Industry)	Feb. 10	341
272	Unit Heater and/or Unit Ventilator Manufacturing	Feb. 10	355
273	Band Instrument Manufacturing	Feb. 10	369
274	Saw and Steel Products Manufacturing	Feb. 10	381
275	Chemical Manufacturing	Feb. 10	393
276	Pleating, Stitching and Bonnaz and Hand Embroidery	Feb. 10	403
277	Gray Iron Foundry	Feb. 10	419
278	Trucking	Feb. 10	431
279	Steam Heating Equipment	Feb. 12	455
280	Retail Solid Fuel	Feb. 14	469
281	Laundry Trade	Feb. 16	487
282	Restaurant	Feb. 16	507
283	Ready-Made Furniture Slip Covers Manufacturing	Feb. 16	527
284	Pottery Supplies and Backwall and Radiant	Feb. 16	539
285	Railway Car Building	Feb. 16	551
286	Beauty and Barber Shop—Mechanical Equipment Manufacturing	Feb. 16	569

(III)

Figure 8.2. Codes of Fair Competition Nos. 245–286

Source: National Recovery Administration (1934).

less likely to raise prices in response to higher NIRA/PRA wages. As was the case in the previous periods, firms in industries that had converted less would have had less of a margin and would as such be more inclined to raise prices in response to higher wages. The real product wage, throughout this period, was increasing in both ELECGROWTH and ELECPERCENT. Payroll, however, was decreasing in both, indicating

Table 8.12.   The NIRA/PRA Period July 1933–June 1935

Industry	ELECGROWTH	ELECPERCENT	Price 7/33-6/35	Wage 7/33-6/35	Empl 7/33-6/35	Hours 7/33-6/35	RPW	Payroll 7/33-6/35
Furniture	6.640	0.662	0.076	0.518	0.160	-0.092	0.441	0.812
Leather	6.452	0.567	0.030	0.317	0.052	-0.237	0.287	0.086
Meat	3.468	0.332	0.890	0.457	-0.019	-0.188	-0.432	0.222
Newsprint	9.135	0.574	0	0.281	0.189	-0.169	0.281	0.296
Paper products	9.135	0.574	0.013	0.281	0.189	-0.169	0.268	0.296
Passenger cars	11.737	0.399	0.032	0.347	0.627	-0.088	0.314	0.915
Rubber	8.644	0.896	0.575	0.365	-0.024	-0.19	-0.209	0.080
Steel sheet	5.049	0.498	0.062	0.302	0.200	-0.259	0.239	0.368
Wool	16.838	0.595	0.094	-0.224	0.062	-0.224	-0.319	0.174
Chemicals	1.575	0.006	0.041	-0.062	0.091	0.289	-0.103	0.683
Cotton	6.153	0.535	-0.450	0.421	-0.189	-0.121	0.872	-0.140
Total shoe	3.490	0.499	0.063	0.403	-0.077	-0.247	0.339	-0.045
Average	7.360	0.511	0.119	0.284	0.105	-0.141	0.165	0.312

Table 8.13.   The NIRA/PRA Period July 1933–June 1935 Correlation Coefficient Matrix

Blank	ELECGROWTH	ELECPERCENT	Wage 7/33-6/35	Price 7/33-6/35	Empl 7/33-6/35	Hours 7/33-6/35	RPW 7/33-6/35	Payroll 7/33-6/35
ELECGROWTH	1.000	0.471	-0.406	-0.122	0.369	-0.345	-0.129	0.054
ELECPERCENT		1.000	0.329	0.061	-0.154	-0.699	0.138	-0.369
Wage 7/33-6/35			1.000	0.137	-0.046	-0.343	0.463	0.020
Price 7/33-6/35				1.000	-0.057	-0.151	-0.813	-0.062
Empl 7/33-6/35					1.000	0.129	0.024	0.801
Hours 7/33-6/35						1.000	-0.066	0.533
RPW 7/33-6/35							1.000	-0.054
Payroll 7/33-6/35								1.000

that firms in industries that had converted to electric unit drive the most experienced lower payroll growth.

8.17 The Aftermath: June 1935–December 1935

This section examines firm behavior in the aftermath of the NIRA — that is, after it was declared unconstitutional (May 27, 1935). Of particular interest is how firms in the 12 industries differed in their response to the lifting of the various measures imposed by the NIRA/PRA. The model would predict that firms in low ELECGROWTH and ELECPERCENT industries would cut wages, increase prices and raise hours while firms in high ELECGROWTH and ELECPERCENT industries would be less likely to lower wages and raise prices given what was greater productivity (higher $s(t)$). The results are presented in Tables 8.14 and 8.15, where the evidence is mixed. In general, prices increased, wages decreased but by very little in both cases, and employment increased as did hours. The correlation coefficients presented in Table 8.15 show that wages were decreasing in ELECGROWTH and ELECPERCENT. Prices were increasing in both, indicating that high ELECGROWTH and ELECPERCENT industries were more likely to raise prices in the wake of the post-NIRA era. Employment was increasing in both ELECGROWTH and ELECPERCENT, indicating that larger firms were more likely to raise employment.[22] Last, the real product wage was decreasing in both ELECGROWTH and ELECPERCENT.

The results can be summarized as follows. First, nominal wage growth was, in most cases, positively correlated with ELECGROWTH and ELECPERCENT. For example, from 1933 to 1935, nominal wages either increased by more, or decreased by less, in industries that had converted to electric unit drive. This could be interpreted as evidence of the presence of greater productivity (higher $s(t)$) in high ELECGROWTH and ELECPERCENT industries, confirming the basic underlying premise of Rexford Tugwell and Harold Moulton's argument in favor of the NIRA and PRA. Second, in both the PRA and NIRA periods, firms in industries that had converted to electric unit drive the most were less likely to increase price. Third, variations in hours were inversely correlated to

---

[22] Smaller competitive firms would have found it harder to raise prices, at least in such a short time span.

Table 8.14.　The Post NIRA/PRA Period June 1935–December 1935

Industry	ELECGROWTH	ELECPERCENT	Price 6/35–12/35	Wage 6/35–12/35	Empl 6/35–12/35	Hours 6/35–12/35	RPW 6/35–12/35	Payroll 6/35–12/35
Furniture	6.640	0.662	0.006	−0.007	0.124	0.033	−0.013	0.115
Leather	6.452	0.567	0.073	0.007	0.080	0.043	−0.065	0.162
Meat	3.468	0.332	0.014	−0.005	−0.063	0.056	−0.019	0.063
Newsprint	9.135	0.574	0	0.005	0.005	0.064	0.005	0.098
Paper products	9.135	0.574	−0.007	0.005	−0.015	0.064	0.012	0.098
Passenger cars	11.737	0.399	−0.016	−0.011	0.101	0.002	0.005	0.240
Rubber	8.644	0.896	0.047	0.024	0.004	0.123	−0.022	0.154
Steel sheet	5.049	0.498	0	0.009	0.071	0.114	0.009	0.25
Wool	16.838	0.595	0.083	0	0.071	0	−0.083	0.081
Chemicals	1.575	0.006	0.044	0.025	0.025	0.006	−0.019	0.058
Cotton	6.153	0.535	0.047	−0.017	0.087	−0.161	−0.065	0.253
Total shoe	3.490	0.499	0	0	0.035	−0.026	0	0.045
Average	7.360	0.511	0.024	0.003	0.044	0.026	−0.021	0.134

Table 8.15.   The Post NIRA/PRA Period June 1935–December 1935 Correlation Coefficient Matrix

Blank	ELECGROWTH	ELECPERCENT	Wage 6/35–12/35	Price 6/35–12/35	Empl 6/35–12/35	Hours 6/35–12/35	RPW 6/35–12/35	Payroll 6/35–12/35
ELECGROWTH	1.000	0.471	−0.214	0.208	0.252	0.032	−0.297	0.141
ELECPERCENT		1.000	−0.056	0.097	0.142	0.254	−0.121	0.220
Wage 6/35–12/35			1.000	0.241	0.133	−0.209	−0.921	−0.071
Price 6/35–12/35				1.000	0.133	−0.209	−0.921	−0.308
Empl 6/35–12/35					1.000	−0.368	−0.283	0.540
Hours 6/35–12/35						1.000	0.460	−0.153
RPW 6/35–12/35							1.000	−0.051
Payroll 6/35–12/35								1.000

Table 8.16.   Index of Factory Payrolls by Industry

Industry	Payroll 1/29	Payroll- 1/33	Payroll 7/33	Payroll 12/33	Payroll- 6/35	Payroll 12/35
Furniture	119.1	28.7	46.9	33.1	60	66.9
Leather	88	50.2	74.2	70.9	77	89.5
Meat	107.1	60.6	83.9	67.4	82.4	87.6
Newsprint	115.2	66	76.5	66.8	86.6	95.1
Paper products	115.2	66	76.5	66.8	86.6	95.1
Passenger cars	107.3	34.5	41.2	43.7	83.7	103.8
Rubber	122.3	38.7	66.9	70.5	76.2	88
Steel sheet	102.5	26	47.6	45	61.6	77
Wool	75	34.6	48.4	55.7	65.4	70.7
Chemicals	115.2	60.1	86.7	59	99.3	105.1
Cotton	93.7	43.7	69.7	67.1	57.7	72.3
Total shoe	92	47.6	55.3	71	67.8	70.9

Source: NBER Macrohistory Data (2014).

ELECGROWTH and ELECPERCENT (except for in early 1933), indicating the more productive firms reduced hours by more than smaller firms. Fourth, in the NIRA/PRA period (July 1933–June 1935), hours and employment were positively correlated across the 12 sample industries. Hence, while nominal wages had increased in high ELECGROWTH and ELECPERCENT industries, hours worked and employment decreased, on average, which had an adverse effect on payroll and, hence, on overall purchasing power. Fifth, while payroll did increase throughout the 12 industries, it bears noting that at the end of the NIRA/PRA (June 1935), it was still far below the 1929 levels. Referring to Table 8.16, we see that in the Furniture industry, it stood at 50 percent of its 1929 level. In all 12 industries, payroll in June 1935 stood at 72 percent of its January 1929 level.

Last, it is important to put these results in perspective. Specifically, given (i) the limited purview of our data set (12 manufacturing industries that had, for the most part, converted to electric unit drive), (ii) the presence of considerable heterogeneity among firms within industries, and (iii) the problem with the industry nomenclature, it stands to reason that these results are suggestive at best. As firms differed in terms of size, technique (i.e., electrification), degree of vertical integration, and the breadth of their activities, more detailed analysis of all sectors of the economy (especially those not touched by electrification) would be in order.

Wage, price, hours, employment and payroll variations varied substantially across firms within a given industry (and across industries and sectors). Clearly, the PRA and the NIRA, specifically the Code of Fair Competition approach to raising payrolls, and in so doing raising purchasing power in line with productivity, was fundamentally flawed and, to put it mildly, a monumental failure. As the 1937 Committee of Industrial Analysis pointed out in its report, industries differed widely in terms of their experience with the NIRA and PRA. Specifically, it pointed to the existence of two distinct groups of industries. The first consisted of industries where codes of fair competition were successfully administered. These were industries where firms were relatively few, large and "heavily equipped." The second group consisted of industries with many firms, most of which were small. More importantly, however, was the presence of considerable differences in "methods of operation" and in size.

If nothing else, these results corroborate the role of technique, notably the adoption and use of electric unit drive, as a statistically significant factor influencing firm behavior. In fact, one could go so far as to argue that the compliance crisis (Taylor and Klein, 2008) was, at least in part, the result of firm and industry heterogeneity (Alexander, 1997). In other words, given firm and industry heterogeneity, some firms found it more challenging to comply to the PRA and NIRA. It bears noting that it was a small kosher poultry company in New York City, the Schechter Poultry Corporation, that was ultimately responsible for its demise (Schechter Poultry Corp. versus the United States Government (295US495)). As it turned out, the U.S. Committee of Industrial Analysis 1937, commissioned by President Roosevelt to study the effects of the NIRA, also pointed to firm heterogeneity as a key factor in its demise. In its recommendations for future policy measures aimed at controlling wages and prices (The Problem of Standards to Guide Policy), it declared that: "Such standards must consider not only the money cost of an adequate standard of living, but the ability of industry to pay the wage without the necessity of raising prices or of raising them unduly" (U.S. Committee of Industrial Analysis, 1937, p. 236).

In short, the evidence presented here suggests that the NIRA was a well-intentioned but fundamentally flawed piece of legislation. The overriding objective of closing the wage–productivity gap was overshadowed by (i) the heterogeneity of firms and industries in the 1920s (ii) incomplete limited information on the part of the National Recovery Administration and (iii) the lack of coordination. While the solution may have appeared to be obvious on paper to Tugwell, Wagner and Roosevelt, the design of and execution of *bona-fide* policy measures was, in the presence of heterogeneity and incomplete information, severely compromised.

8.18 Summary and Conclusions

With the benefit of hindsight, it is abundantly clear that despite being well-intentioned, the Roosevelt Administration was over its head in its attempt to restore balance to the U.S. economy. Not helping matters was the fact that by the time it took office, the U.S. was facing two gaps, namely the structural gap, referred to by President Herbert Hoover's *Committee on Recent Economic Changes* as "the imbalance," and the contractionary gap, the result of the precipitous downturn from 1930 to 1933. To its way of thinking, closing the structural gap would be the key to recovery. In other words, by addressing the root cause of the downturn, it would kill the proverbial two birds with one stone. Getting wages and prices right (relative to 1929) would close the contractionary output gap. The focus of the NIRA was the underlying structural problem.

However, there were serious problems with not only its understanding of the underlying structural problem, but with the proposed solution. While it was true that electric unit drive-based acceleration had increased productivity in many manufacturing and mining firms, others were unaffected as were whole sectors of the economy. Any one-size-fits-all solution would be bound to fail. Second, the Administration, specifically, had limited — virtually none — information regarding productivity at the firm or industry level.

Seeing this, it turned to industry to implement the policy via Codes of Fair Competition where cartel-like industry associations would set wages and prices. In the summer of 1933, seeing little progress on the Code front, the President issued an executive order, known as the President's Reemployment Agreement, calling for an across-the-board wage increase of 15 percent. Over the course of the next two years, it would see a total of 557 Codes of Fair Competition signed. These, however, would be of little to no consequence as the Act itself was struck down by the Supreme Court, which raises the counterfactual question of whether it would have, over time, been successful?

The results presented in this chapter suggest that it would not, as it was poorly conceived and executed. The task of moving an industrial economy onto a higher growth path in response to what the report of President Herbert Hoover's Committee on Recent Economic Changes referred to as acceleration, while mired in a historic downturn, was a daunting one, one that was virtually impossible without a thorough understanding of the technology shock in question and extensive data, both of which were sorely lacking in the Roosevelt Administration.

Appendix: Keynes, Acceleration and the National Industrial Recovery Act

As pointed out in this chapter, the National Industrial Recovery Act, enacted in the midst of the worse economic downturn in history, was largely misunderstood. After all, Roosevelt and the Brains Trust were attempting to solve what was a structural problem that predated the downturn by years. In their view, the contraction was merely a symptom that would disappear once the underlying structural problem was solved. As it turned out, this was widely misunderstood, both among laymen and experts. One such expert was British economist John Maynard Keynes. Consider, for example, the contents of a letter he sent to President Roosevelt on the subject of the NIRA on December 16, 1933.

An Open Letter to President Roosevelt, by John Maynard Keynes

Dear Mr. President,
You have made yourself the Trustee for those in every country who seek to mend the evils of our condition by reasoned experiment within the framework of the existing social system. If you fail, rational change will be gravely prejudiced throughout the world, leaving orthodoxy and

revolution to fight it out. But if you succeed, new and bolder methods will be tried everywhere, and we may date the first chapter of a new economic era from your accession to office. This is a sufficient reason why I should venture to lay my reflections before you, though under the disadvantages of distance and partial knowledge.

At the moment your sympathisers in England are nervous and some-times despondent. We wonder whether the order of different urgencies is rightly understood, whether there is a confusion of aim, and whether some of the advice you get is not crackbrained and queer. If we are dis-concerted when we defend you, this may be partly due to the influence of our environment in London. For almost everyone here has a wildly distorted view of what is happening in the United States. The average City man believes that you are engaged on a hare-brained expedition in face of competent advice, that the best hope lies in your ridding yourself of your present advisers to return to the old ways, and that otherwise the United States is heading for some ghastly breakdown. That is what they say they smell. There is a recrudescence of wise head-waging by those who believe that the nose is a nobler organ than the brain. London is convinced that we only have to sit back and wait, in order to see what we shall see. May I crave your attention, whilst I put my own view?

You are engaged on a double task, Recovery and Reform: — recovery from the slump and the passage of those business and social reforms which are long overdue. For the first, speed and quick results are essential. The second may be urgent too: but haste will be injurious, and wisdom of long-range purpose is more necessary than immediate achievement. It will be through raising high the prestige of your admin-istration by success in short-range Recovery, that you will have the driv-ing force to accomplish long-range Reform. On the other hand, even wise and necessary Reform may, in some respects, impede and compli-cate Recovery. For it will upset the confidence of the business world and weaken their existing motives to action, before you 2 have had time to put other motives in their place. It may over-task your bureaucratic machine, which the traditional individualism of the United States and the old "spoils system" have left none too strong. And it will confuse the thought and aim of yourself and your administration by giving you too much to think about all at once.

Now I am not clear, looking back over the last nine months, that the order of urgency between measures of Recovery and measures of Reform has been duly observed, or that the latter has not sometimes been mistaken for the former. In particular, I cannot detect any material aid to recovery in N.I.R.A., though its social gains have been large. The driving force which has been put behind the vast administrative task set by this Act has seemed to represent a wrong choice in the order of urgencies. The Act is on the Statute Book: a considerable amount has been done towards implementing it: but it might be better for the present to allow experience to accumulate before trying to force through all its details. That is my first reflection — that N.I.R.A., which is essentially Reform and probably impedes Recovery, has been put across too hastily, in the false guise of being part of the technique of Recovery.

My second reflection relates to the technique of Recovery itself. The object of recovery is to increase the national output and put more men to work. In the economic system of the modern world, output is primarily produced for sale: and the volume of output depends on the amount of purchasing power, compared with the prime cost of production, which is expected to come in the market. Broadly speaking, therefore, and increase of output depends on the amount of purchasing power, compared with the prime cost of production, which is expected to come on the market. Broadly speaking, therefore, an increase of output cannot occur unless by the operation of one or other of three factors. Individuals must be induced to spend more out of their existing incomes: or the business world must be induced, either by increased confidence in the prospects or by a lower rate of interest, to create additional current incomes in the hands of their employees, which is what happens when either the working or the fixed capital of the country is being increased: or public authority must be called in aid to create additional current incomes through the expenditure of borrowed or printed money. In bad times the first factor cannot be expected to work on a sufficient scale. The second factor will come in as the second wave of attack on the slump after the tide has been turned by the expenditures of public authority. It is, therefore, only from the third factor that we can expect the initial major impulse.

Now there are indications that two technical fallacies may have affected the policy of your administration. The first relates to the part played in recovery by rising prices. Rising prices are to be welcomed because they are usually a symptom of rising output and employment. When more purchasing power is spent, one expects rising output at rising prices. Since there cannot be rising output without rising prices, it is essential to ensure that the recovery shall not be held back by the insufficiency of the supply of money to support the increased monetary turnover. But there is much less to be said in favour of rising prices, if they are brought about at the expense of rising output. Some debtors may be helped, but the national recovery as a whole will be retarded. Thus, rising prices caused by deliberately increasing prime costs or by restricting output have a vastly inferior value to rising prices which are the natural result of an increase in the nation's purchasing power.

I do not mean to impugn the social justice and social expediency of the redistribution of incomes aimed at by N.I.R.A. and by the various schemes for agricultural restriction. The latter, in particular, I should strongly support in principle. But too much emphasis on the remedial value of a higher price-level as an object in itself may lead to serious misapprehension as to the part which prices can play in the technique of recovery. The stimulation of output by increasing aggregate purchasing power is the right way to get prices up: and not the other way round.

Thus, as the prime mover in the first stage of the technique of recovery I lay overwhelming emphasis on the increase of national purchasing power resulting from governmental expenditure which is financed by Loans and not by taxing present incomes. Nothing else counts in comparison with this. In a boom inflation can be caused by allowing unlimited credit to support the excited enthusiasm of business speculators. But in a slump governmental Loan expenditure is the only sure means of securing quickly a rising output at rising prices. That is why a war has always caused intense industrial activity. In the past orthodox finance has regarded a war as the only legitimate excuse for creating employment by governmental expenditure. You, Mr President, having cast off such fetters, are free to engage in the interests of peace and prosperity the technique which hitherto has only been allowed to serve the purposes of war and destruction.

The set-back which American recovery experienced this autumn was the predictable consequence of the failure of your administration to organise any material increase in new Loan expenditure during your first six months of office. The position six months hence will entirely depend on whether you have been laying the foundations for larger expenditures in the near future.

I am not surprised that so little has been spent up-to-date. Our own experience has shown how difficult it is to improvise useful Loan-expenditures at short notice. There are many obstacles to be patiently overcome, if waste, inefficiency and corruption are to be avoided. There are many factors, which I need not stop to enumerate, which render especially difficult in the United States the rapid improvisation of a vast programme of public works. I do not blame Mr. Ickes for being cautious and careful. But the risks of less speed must be weighed against those of more haste. He must get across the crevasses before it is dark.

The other set of fallacies, of which I fear the influence, arises out of a crude economic doctrine commonly known as the Quantity Theory of Money. Rising output and rising incomes will suffer a set-back sooner or later if the quantity of money is rigidly fixed. Some people seem to infer from this that output and income can be raised by increasing the quantity of money. But this is like trying to get fat by buying a larger belt. In the United States to-day your belt is plenty big enough for your belly. It is a most misleading thing to stress the quantity of money, which is only a limiting factor, rather than the volume of expenditure, which is the operative factor.

It is an even more foolish application of the same ideas to believe that there is a mathematical relation between the price of gold and the prices of other things. It is true that the value of the dollar in terms of foreign currencies will affect the prices of those goods which enter into international trade. In so far as an over-valuation of the dollar was impeding the freedom of domestic price-raising policies or disturbing the balance of payments with foreign countries, it was advisable to depreciate it. But exchange depreciation should follow the success of your domestic price-raising policy as its natural consequence, and should not be allowed to disturb the whole world by 4 preceding its justification at an entirely arbitrary pace. This is another example of trying to put on flesh by letting out the belt.

These criticisms do not mean that I have weakened in my advocacy of a managed currency or in preferring stable prices to stable exchanges. The currency and exchange policy of a country should be entirely subservient to the aim of raising output and employment to the right level. But the recent gyrations of the dollar have looked to me more like a gold standard on the booze than the ideal managed currency of my dreams.

You may be feeling by now, Mr President, that my criticism is more obvious than my sympathy. Yet truly that is not so. You remain for me the ruler whose general outlook and attitude to the tasks of government are the most sympathetic in the world. You are the only one who sees the necessity of a profound change of methods and is attempting it without intolerance, tyranny or destruction. You are feeling your way by trial and error, and are felt to be, as you should be, entirely uncommitted in your own person to the details of a particular technique. In my country, as in your own, your position remains singularly untouched by criticism of this or the other detail. Our hope and our faith are based on broader considerations.

If you were to ask me what I would suggest in concrete terms for the immediate future, I would reply thus.

In the field of gold-devaluation and exchange policy the time has come when uncertainty should be ended. This game of blind man's buff with exchange speculators serves no useful purpose and is extremely undignified. It upsets confidence, hinders business decisions, occupies the public attention in a measure far exceeding its real importance, and is responsible both for the irritation and for a certain lack of respect which exists abroad. You have three alternatives. You can devalue the dollar in terms of gold, returning to the gold standard at a new fixed ratio. This would be inconsistent with your declarations in favour of a long-range policy of stable prices, and I hope you will reject it. You can seek some common policy of exchange stabilisation with Great Britain aimed at stable price-levels. This would be the best ultimate solution: but it is not practical politics at the moment unless you are prepared to talk in terms of an initial value of sterling well below $5 pending the realisation of a marked rise in your domestic price-level. Lastly you can announce that you will definitely control the dollar exchange by buying and selling gold and foreign currencies so as to avoid wide or meaningless fluctuations, with a right to shift the parities at any time but with a declared intention only so to do either to correct a serious want of balance in America's international receipts and payments or to meet a shift in your domestic price level relatively to price-levels abroad. This appears to me to be your best policy during the transitional period. In other respects, you would regain your liberty to make your exchange policy subservient to the needs of your domestic policy–free to let out your belt in proportion as you put on flesh.

In the field of domestic policy, I put in the forefront, for the reasons given above, a large volume of Loan-expenditures under Government auspices. It is beyond my province to choose particular objects of expenditure. But preference should be given to those which can be made to mature quickly on a large scale, as for example the rehabilitation of the physical condition of the railroads. The object is to start the ball rolling. The United States is ready to roll towards prosperity, if a good hard shove can be given in the next six months. Could not the energy and enthusiasm, which 5 launched the N.I.R.A. in its early days, be put behind a campaign for accelerating capital expenditures, as wisely chosen as the pressure of circumstances permits? You can at least feel sure that the country will be better enriched by such projects than by the involuntary idleness of millions.

I put in the second place the maintenance of cheap and abundant credit and in particular the reduction of the long-term rates of interest. The turn of the tide in Great Britain is largely attributable to the reduction in the long-term rate of interest which ensued on the success of the conversion of the War Loan. This was deliberately engineered by means of the open-market policy of the Bank of England. I see no reason why you should not reduce the rate of interest on your long-term Government Bonds to 2 percent or less with favourable repercussions on the whole bond market, if only the Federal Reserve System would replace its present holdings of short-dated Treasury issues by purchasing long-dated issues in exchange. Such a policy might become effective in the course of a few months, and I attach great importance to it.

With these adaptations or enlargements of your existing policies, I should expect a successful outcome with great confidence. How much that would mean, not only to the material prosperity of the United States and the whole World, but in comfort to men's minds through a restauration of their faith in the wisdom and the power of Government!

With great respect,
Your obedient servant
J M Keynes

To his credit, he was able to distinguish between structural and contractionary issues. However, to his discredit, he clearly failed to understand the underlying logic and premises of the NIRA, namely being an attempt to address a structural problem (i.e., the structural output gap — or imbalance) and in so doing, address — even solve — the contractionary problem (i.e., the contractionary output gap). Not mincing words, he referred to the former in extremely demeaning terms, referring to it as "queer and hare-brained." Clearly, the issues being addressed by Roosevelt and the Brains Trust were either unbeknownst to Keynes, or beyond his intellectual capabilities — it bears noting that he was not a formally-trained economist. In fact, it is alleged that as a student, he did not study economics or political economy. Thus, it is not at all surprising that he would have failed to understand the logic behind the NIRA, not helping matters.

Chapter 9

Why So Slow? The Role of Ongoing Conversion/Acceleration in Delaying the Recovery[*]

Manufacturers throughout the country must proceed to modernize their plants "to put themselves in readiness for the return of better days that are near at hand." According to a recent survey of the *American Machinist*, 48 percent of the entire machine-tool equipment of American industry is more than ten years old. In that period the productive efficiency of machine tools has been improved something like 300 percent.

New York Times, December 8, 1932

Faster Machines Sought: Manufacturers Demanding Speed Attachments for Equipment.

New York Times, December 1, 1935

---

[*] This chapter is based on Beaudreau, Bernard C. Why So Slow: The Role of Continued Conversion to Electric Unit Drive in Delaying the Recovery in the 1930s, 2019, Manuscript. Département d'économique, Université Laval.

9.1 Introduction

As shown in the last chapter, the NIRA failed to close the output gap that had been opened by the widespread adoption of electric unit drive and the resulting acceleration of production. Hours and employment continued to display weakness throughout the 1930s, making the downturn somewhat historic as previous downturns had lasted, on average, 18 months. This raises the obvious question of why? Why was the U.S. economy mired in a full-blown depression for a decade? Why did the various government policies fail to restore full employment? In this chapter, it will be argued that a contributing factor was the continuing, ongoing conversion to electric unit drive throughout the 1930s as described by the two above quotations. As shown earlier, adopting electric unit drive in the face of falling sales and revenues was a profit-increasing strategy.

Further, the high-wage provisions of the PRA and NIRA would have incited laggard firms to adopt the new technology in order to minimize labor costs, thus widening even further the already substantial output gap — or imbalance. Finally, the Roosevelt Administration's policy of investing massively in power generation (and electrical grids) throughout the 1930s increased the supply and availability of low-cost electricity, which would have contributed further to accelerating the shift to electric unit drive.

Combined, these factors would have exacerbated the problem the Roosevelt Administration was attempting to solve. Metaphorically, the policy target (i.e., full capacity utilization) was constantly shifting (i.e., increasing) throughout the 1930s as firms continued to adopt the new power drive technology. However, this paradox was lost on the Brains Trust as it had a very rudimentary understanding of the technology shock that had hit the U.S. economy in the 1910s and especially in the 1920s.

9.2 The Ongoing Conversion to Electric Unit Drive during the Downturn

As was shown in Chapters 3 and 4, converting to unit drive increases a firm's rated capacity, thus enabling it to produce more with what is essentially the same labor and capital, making it a highly profitable investment.

In addition to increasing potential output, it reduces the cost of producing any given level of output by lowering the variable costs. More specifically, by accelerating the relevant material processes, a given quantity of output can be produced in less time, which has the effect of lowering per unit cost. In more practical terms, less labor ($h(t)$) is needed to produce the same level of output.

This chapter maintains that one of the key factors prolonging the downturn was the ongoing conversion to electric unit drive, itself the result of two developments, namely declining sales which increased the probability of conversion to electric unit drive and the increasing availability and affordability of low-cost, utility-generated electricity. Throughout the 1930s, the development of large- and small-scale power sources (e.g., TVA and Hoover Dam) increased availability and affordability throughout America. Paradoxically, the myriad power-related projects of the New Deal, while creating employment in the short run, contributed to prolonging the recession by accelerating the conversion to electric unit drive in U.S. industry. The demand for labor and thus, wage income in general, weakened, thus prolonging the downturn. Again, paradoxically, U.S. potential rated GDP increased throughout the Great Depression. While income and expenditure had contracted, the ongoing conversion to electric unit drive served to increase potential output.

9.3 The New Deal and the Growth of the U.S. Power Supply

The conversion to electric unit drive in the 1920s had been concentrated in the industrialized North-East, owing largely to a number of developments in the supply of low-cost electric power. These include the increasing presence of integrated power grids as well as the bringing on-line of new power sources (e.g., the Conowingo Dam in New Jersey). The 1930s, however, witnessed a slew of new projects throughout the country as the U.S. engineering profession gauged the potential of various hydroelectric sites. One such project was the Tennessee Valley Authority and its myriad hydroelectric dams. As such, the U.S. supply of electric power literally exploded. As a result, firms throughout the country had access to cheap power with predictable results, namely the further conversion to electric unit drive.

9.4   How New Deal Policies Exacerbated the Problem of Excess Capacity

Previously, it was shown that the Smoot–Hawley Tariff Bill, by promising greater sales for U.S. firms, accelerated the conversion to electric unit drive and mass production. This was also the case with the New Deal whose policies contributed to accelerating the conversion, but for a whole different set of reasons. Specifically, the specter of higher wages (and perhaps higher sales) would have incited firms to adopt the new power drive technology. Second, the various public works programs, by fostering widespread public investment in large-scale electricity-generating public works, including the Tennessee Valley Authority and the Hoover Dam, increased the supply of cheap, abundant electric power.

As shown in the previous chapter, firms that had invested in electric unit drive were able to pay the higher wages in the President's Reemployment Agreement and the various Codes of Fair Competition, given the resulting higher machine speed (i.e., $s(t)$) and overall productivity. Such was not the case for laggard firms, for whom the specter of higher wages could result in losses and even bankruptcy. However, this could be averted by investing in the new power drive technology that was electric unit drive. Existing machinery and equipment would be speeded up, thus increasing productivity.

Further contributing to the accelerated conversion to electric unit drive-based production technology was the massive New Deal-inspired investment in electricity-generating public works which served to increase the supply of cheap electric power especially in isolated regions (e.g., the Tennessee Valley, the Pacific Northwest and the Southwest). A good example of this is the Tennessee Valley Authority that provided cheap electric power to the whole Tennessee Valley region, making the conversion by area firms to electric unit drive economically viable. Other such projects include the Hoover Dam, the Grand Coulee Dam and the Bonneville Dam (see Figure 9.1).

Table 9.1 presents data on the increase in federal publicly owned utility-based electricity-generating capacity in the New Deal era (1933–1939). We see that it went from 458,000,000 kWh to 5,476,000,000 kWh, a 12-fold increase. This does not include all municipal PWA electric power projects, which went from 5,072,000,000 kWh to 12,564,000,000 kWh, a 147 percent increase.

Figure 9.1.   Hoover Dam and TVA

Another key New Deal era development was the enactment of the Public Utility Holding Company Act of 1935 (PUCHA) which put an end to a number of questionable practices in the utility sector, notably the pyramidal structures that crossed state lines, making regulation challenging if not altogether impossible. By establishing clear rules for state and

Table 9.1.   Net Production of Electric Energy, by Class of Ownership 1933–1939*

Year	Total-Utility and Industrial	Total-Publicly Owned	Federal
1933	102,655	5,072	458
1934	110,404	5,179	357
1935	118,935	5,957	555
1936	136,006	7,023	1,072
1937	146,476	8,449	1,843
1938	141,955	9,722	3,029
1939	161,308	12,564	5,476

Source: U.S. Department of Commerce (1975), S-44-52 (*000,000 of kWh).

Table 9.2.   New Deal Policy Measures and Effects

Measure	Effect(s)
President's reemployment agreement	Increase wages, labor costs: Accelerating conversion to electric unit drive
Codes of fair competition	Increase wages for laggard firms, accelerating conversion to electric unit drive
Tennessee valley authority (TVA)	Increasing supply of low-cost electric power
Rural electrification	Increase supply of low-cost power
PWA	Increase supply of low-cost power
Public utility holding company act of 1935	Lowered price of electric power

interstate regulation, the PUCHA ushered in a period of unprecedented growth in the provision of electric power.

Hence, much like the Republican tariff-based attempt to close the output gap, the New Deal contributed to widening it (see Table 9.2). While ironic, this stemmed from a poor understanding on the part of the National Recovery Administration of the underlying changing fundamentals, namely the initial and ongoing shift from conventional belting and shafting to electric unit drive. In their view, productivity had simply increased. Their wage provisions (PRA, Codes of Fair Competition, right to unionize), by raising wages, contributed to accelerating the conversion to electric unit drive, thus widening the output gap.

9.4.1 *Anecdotal evidence*

It is important to bear in mind that despite the negative levels of investment reported in Bernstein (1987), investment in electric unit drive-based technology continued unabated throughout the 1930s, increasing firms' rated capacity. Laggard firms in industries that had experienced above average growth in electric power usage, as well as firms in other industries and industry as a whole, converted to the new technology throughout the 1930s. The reason was relatively simple, namely that great increases in rated capacity and ultimately output could be achieved at very little cost to the firm, thus increasing productivity, lowering the demand for labor per unit output, lowering costs and increasing profits. Consider the following article that appeared in the *New York Times* on December 1, 1935, under the headline "Faster Machines Sought: Manufacturers Demanding Speed Attachments for Equipment," which captures well our essential argument: "Demands made upon machine tool builders for special attachments to increase productive speed and accuracy are becoming an increasing problem to producers, it was pointed out here yesterday (*New York Times*, December 1, 1935)."

9.5 Ongoing Conversion and Employment: Simulation Analysis

To illustrate the essence of the argument presented here, a 3 percent annual growth rate in machine speed $s(t)$ is introduced in the numerical example presented in Chapter 4. Referring to Table 9.3, the ongoing increases in average machine speed serve to reduce $h(t)$, the average number of hours capital is utilized. At $t = 0$, capital is fully utilized as $h(t) = 24$, and GDP, national income and expenditure are all equal to 1200. In the first and subsequent periods, $s(t)$ increases by 2.5 percent annually, resulting in an increase in rated capacity, which cannot be supported by existing income and expenditure levels. As such, in the next period $h(t)$ is adjusted downward, resulting in a decrease in aggregate demand as fewer hours are worked. This process continues for 19 periods over which time $h(t)$

Table 9.3.   Ongoing Conversion to Electric Unit Drive
and Employment: Simulation Analysis

t	$s(t)$	$h(t)$	$y(t)$	$w(t)k(t)h(t)+\pi^v(t)$
0	5.00	24.00	1200.00	1200.00
1	5.03	23.88	1206.00	1200.00
2	5.05	23.68	1206.00	1195.82
3	5.08	23.42	1201.80	1188.77
4	5.10	23.13	1194.71	1179.78
5	5.13	22.81	1185.68	1169.53
6	5.15	22.49	1175.38	1158.51
7	5.18	22.15	1164.30	1147.05
8	5.20	21.82	1152.78	1135.38
9	5.23	21.49	1141.06	1123.68
10	5.26	21.16	1129.30	1112.05
11	5.28	20.84	1117.61	1100.56
12	5.31	20.52	1106.07	1089.27
13	5.33	20.21	1094.71	1078.19
14	5.36	19.91	1083.58	1067.35
15	5.39	19.61	1072.69	1056.76
16	5.42	19.32	1062.04	1046.41
17	5.44	19.04	1051.64	1036.30
18	5.47	18.77	1041.48	1026.44
19	5.50	18.50	1031.57	1016.81

Note: $w(t) = 3.5$, $k(t) = 10$, $\pi(t) = 360$.

decreases monotonically reaching 18.50 at $t = 19$. Also decreasing are aggregate output, income and expenditure, illustrating the contractionary effect of continuous productivity growth over time.

9.6 Macroeconomic Evidence

In this section, evidence that the diffusion/adoption of the new technology (electric unit drive) was affected by New Deal policy measures is presented. To this end, two sources of data were employed, namely employment data for the electrical equipment industry, which is used as a proxy for sales, and second, data on the supply of publicly funded electric power utilities, the latter being a proxy for New Deal policy-based additions to capacity. Put differently, not only did the various New Deal policies accelerate conversion to electric unit drive, they contributed to provide more available and affordable kilowatts.

To begin with, monthly NBER macrohistory data on employment in the electrical equipment (m08213a) and machinery (m08224) industries were used to examine investment in electrical equipment over the period in question (see Appendix for data). Data on employment in the machinery industry was used as a benchmark, the idea being that the two should display a certain degree of co-movement. The results are shown in Figure 9.1 where the two series (Employment–Electrical Equipment, Employment–Total Manufacturing) are presented. Using employment as a proxy for sales, we see that sales of electrical equipment in 1925 was greater throughout the 1930s than overall expenditure in manufacturing.

From then on, both series decreased until June 1933, which corresponds to the signing of the National Industrial Recovery Act. Employment in both the electrical equipment industry and the machinery industry increased monotonically until the downturn in 1937. What is noteworthy in Figure 9.2 is the fact that the employment index in the electrical equipment industry throughout the period in question was greater than the

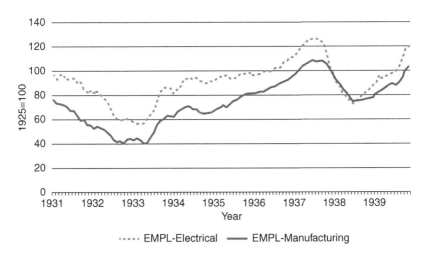

Figure 9.2. Employment — Electrical Equipment and Total Machinery

Source: NBER Macrodata (2014), Series m08213a, 08224.

Table 9.4.   Census Data for the Electrical Machinery Industry 1899–1939

Year	Value-added (% of Man.) millions	All Employees (% of Man., % of Tot. Empl.)	Value of Products (000,000)	Number of Establishments
1899	44 (0.9)	48,491 (1.0,na)	94.7	592
1904	80 (1.3)	75,019 (1.3,0.2)	151.0	798
1909	121 (1.5)	111,067 (1.6,0.3)	233.0	1,027
1914	201 (2.1)	155,699 (2.1,0.4)	362.3	1,048
1919	672 (2.8)	305,222 (3.1,0.7)	1,156.5	1,570
1921	547 (3.2)	239,944 (3.2,0.6)	932.2	1,487
1923	806 (3.3)	331,505 (3.5,0.8)	1,400.3	1,782
1925	940 (3.7)	308,592 (3.4,0.7)	1,601.1	1,807
1927	1,049 (4.0)	322,397 (3.6,0.7)	1,743.6	1,837
1929	1,389 (4.5)	421,283 (4.4,0.9)	2,397.8	1,861
1931	763 (4.1)	—	—	1,596
1933	404 (2.9)	202,129 (3.1,0.5)	—	1,365
1935	686 (3.7)	275,343 (3.8,0.7)	—	1,589
1937	1,102 (4.4)	374,290 (3.8,0.8)	—	1,597
1939	941 (3.8)	—	1,727.4	1,979

Source: Backman (1962, p. 46, 77, 204).

employment index in manufacturing as a whole, despite starting at roughly the same level — index wise — in 1925.

Table 9.4 presents *Census of the Manufactures* data on the electrical machinery industry from 1899 to 1939. Column 1 presents the level of value-added in absolute terms as well as a percentage of overall value-added in manufacturing, while Column 2 presents employment: Column 3, the value of products and Column 4, the number of establishments. What is noteworthy here is the extent to which the electrical machinery industry increased its overall share of value-added, employment and value in the manufacturing sector prior to October 1929, followed by a lull until 1937, by which point it had recovered. This would suggest that throughout this period, the conversion to electric unit drive continued, resulting in rising productivity and rated potential capacity.

The marked increase in sales of electrical machinery in the late 1920s and 1930s, it stands to reason, would result in an increase in the use of

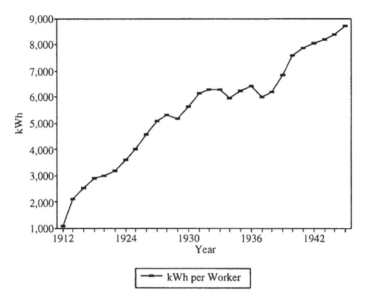

Figure 9.3.   U.S. Electric Power Consumption per Worker — Manufacturing, 1912–1945
Source: Beaudreau (1996, p. 14).

electric power in industry. Specifically, greater machine speeds would result in higher electric power per employee ratios. Put differently, employees would be made to oversee faster, more electric power-using machines. Figure 9.3, taken from *The Historical Statistics of the United States* (Department of Commerce 1975), plots electric power and employment in manufacturing from 1925 to 1939, along with the ratio of the two. Electric unit drive and the associated increase in electric power per employee are apparent from 1926 on. What is particularly noteworthy, however, is the increase in electric power per employee in the downturn, specifically from 1929 onward, a trend that shows consistent speed-ups or acceleration. In other words, in the downturn, conventionally measured labor productivity was increasing as firms that had previously resisted decided to convert to electric unit drive, resulting in faster machine speeds. What is also noteworthy is the fact that electric power per employee appears to be increasing in the late 1930s, once the cyclical variation is factored out, a result that is consistent with increasing conversion to electric unit drive.

According to Devine (1983), Sonenblum (1990) and David (1990), the increase in electric power use came as the result largely of the bringing on-line of cheap, public utility generated power. Table 9.5 illustrates this very fact in the late 1920s and early 1930s, where public utility electric energy as a share of total electric energy (public utility and industrial) increased from 72 percent in 1925 to 79 percent in 1939. The federal government's share of public utility-provided electric energy went from one-tenth of a percent in 1925 to 12 and a half percent in 1945, the result of the many New Deal-related projects that came on-stream in the late 1930s/early 1940s. What is astonishing is the extent to which power generation and sales increased throughout the Great Depression. What is also

Table 9.5.   Total Electric Energy-Utility, Federal and Industrial (kWh)

Year	Total	PUE	Federal	Industrial	PUE/ Total	Federal/ Utilities
1925	84,666	61,451	103	23,215	0.72	0.001
1926	94,222	69,363	518	24,869	0.73	0.007
1927	101,390	75,418	668	25,972	0.74	0.008
1928	108,069	82,794	356	25,275	0.76	0.004
1929	116,747	92,180	300	24,567	0.78	0.003
1930	114,637	91,112	465	23,525	0.79	0.005
1931	109,373	87,350	497	22,023	0.79	0.005
1932	99,359	79,393	445	19,966	0.79	0.005
1933	102,655	81,740	458	20,915	0.79	0.005
1934	110,404	87,258	357	23,146	0.79	0.004
1935	118,935	95,289	555	23,648	0.80	0.005
1936	136,006	109,316	1,072	26,690	0.80	0.009
1937	146,476	118,213	1,843	27,563	0.80	0.015
1938	141,955	113,812	3,029	28,143	0.80	0.026
1939	161,308	127,642	5,476	33,666	0.79	0.042
1940	179,907	141,837	8,584	38,070	0.82	0.060
1941	208,306	164,788	10,793	43,518	0.78	0.065
1942	233,146	185,979	16,893	47,167	0.79	0.090
1943	267,540	217,759	24,485	49,781	0.79	0.112
1944	279,525	228,189	28,867	51,336	0.81	0.126
1945	271,255	222,486	28,000	48,769	0.81	0.125

Source: U.S. Department of Commerce (1975), Series S44, S45 and S52.

astonishing is the fact that the generation of electric power in the war years (1939–1945) was achieved with essentially the same stock of electric power generating capacity as before the war, which is indicative of the extent of excess capacity in the system.

9.7 Evidence from Industry and Country Data

In earlier work (Beaudreau, 2019), evidence of the role of the on-going conversion to electric unit drive in prolonging the downturn using industry and country data was presented. Specifically, the hypothesis that those industries that had converted the most to electric unit drive would have been slower to return to pre-downturn levels of employment was tested using data on the level and rate of growth of electrical horsepower as well as the level of employment. A similar test was conducted using country data, the idea being that at the aggregate level, countries that had invested massively in electric unit drive (i.e., the U.S., Canada and Germany) would be mired in the downturn longer than countries that converted the least.

9.7.1 *Industry data*

The model presented in Chapter 4 predicts that industries that invest heavily in electric unit drive (i.e., $s(t)$) would witness an important decrease in employment (i.e., $h(t)$) as the resulting greater machine speeds would, by increasing productivity, reduce the demand for work hours. For example, greater machine speeds could conceivably lead a firm to cut an entire eight-hour shift, while not sacrificing output. Henry A. Porter, in *Technocracy and Roosevelt,* published in 1932, came to a similar conclusion, namely that "if, by some miracle, the United States could return to the same degree of industrial prosperity which prevailed in 1929, employment would be provided for less than 50 percent of the 14,000,000 now unemployed, due to mechanical improvements." He went on to note that "in the past 10 years, the General Electric Company created new machinery capable of producing four times as much man-power (160,000,000) as the total wage-earning population of the United States (Porter, 1932, p. 18)."[15]

To test this hypothesis, data on installed horsepower by industry and wage earners were obtained from the Census of Manufactures for three years, namely 1919, 1929 and 1939. Specifically, data on installed horsepower by industry for 1919 and 1929 were used to generate HP29/19, the rate of growth of installed horsepower at the industry level (see Column 2 in Table 9.6). For example, we see that the growth of installed horsepower varied considerably among industries, from a low of 14 percent in the Leather and its Manufactures industry, to 147 percent in the Products of Petroleum and Coal industry. Also presented are the following variables, ESTB35/29, the ratio of the number of establishments in the industry in 1935 relative to 1929, ESTB 39/29, the ratio of the number of establishments in the industry in 1939 relative to 1929, WE35/29, the ratio of the number of wage earners in the industry in 1935 relative to 1929,

Table 9.6.   Census of Manufacturing Data, U.S., 1919, 1929, 1935, 1939

Industry	HP29/ 19	ESTB35/ 29	ESTB39/ 29	WE35/ 29	WE39/ 29	VA35/ 29	VA39/ 29
Food and kindred products	1.439	0.869	0.913	1.059	1.100	0.822	1.049
Textiles and their products	1.276	0.815	0.972	0.988	1.074	0.619	0.525
Forest products	1.078	0.599	0.742	1.006	1.135	0.167	0.780
Paper and allied products	1.617	0.942	1.049	1.010	1.134	0.797	1.088
Printing, publishing and allied industries	1.712	0.821	0.904	0.852	0.907	0.265	0.735
Chemicals and allied products	1.344	0.896	1.112	0.984	1.022	0.777	1.051
Products of petroleum and coal	2.474	0.807	0.661	0.789	0.716	0.621	0.614
Rubber products	1.214	0.888	1.133	0.769	0.810	0.574	0.754
Leather and its manufactures	1.141	0.820	0.820	0.976	1.029	0.690	0.754
Stone, clay and glass products	1.801	0.672	0.825	0.710	0.875	0.574	0.880
Iron, steel and their products	1.431	0.970	1.355	2.345	2.921	0.577	0.902
Non-ferrous metals and their products	1.647	0.719	0.744	0.683	0.727	0.512	0.728
Machinery, not including transportation	1.779	0.909	0.889	0.725	0.714	0.528	0.683
Transportation equipment, air, Land Water	1.562	0.730	0.821	0.902	1.043	0.572	0.779

WE39/29, the number of wage earners in the industry in 1939 relative to 1929, VA35/29, the ratio of value-added in the industry in 1935 relative to 1929, and VA39/29, the ratio of wage earners in the industry in 1939 relative to 1929.

Macroeconomic recovery was measured by two variables, WE35/29 and WE39/29, the ratio of wage earners in the industry in 1935 and 1939, respectively, relative to 1929. Thus, the greater this ratio, the quicker or faster the recovery, abstracting from any growth considerations. Referring to Columns 5 and 6 in Table 9.6, we see that recovery varied considerably across industries. For example, by 1939 — a decade later — the number of wage earners in the Machinery Equipment industry was 71.4 percent of its 1929 level.

The model presented in Chapter 4 predicts that WE35/29 and WE39/29 will be decreasing in HP29/19. That is, the extent of the recovery as measure by the ratio of wage earners in 1935 and 1939, respectively, will be decreasing in $s(t)$, machine speed, itself proxied by the rate of growth of installed capacity in the 1920s, HP29/19. It also predicts that there will be fewer workers per establishment, the result of acceleration.

Referring to Table 9.7, which reports the findings, we see that WE35/29 and WE39/29 are in fact decreasing in HP29/19, and that WEEST39/29, wage earners per establishment, is also decreasing in HP29/19. In other words, the extent of recovery as measured by the number of wage earners in the industry in 1935 and 1939 relative to 1929,

Table 9.7.   U.S. Census of Manufacturing Data, Correlation Matrix

	HP29/ 19	WEEST 39/29	ESTB 35/29	ESTB 39/29	WE 35/29	WE 39/29	VA 35/29	VA 39/29
HP29/19	1.000	−0.248	0.0662	0.443	0.527	0.617	0.064	0.180
WEEST39/29		1.000	0.620	0.535	0.579	0.653	0.246	0.052
ESTB35/29			1.000	0.684	0.169	0.047	0.633	0.281
ESTB39/29				1.000	0.276	0.27	0.411	0.430
WE35/29					1.000	0.920	0.275	0.416
WE39/29						1.000	0.162	0.468
VA35/29							1.000	0.480
VA39/29								1.000

respectively, was decreasing in the industry's conversion to electric unit drive as measured by the growth of installed horsepower in the 1920s. As a corollary, industries that adopted electric unit drive the most also saw the number of wage earners per establishment decrease the most in the 1930s.

9.8 Evidence: Cross-Country Data

When extrapolated to the country level, the electric unit drive hypothesis maintains that countries whose companies and industries converted the most to electric unit drive were more likely to experience a slow recovery, employment wise, than those that were slow to convert. That is, countries whose firms converted to electric unit drive and thus whose potential output had increased as a result, were more likely to report negative employment growth, and would as such be slower to return to 1929 levels of employment.

9.8.1 *Country data*

The data were obtained from two sources, namely Grytten (2006) and Mitchell (2003). Referring to Table 9.8, FGDPCAP, the fall in GDP per capita from 1920 to 1930, and U1929-U1938, unemployment rates from 1930 to 1938, were used to proxy the extent and duration of the downturn, while ELEC1920, ELEC1930, ELEC1935, ELEC1940, ELECPC1920 and ELECPC1930, electricity consumption in 1920, 1930, 1935 and 1940 as well as electricity consumption per capita for 1920 and 1930, respectively, were used to proxy the country's conversion to electric unit drive. Not surprisingly, the U.S., Canada and Germany were by far the leaders in so far as the adoption of the new power drive technology was concerned. Canada's experience with the new technology owed, in large measure, to the increasing presence of U.S.-based multinationals, both in power generation and industry in general. The relatively poor performance of countries such as Denmark and the Netherlands owed to, among other factors, the absence of abundant fossil fuels and hydro resources. On the other hand, countries like Norway and Switzerland with their abundant hydraulic resources were among the leaders.

Analysis of variance was performed on these variables, the results of which are presented in Table 9.9. We see that FGDP, the decrease in GDP

Table 9.8. Country Per-capita GDP, Unemployment and Electrification Data

Country	FGDPCAP	U1929	U1931	U1933	U1935	U1937	KWHCAP20	KWHCAP30	GKWH	GKWHCAP
Austria	23.4	5.5	9.7	16.3	15.2	13.7	270.85	377.22	1.44	1.39
Belgium	10.0	0.8	6.8	10.6	11.1	7.2	559.01	148.29	0.29	0.27
Canada	34.8	72.9	11.6	19.3	14.2	9.1	688.87	1791.01	3.05	2.60
Germany	25.0	5.9	13.9	14.8	6.5	2.7	245.33	440.07	1.87	1.79
Italy	6.4	71.7	4.3	5.9	5.4	5.0	109.87	233.87	2.41	2.13
Netherlands	16.0	1.7	4.3	9.7	11.2	10.5	103.42	311.24	3.48	3.01
Switzerland	6.7	0.4	1.2	3.5	4.2	3.6	721.65	1318.02	1.89	1.83
UK	6.6	7.5	15.1	14.1	11.9	7.8	142.53	425.01	3.14	2.98
USA	30.8	3.2	15.3	20.6	14.2	9.1	7531.26	958.77	2.06	1.80
Denmark	3.6	7.0	8.2	9.3	7.7	8.0	80.54	157.70	2.24	1.96
Finland	6.3	4.1	6.7	7.6	5.4	3.8	104.83	288.77	3.03	2.75
Sweden	6.5	4.2	6	6.2	4.5	442.00	1.90	1.83		

Table 9.9.　Correlation Matrix

	FGDPCAP	U1929	U1931	U1933	U1935	U1937	KWHCAP20	KWHCAP30	GKWH	GKWHCAP
FGDPCAP	1.000	-0.117	0.516	0.849	0.798	0.631	0.454	0.578	0.076	0.017
U1929		1.000	0.606	0.321	0.228	0.290	-0.515	-0.264	0.258	0.301
U1931			1.000	0.871	0.718	0.456	0.013	0.143	0.135	0.135
U1933				1.000	0.909	0.687	0.245	0.343	0.044	0.009
U1935					1.000	0.880	0.159	0.157	-0.038	-0.075
U1937						1.000	-0.111	-0.075	-0.011	-0.048
KWHCAP20							1.000	0.787	-0.428	-0.435
KWHCAP30								1.000	0.163	0.154
GKWH									1.000	0.992
GKWHCAP										1.000

per capita, and all four proxies for electrification were highly correlated. In other words, the greater a country's experience with electric unit drive, the greater the decrease in GDP per capita from 1929 to 1932. This owed to the fact that companies in countries that had adopted electric unit drive were more likely to decrease employment in response to a decrease in aggregate demand (i.e., ϕ) given the resulting higher output per unit labor (Equation (4.9)). Ergo, countries that had not done so experienced less of a decrease in overall output, and hence in per-capita GDP. For example, the U.S. and Canada, two countries with similar experiences with electric unit drive, experienced a 30.8 and 34.8 percent decrease in GDP per capita, respectively. At the other end of the spectrum were countries like Denmark, Italy and Belgium, whose experience with electric unit drive was minimal, and which experienced comparatively mild decreases in GDP per capita.

Similar results were obtained for unemployment. For each of the years extending from 1930 to 1938, the level of unemployment in our sample countries was positively correlated with all four measures of electrification. For example, correlation coefficients between KWHCAP20, the level of kwh per capita in 1920, and each of the eight measures of unemployment in the 1930s, ranged from a low of −0.5159 in 1929 to a high of 0.2454 in 1933. In other words, prior to the downturn, countries that had adopted electric unit drive experienced lower unemployment. However, this changed with the downturn as these same countries experienced greater unemployment, consistent with Equation (4.9) according to which $h(t)$, the proxy for the level of employment is decreasing in $s(t)$, average machine speed. The results for KWHCAP30, the same variable except for 1930, were even more pronounced, with correlation coefficients that are even greater (Column 9).

What is clear from these estimates is the overridingly positive relationship between the conversion to electric unit drive, on the one hand, and unemployment in the downturn, on the other, specifically from 1929 to 1935. Afterwards, the relationship, especially for GKWH and GKWHCAP, is more tenuous, which can be attributed to the various policy measures put in place by governments.

9.9 Acceleration: The Source of Alexander Field's Most Productive Decade Ever?

In 2003, Santa Clara University economics professor Alexander Field published a paper titled "The Most Technologically Progressive Decade of the Century" in which he argued that contrary to conventional beliefs, the Great Depression decade (1929–1939) was characterized by unprecedented productivity growth as measured by MFP, multi-factor productivity (aka the Solow residual). Throughout the decade, MFP levels averaged 2.46 percent.

The results presented here provide a refinement of his findings by explicitly identifying the underlying cause, namely the continued, ongoing conversion to electric unit drive, which as pointed out throughout this book accelerated production processes and sub-processes, increasing conventionally measured labor and capital productivity. However, as pointed out in Chapter 4, neither labor nor capital was ultimately responsible for the increase. Rather, electric power — specifically, more of it per machine — was the underlying cause.

Our work also provides an alternative narrative of the massive increase in output achieved by the end of World War II. As Field pointed out "Either the growth in MFP is primarily attributable to an exceptional concatenation of technical advances across a broad frontier of the American economy during the 1930s, building on unexploited opportunities at the end of the 1920s, or it is principally the consequence of the production experience of World War II (Field, 2003, p. 1401). Our findings suggest that it was the result of (i) the acceleration-based gains made throughout this period and (ii) the massive increase in government expenditure (defense spending) that permitted U.S. firms to operate, for the first time in decades, at full capacity. In other words, wartime expenditure levels vitiated in the sense of giving full expression to an economy that had been touched by the "magic hand of speed."

9.10 The New Deal: Failure on All Fronts

Despite having accurately diagnosed both the cause of the structural output gap in the 1920s and the underlying cause of the Great Depression, the Roosevelt Administration's policy response, namely the National Industrial Recovery Act, was a failure. Table 9.10 lists its shortcomings.

What explains this incongruity? Foremost among the causes, we maintain, was the lack of information. The NIRA was based on a set of generalizations regarding the U.S. economy in the 1920s. As is the case with generalizations, they fail to capture the complexity of a situation. Not all sectors of the U.S. economy had been affected by electric unit

Table 9.10. Shortcomings of the National Industrial Recovery Act of 1933

1-Failed to increase purchasing power owing to heterogeneous firms and industries.

2-Accelerated conversion to electric unit drive by raising wages, thus widening, not narrowing, the output gap.

3-By investing massively in electric power generation, it accelerated conversion to electric unit drive by providing low-cost electricity.

4-By attempting to stabilize prices, it de facto prevented a Veblen-type product price deflation-based recovery.

drive-based acceleration. Yet, policy was drafted as if that was the case. Further, while its architects referred to increased efficiency, little was known of the underlying causes. As such, many of its policies were detrimental to the recovery as they encouraged further adoption of the new technology, thus exacerbating the problem at hand. In short, the means to implement what was a radical overhaul of the wage and price structure were painfully inadequate. The Brains Trust was charged with a colossal task, one that was, to put it mildly, impossible at the time.

9.11 Summary and Conclusions

In this chapter, it was shown that not only was the conversion to electric unit drive the underlying cause of the Great Depression by increasing potential rated capacity beyond the ability to "take the additional goods off of the market," it served to prolong it as investment in the new drive technology continued unfettered throughout the downturn. Much like automation today, it allowed firms to reduce their variable costs per unit of output, making it a dominant strategy both before and after the stock market crash.

It was also argued that electric unit drive, more specifically, a country's experience with electric unit drive, was a key determinant in the severity of the downturn, with the U.S., Canada and Germany, the three countries that had invested the most in the new technology, being the hardest hit. In fact, one could go as far as to argue that the Great Depression was only truly great in these countries as others only experienced a mild (in comparison) downturn.

These findings are important for a number of reasons. First, they highlight the fact that while well-intentioned, the New Deal policy of investing massively in power generation and power grids was, in many ways, ill-advised as it prolonged the downturn. As shown in Chapter 3, the rapid growth of electric power and electric power grids are what led to the initial output gap. More power and grids would only serve to widen it, and make recovery an even greater challenge.

The upshot, however, was the WWII dividend, namely the fact that the United States was able to essentially double its GDP from 1939 to 1945, thus providing the material wherewithal to defeat the Axis powers. While less public investment in electric generating capacity would have undoubtedly shortened the downturn, it proved to be a godsent in the early 1940s.

This, we argue, goes a long way in explaining why it took government expenditure of roughly $90 billion in 1944 (equivalent to U.S. GDP in 1939) to close the gap. Not only did this new technology increase the rated capacity of existing machinery and equipment, it decreased the demand for new machinery and equipment. Firms could meet actual or anticipated increases in demand by simply converting to this new technology. Similarly, it decreased the demand for labor per unit output as machine speeds and hence conventionally defined labor productivity increased.

Attempts to address the resulting disequilibrium (i.e., excess capacity) only served to exacerbate the problem by accelerating the rate of conversion. This occurred in two ways, namely by accelerating the adoption of electric unit drive among laggard firms and industries (high-wage policies), and second, by increasing the electric power generating capacity from the large-scale public work programs of the New Deals, notably the TVA, the Hoover Dam and the Grand Coulee and Bonneville Dams, not to mention the hundreds of other WPA-inspired electric power generating projects throughout the country. Ironically, what was seen as a solution to the problem (i.e., massive public works programs) contributed ultimately to worsening the problem.

Throughout the 1930s, productive capacity continued to increase, with the result that by 1944, following massive war-related government expenditure, the U.S. economy was able to double its output relative to 1929. Put differently, the war with its unprecedented expenditure levels unleashed the "unbound prometheus" that had been building throughout the worst industrial depression in history.

Like Vedder and Galloway (1993) and Cole and Ohanian (2004), we showed that the policy measures put in place in the 1930s contributed to delaying the recovery but for fundamentally different reasons. Whereas they focused on the consequences of the high wage policies of the Roosevelt Administration on labor demand, we focused on the effects these policies had on the underlying problem, namely increasing excess rated capacity.

Our analysis shows that the Great Depression itself and the delayed recovery can and should be seen as pieces/parts of a greater whole, one whose defining feature was a revolutionary power drive technology that increased machine speeds throughout the U.S. economy, thus increasing output per unit capital/labor. While such an increase failed to appear on the conventional radar screen(s), it wreaked havoc in policy circles as Republicans and Democrats scrambled to find a way to deal with the fallout.

As we pointed out, it could be argued that while the looming depression in the late 1920s was "great," there is every reason to believe that it was worsened by the various policy measures enacted by both political parties.

These findings have important implications for the debate surrounding the efficacy of policy instruments in the 1930s in general. Consider, for example, monetary policy. In light of our findings, it is highly unlikely that "quantitative easing" or a zero interest rate would have restored investment levels to pre-1930s levels, given the increased presence of electric unit drive-based rated capacity growth. Throughout the 1930s, the rated capacity of existing capital was increasing, the result of machine speed-ups, or what many authors referred to as "acceleration." Put differently, electric unit drive provided firms with a cost-effective way to increase rated capacity.

Next, consider wage policy or, specifically, a policy aimed at lowering wages. Again, it is by no means obvious that such a policy would have increased employment given the increase in conventionally defined labor productivity. Lower wages would have increased profitability, but would have wreaked havoc on product markets. Furthermore, given the fact that productivity had increased, to argue that high wages were responsible for unemployment would be fallacious.

Other policy measures of questionable value include free trade, and private debt-financed government expenditure. The former owes to the zero-sum nature of trade, while the latter owes to the fact that the increase in rated capacity described in this chapter was not monetized. Put differently, money income did not increase commensurately with rated capacity. As such, private debt-financed government expenditure could and would replace falling private investment expenditure, but would be insufficient to raise overall GDP–that is, produce at the new rated capacity.

Last, our analysis has important implications for the debate over the effect of World War II on productivity, as measured by TFP (Gordon, 2014; Field, 2018). Robert Gordon maintains that WWII, via learning effects, increased TFP, while Alexander Field maintains that if anything, TFP fell from 1941 to 1948, arguing instead that the phenomenal productivity growth of the period owed to innovations in the 1930s. Our analysis points to two things, namely the growing excess rated capacity of the U.S. capital stock over a decade (1930–1940), combined with the unprecedented increase in overall expenditure, led to a marked increase in output and productivity as capital utilization rates were pushed to the limit, thus allowing firms, many for the first time, to effectively produce at their new, higher electric unit drive-based rated capacity. In other words, WWII unshackled the potential that had been building throughout the 1930s.

Thus, in answer to the question, "why was the U.S. economy so slow to reach the full utilization of its productive capacity," the reason lies paradoxically in the "speed" or "acceleration" of the nation's $k(t)$, its productive capacity. As $s(t)$ increased, *ceteris paribus*, so too would the duration of the downturn/recovery.

Chapter 10

Summary and Conclusions

To many, the view of the events leading up to and including the Great Depression presented here will appear to be novel. However, I want to reassure them that it is not. In fact, it can be found, explicitly or implicitly, in the writings of period scholars, in the writings of period analysts, in the press reports of period journalists, in the speeches of congressmen, and in the policies of presidents. Which begs the question, why then has it been absent from the literature on the Great Depression? Why has the wisdom and insights of these period writers been ignored?

There are at least two reasons, namely the state of production theory in the 1920s, on the one hand, and the cognitive dissonance that character-ized the profession following the stock market boom and crash, the pro-hibitive Smoot–Hawley Tariff Bill, the precipitous decline in investment and the attempt on the part of the federal government to radically alter the very foundations of American society, on the other.

As President Hoover's *Committee on Recent Economic Changes of the President's Conference on Unemployment* pointed out, electric unit drive-based acceleration was the underlying cause of the growing imbal-ance in the economy and the weakening employment growth. However, this very fact was lost on the economics profession whose formalization of production processes and, thus, whose very understanding of wealth creation were devoid of energy, speed and acceleration. It bears noting that all references to electric unit drive in the *Report* were made by engi-neers and not economists.

This explains the profession's failure to get a handle on the veritable causes of the Smoot–Hawley Tariff Bill, as well as the underlying logic behind Roosevelt's National Industrial Recovery Act. Engineers, journalists and politicians were reveling in the new power drive technology and its ability to increase wealth: ironically, this was all but lost on the economics profession.

Not being able to understand the role of the new technology on productivity and the Republican response led the profession down an altogether different path, one couched in randomness, in bubbles and animal spirits. The events of the late 1920s and early 1930s were attributed to just about anything and everything but the true underlying cause. The stock market crash was seen as a bubble, the result of irrationality on the part of investors and bankers. Investment expenditure was alleged to be guided by animal spirits.

In a back-to-the future way, this book gives a voice to those whose voices were ignored or forgotten in the early 1930s. It provides an alternative account of the Great Depression, one that is based on a thorough understanding of the role of power in general and electric power in particular in productivity both at the plant and economy-wide levels. By accelerating existing machinery and equipment, electric unit drive increased a plant's rated capacity, which at the aggregate level increased the ability of the U.S. economy as a whole to create wealth.

In short, it is the fruit of the application of basic science to production and to the events of the 1920s and 1930s. Production theory then as now was devoid of references to the science of material processes. Instead, wealth was seen as an increasing function of capital and labor. An increase in machine speed would, as such, have gone unnoticed. After all, to the naked eye, nothing would have changed. This is somewhat ironic as the decade of the 1920s was referred to as the "Roaring Twenties" in reference to the dynamos that were driving the economy. Even Charlie Chaplin, the author and producer (and actor) of the film *Modern Times*, had understood that acceleration was the key to understanding the 1920s and 1930s (see Figure 10.1).

The main contribution of this book, it therefore follows, consists of having re-examined the events of the 1920s and 1930s through the prism of the material sciences. The result is a coherent, empirically consistent account of a series of events and developments in this period, events and developments that, until now, were seen as being largely unrelated. For example, the stock market boom and crash was shown not to be a speculative bubble, but rather the result of failed government policy against a background of rapidly increasing productivity. The precipitous fall in

Figure 10.1. *Modern Times* — Management Instructing Technician to Increase Speed

investment that followed owed to the increasing presence of excess rated capacity.

The end result is a view of both the Smoot–Hawley Tariff Act and the National Industrial Recovery Act that is more in keeping with the objectives of their framers. This stands in contrast with the existing literature which sees both as being unwarranted, ill-advised and misguided. The fact of the matter is that the U.S. in the 1920s faced a crisis of unknown cause (acceleration) with virtually no policy instruments. This led invariably to improvization and experimentation. The problem, from a policy design point of view, was the near-total absence of information. Hunches, generalizations, and common sense replaced fact-based analysis and policy. For example, Rexford G. Tugwell, one of the main architects of the National Industrial Recovery Act, referred correctly to electric unit drive and electrification as the cause but had little idea whatsoever of the underlying mechanics (acceleration), of its breadth or its impact on productivity and rated capacity. Put differently, its one thing to identify a shock, and another to design the appropriate policy.

The fact of the matter is that the Hoover Administration and the Roosevelt Administration were very much in the dark regarding the very nature of the new technology and its impact on the U.S. economy. Add to this the failure on the part of officials to understand its role in the stock market boom and crash and you get the perfect storm. That both the Smoot–Hawley Tariff Act and the National Industrial Recovery Act failed comes as little surprise. Both were shots in the dark, so to speak, based on a set of impressionistic notions of increased efficiency and excess capacity but no hard data or estimates (electrification, excess rated capacity). In fact, only in the mid-1930s would estimates of the output gap appear as a result of broad national surveys (Brookings Institution and Harold Loeb).

The upshot of this book is straightforward: the greatest economic downturn in history was the result of an unprecedented technology shock, one that increased the productivity of existing plant and equipment, and one that would paradoxically result in a 50 percent decrease in output and a 30 percent rate of unemployment. In many regards, it was a replay of Adam Smith's famous proverb of specialization being determined by the extent of the market with a twist, namely that in the late 1920s, the full utilization of the new rated capacity would be determined by the extent of the market. And the latter was dearly lacking, which explains both the Republican Party's attempt to secure more of the domestic market for U.S. firms, and the Democratic Party's attempt at extending the market by raising wages and purchasing power. In short, the Great Depression was the result of forces that have plagued market economies from 1776 on, namely the inability of income and expenditure to increase in lockstep with rated capacity.

Time and the outbreak of a world war would do what a misguided tariff policy, a bold attempt to reform American capitalism, and a second New Deal had failed to do, namely close what was by then a $100 billion output gap. Given that 1929 GNP stood at $100 billion, it stands to reason that the output gap throughout the 1930s was greater than either the Brookings Institution or Harold Loeb had estimated.

Bibliography

Alexander, B. (1997). Failed cooperation in heterogeneous industries under national recovery administration. *The Journal of Economic History*, 57, 322–344.

Babbage, C. (1832). *On the Economy of Machinery and Manufactures*. London: Charles Knight.

Backman, J. (1962). *The Economics of the Electrical Machinery Industry*. New York, NY: New York University Press.

Bakker, G., Crafts, N. and Woltjer, P. (2015). A vision of the growth process in a technologically progressive economy: The United States, 1929–1941. CEPR, Discussion Paper No. 10995.

Beard, C. (1933). Review of the industrial discipline and the governmental arts. *American Political Science Review*, 27, 833–835.

Beaudreau, B. C. (1995). The impact of electric power on manufacturing productivity: The case of U.S. manufacturing. *Energy Economics*, 17(3), 231–236.

Beaudreau, B. C. (1996). *Mass Production, The Stock Market Crash, and The Great Depression: The Macroeconomics of Electrification*. Westport, CT: Greenwood Press.

Beaudreau B. C. (1998). *Energy and Organization: Growth and Distribution Reexamined*. Westport, CT: Greenwood Press.

Beaudreau, B. C. (1999). *Energy and the Rise and Fall of Political Economy*. Westport, CT: Greenwood Press.

Beaudreau, B. C. (2005). *The National Industrial Recovery Redux: Technology and Transitions*. New York, NY: iUniverse.

Beaudreau, B. C. (2014a). Electrification, tractorization and motorization: Revisiting the Smoot–Hawley Tariff Act. *Journal of Economic Issues*, 48(4), 1–33.

Beaudreau, B. C. (2014b). Discriminating among tariff-based theories of the stock market crash. *Essays in Economic and Business History*, 32(3), 80–99.

Beaudreau, B. C. (2016a). Why did the National Industrial Recovery Act fail? *European Review of Economic History*, 20(1), 79–101. Oxford University Press.

Beaudreau, B. C. (2016b). The petition against the Smoot–Hawley Tariff Act: What 1,028 economists overlooked. *Real World Economics Review*, 74(2), 124–138.

Beaudreau, B. C. (2017a). Economies of speed, KE=1/2mv2 and the productivity slowdown. *Energy*, April, 124, 100–113.

Beaudreau, B. C. (2017b). Reexamining the origins of the Smoot–Hawley Tariff Act. *Research in Economic History*, 33, 1–22.

Beaudreau, B. C. (2017c). Electrification, the Smoot–Hawley Tariff Act and the decline in investment expenditure in 1931–1932: Testing the excess capacity hypothesis. *International Advances in Economic Research*, 23(3), 295–308.

Beaudreau, B. C. (2018). Electrification, the Smoot–Hawley Tariff Act and the stock market boom and crash; evidence from longitudinal data. *Journal of Economics and Finance*, 42(3), 631–650.

Beaudreau, B. C. and Taylor, J. (2018). Why did the Roosevelt administration think cartels, higher wages and shorter workweeks would promote recovery from the Great Depression? *The Independent Review*, 23(1).

Beaudreau, B. C. (2019). Why so slow: The role of continued conversion to electric unit drive in delaying the recovery in the 1930s. Manuscript. Département d'économique, Université Laval.

Beaudreau, B. C. (2020). *The Economics of Speed: Machine Speed as the Key Factor in Productivity*. Zurich: Springer.

Bell, S. (1940). *Productivity, Wages and National Income*. Washington, DC: Brookings Institution.

Bernanke, B. S. (1986). Employment, hours, and earnings in the depression: An analysis of eight manufacturing industries. *American Economic Review*, 76(1), 82–109.

Bernstein, M. (1987). *The Great Depression: Delayed Recovery and Economic Change in America, 1929–1939*. London: Cambridge University Press.

Bresnahan, T. F. and Trajtenberg, M. (1995). General purpose technologies engines of growth? *Journal of Econometrics*, 65(1), 83–108.

Brookings, R. E. (1932). *The Way Forward*. New York: The MacMillan Co.

Bohn, F. and Ely, R. T. (1935). *The Great Change: Work and Wealth in the New Age*. New York, NY: T. Nelson and Sons.

Callahan, C., McDonald, J. A. and O'Brien, A. P. (1994). Who voted for Smoot–Hawley? *The Journal of Economic History*, 54(3), 683–690.

Carver, T. N. (1925). *The Present Economic Revolution in the United States*. Boston: Little, Brown and Company.

Chandler, A. D. (1977). *The Visible Hand: The Managerial Revolution in American Business*. Cambridge, MA: Harvard University Press.

Chase, S. (1934). *The Economy of Abundance*. New York, NY: The John Day Company.

Cohen, M. R. (1933). Review of the industrial discipline and the governmental arts. *Columbia Law Review*, 33(7), 1273–1277.

Cohen, A. (1984). Technical change as historical process: The case of the U.S. pulp and paper industry, 1915–1940. *Journal of Economic History*, 44(3), 775–799.

Cole, H. L. and Ohanian, L. E. (2004a). New deal policies and the persistence of the great depression. *Journal of Political Economy*, 112(3), 779–816.

Cole, H. L. and Ohanian, L. E. (2004b). New deal policies and the persistence of the great depression: A general equilibrium analysis. *Journal of Political Economy*, 114(4), 779–816.

Conference on Unemployment. (1929). Report of the Committee on Recent Economic Changes of the President's Conference on Unemployment, Herbert Hoover, Chairman, Including the Reports of a Special Staff of the National Bureau of Economic Research, Inc. Washington, D.C., Committee on Recent Economic Changes, New York, NY: McGraw-Hill.

Congressional Record (various volumes). U.S. Congressional Record-Senate and House of Representatives. Washington, DC: U.S. Government Printing Office.

Crocker, F. B. (1901). The electric distribution of power in the workshops. *Journal of the Franklin Institute*, 151(1), 2–9.

Crocker, F. B., Benedikt, V. M. and Ormsbee, A. F. (1895). Electric power in factories and mills. Transactions of the American Institute of Electrical Engineers. June 12.

Cupitt, R. T. and Elliott, E. (1994). Schattschneider revisited: Senate voting on the Smoot–Hawley Tariff Act of 1930. *Economics and Politics*, 6(3), 187–199.

David, P. (1990). The dynamo and the computer: An historical perspective on the modern productivity paradox. *The American Economic Review*, 80(2), 355–361.

David, P. A. and Wright, G. (2003). General purpose technologies and productivity surges: Historical reflections on the future of the ICT revolution. In David, P. A. and Thomas, M. (Eds.), *The Economic Future in Historical Perspective*. Oxford University Press.

Day, C. (1904). Discussion on the individual operation of machine tools by electric motors. *Journal of the Franklin Institute*, 158(5), (November).

Devine, W. D. Jr. (1983). From shafts to wires: Historical perspective on electrification.

Devine, W. D. Jr. (1990). Electrified mechanical drive: The historical power distribution revolution. In Schurr, S. H., Burwell, C. C., Devine, W. D. Jr. and Sonenblum, S. (eds.), *Electricity in the American Economy: Agent of Technological Progress*. Westport, CT: Greenwood Press.

Dice, C. A. (1929). *New Levels in the Stock Market*. New York, NY: McGraw-Hill.

Douglas, P. H. (1927). The modern technique of mass production and its relation to wages. *Proceedings of the Academy of Political Science in the City of New York*, 12(3), 17–42.

Eggertsson, G. (2008). Great expectations and the end of the depression. *American Economic Review*, 98(4), 1476–1516.

Eichengreen, B. (1989). The political economy of the Smoot–Hawley Tariff. In R. L. Ransom, P. H. Lindert and R. Sutch (eds.), *Research in Economic History*, Vol. 12, pp. 1–43.

Eichengreen, B. (1992a). *Golden Fetters: The Gold Standard and the Great Depression, 1919–1929*. Oxford: Oxford University Press.

Eichengreen, B. (1992b). The origins and nature of the great slump revisited. *The Economic History Review*, 45(2), 213–239.

Eichengreen, B. and O'Rourke, K. H. (2009). A tale of two depressions. *Advisor Perspectives*, April 21. https://citeseerx.ist.psu.edu/viewdoc/download?doi=10.1.1.520.3990&rep=rep1&type=pdf.

Ezekiel, M. (1936). Population and unemployment. *The Annals of the American Academy of Political and Social Science*, 188, 230–242.

Faulkner, H. U. (1950). *From Versailles to the New Deal*. New Haven, CT: Yale University Press.

Field, A. J. (2003). The most technologically progressive decade of the century. *American Economic Review*, 93(4), 1399–1413.

Field, A. J. (2018). The impact of World War II on growth of U.S. potential output. Santa Clara University Working Paper.

Filene, E. A. (1923). The minimum wage and efficiency. *American Economic Review*, 13, 411–415.

Filene, E. A. (1924). *The Way Out: A Forecast of Coming Changes in American Business and Industry*. New York: Doubleday, Page and Co.

Filene, E. A. (1929). Mass production makes a better world. *Atlantic Monthly*, 143, 625–631.

Filene, E. A. (1931). *Successful Living in This Machine Age*. New York: Simon and Schuster.

Fisher, I. (1930). *The Stock Market Crash–and After*. New York, NY: The Macmillan Company.

Ford, H. (1922). *My Life and Work*. Garden City, NY: Garden City Publishing Co.

Ford, H. (1926a). *Today and Tomorrow*. New York, NY: Doubleday.

Ford, H. (1926b). Mass production. *Encyclopaedia Britannica*, 13, 821–823.
Foster, W. T. and Catchings, W. (1927). *Business Without a Buyer*. New York, NY: Houghton Mifflin.
Friedman, M. and Schwartz, A. J. (1963). *A Monetary History of the United States 1867–1960*. New York, NY: National Bureau of Economic Research.
Galbraith, J. K. (1954). *The Great Crash of 1929*. New York: Houghton Mifflin.
General Electric Company, (1937). Machine tool speed show. https://www.youtube.com/watch?v=CUYajEF7X-U&t=344s.
Giedion, S. (1948). *Mechanization Takes Command, A Contribution to Anonymous History*. Oxford University Press.
Gordon, R. J. (1961). *Business Fluctuations*. New York: Harper & Brothers.
Gordon R. J. (2014). The Demise of U.S. Economic Growth: Restatement, Rebuttal, and Reflections, NBER Working Paper 19895, Cambridge.
Gordon, R. J. (2016). *The Rise and Fall of American Growth: The U.S. Standard of Living since the Civil War*. Princeton, NJ: Princeton University Press.
Grytten, O. H. (2008). Why was the Great Depression not so great in the Nordic countries?: Economic policy and unemployment. *The Journal of European Economic History*, 369–403.
Hansen, A. (1977). *The American Economy*. Westport, CT: Greenwood Press.
Hawley, E. (1974). Herbert Hoover, the Commerce Secretariat, and the Vision of an "Associative State," 1921–1928. *Journal of American History*, 61(1), 116–140.
Hopkins, W. (1933). Review of the industrial discipline and the governmental arts. *Economic Journal*, 33(9), 500–502.
Hounshell, D. A. (1984). *From the American System to Mass Production 1800–1932*. Baltimore, MD: The Johns Hopkins University Press.
Hughes, T. P. (1976). Technology and public policy: The failure of giant power. *Proceedings of the IEEE*, 64(9), 1361–1371.
Hughes, T. P. (1983). *Networks of Power: Electrification in Western Society 1880–1930*. Baltimore, MD: The Johns Hopkins University Press.
Hunter, L. and Bryant, L. (1991). *A History of Industrial Power in the United States 1780–1930 Volume 3, The Transmission of Power*. Cambridge, MA: MIT Press.
Irwin, D. A. (2011). *Peddling Protectionism: Smoot–Hawley and the Great Depression*. Princeton, NJ: Princeton University Press.
Irwin, D. A. and Kroszner, R. S. (1996). Log-rolling and economic interests in the passage of the Smoot–Hawley Tariff. *Carneige–Rochester Conference Series on Public Policy*, 45, 173–200.
Jerome, H. (1934). *Mechanization in Industry*. Cambridge, MA: National Bureau of Economic Research.
Jevons, W. S. (1865). *The Coal Question*. London: Macmillan and Co.

Jevons, W. S. (1871). *The Theory of Political Economy*. London: Macmillan and Co.

Kahn, R. F. (1931). The relation of home investment to unemployment. *The Economic Journal*, 41, 173–198.

Keynes, J. M. (1936). *The General Theory of Employment, Output and Money.* London: Palgrave Macmillan.

Kimball, D. (1929). Changes in New and Old Industries, in Conference on Unemployment 1929 Report of the Committee on Recent Economic Changes of the President's Conference on Unemployment, Herbert Hoover, Chairman, Including the Reports of a Special Staff of the National Bureau of Economic Research, Inc. Washington, D.C., Committee on Recent Economic Changes, New York, NY: McGraw-Hill.

Klein, M. (2001). The stock market crash of 1929: A review article. *Business History Review*, 75(2), 325–351.

Knight, F. (1921). *Risk, Uncertainty and Profit*. New York, NY: Houghton Mifflin Co., The Riverside Press.

Kummel, R., Henn, J. and Lindenberger, D. (2002). Capital labor, energy and productivity: Modeling innovation diffusion. *Structural Change and Economic Dynamics*, 13(1), 41–53.

Lacey, R. (1986). *Ford: The Men and the Machine*. Boston, MA: Little Brown and Company.

Laing, G. (1933). *Towards Technocracy*. New York, NY: Angelus Press.

Loeb, H. (1935). *The Chart of Plenty: A Study of America's Product Capacity Based on the Findings of the National Survey of Potential Product Capacity*. New York, NY: Viking Press.

Lorant, J. H. (1967). Technological change in American manufacturing during the 1920s. *The Journal of Economic History*, 27(2), 243–246.

Lyon, L. S. *et al.* (1935). *The National Recovery Administration: An Analysis and Appraisal*. Washington, DC: Brookings Institution.

Marshall, A. (1890). *Principles of Economics*. London: MacMillan.

Marx, K. (1867). *Das Kapital*. Verlag von Otto Meisner.

McGrattan, E. and Prescott, E. (2004). Irving Fisher was right. *International Economic Review*, 45, 991–1009.

Merrill, M. (1990). *Reed Smoot: Apostle in Politics*. Provo, UT: Utah State University.

Mitchell, B. R. (2003). *International Historical Statistics: Europe, 1750–2000*. New York, NY: Palgrave Macmillan.

Moulton, H. G. (1935). *Income and Economic Progress*. Washington DC: The Brookings Institution.

National Bureau of Economic Research. (1929). *Recent Economic Changes in the United States, Volumes 1 and 2*. Cambridge, MA: National Bureau of Economic Research.

National Bureau of Economic Research. (2014). NBER macrohistory database. http://www.nber.org/databases/macrohistory/contents/index.html.

National Recovery Administration. (1936). *Codes of Fair Competition*, Vol. 6, pp. 245–286. Washington, DC: United States Government Printing Office.

Nevins, A. (1954). *Ford: The Times, The Man, The Company*. New York, NY: Charles Scribner's Sons.

New York Times (various editions). *New York Times*, New York, NY: *New York Times*.

Nourse, E. A. *et al.* (1934). *America's Capacity to Produce*. Washington DC: Brookings Institution.

Nye, D. E. (1990). *Electrifying America: Social Meanings of a New Technology*. Cambridge, MA: MIT Press.

Oshima, H. T. (1984). The growth of U.S. factor productivity: The significance of new technologies in the early decades of the 20th century. *Journal of Economic History*, 44(1), 161–170.

Pastor, R. (1980). *Congress and the Politics of United States Foreign Economic Policy, 1929–1976*. Berkeley, CA: University of California Press.

Pecora, F. (1939). *Wall Street Under Oath: The Story of Our Modern Money Changers*. New York, NY: A.M. Kelley.

Polakov, W. N. (1933). *The Power Age, Its Quest and Challenge*. New York, NY: Covici, Friede Publishers.

Porter, H. A. (1932). *Roosevelt and Technocracy*. Los Angeles, CA: Wetzel Publishing Company.

Powell, J. (2003). *FDR's Folly: How Roosevelt and His New Deal Prolonged the Great Depression*. New York, NY: Three Rivers Press.

Ramey, V. (2011). Can government purchases stimulate the economy? *Journal of Economic Literature*, 49(3), 673–685.

Robinson, J. (1937). *Essays in the Theory of Employment*. London: Macmillan.

Romasco, A. U. (1983). *The Politics of Recovery*. New York, NY: Oxford University Press.

Rosenberg, N. (1972). *Technology and American Economic Growth*. Armonk, NY: M.E. Sharpe.

Rosenberg, N. and Birdzell, L. E. Jr. (1986). *How the West Grew Rich: The Transformation of the Industrial World*. New York, NY: Basic Books.

Schurr, S. H., Burwell, C. C., Devine, W. D. Jr. and Sonenblum, S. (eds.). (1990). *Electricity in the American Economy: Agent of Technological Progess*. Westport, CT: Greenwood Press.

Scott, H. *et al.* (1933). *Introduction to Technocracy*. New York, NY: The John Day Company.

Schattschneider, E. E. (1935). *Politics, Pressures, and the Tariff*. New York, NY: Prentice Hall.

Shiller, R. J. (2000). *Irrational Exuberance*. Princeton, NJ: Princeton University Press.

Sirkin, G. (1975). The stock market of 1929 revisited: A note. *Business History Review*, 44(3), 223–231.

Smith, A. (1976). *An Inquiry into the Nature and Causes of the Wealth of Nations, 1776.* London: W. Strahan and T. Cadell.

Soddy, F. (1922). *Cartesian Economics: The Bearing of Physical Science Upon State Stewardship.* London: Hendersons.

Soule, G. (1947). *Prosperity Decade: From War to Depression 1917–1929.* New York: Rinehart and Company.

Sonenblum, S. (1990). Electrification and productivity growth in manufacturing. In Schurr, S. H., Burwell, C. C., Devine, Jr. W. D. and Sonenblum, S. (eds.), *Electricity in the American Economy: Agent of Technological Progress.* Westport, CT: Greenwood Press.

Soule, G. (1947). *Prosperity Decade: From War to Depression, 1917–1929.* New York: Rinehart and Company.

Steindl, F. G. (2004). *Understanding Economic Recovery in the 1930s: Endogenous Propagation in the Great Depression.* Ann Arbor: University of Michigan Press.

Stresing, R., Lindenberger, D. and Kummel, R. (2008). Cointegration of output, capital, labor and energy. *The European Physical Journal B: Condensed Matter and Complex Systems*, 66(2), 279–287.

Szostak, R. (1996). *Technological Innovation and the Great Depression.* New York, NY: Routledge, Taylor and Francis.

Tapley, W. H. (1899). The practical application of electric motors to printing press machinery. *Journal of the Franklin Institute*, 148(4), 259–279.

Taussig, F. (1930). The Tariff, 1929–1930. *The Quarterly Journal of Economics*, 44(2), 175–204.

Taylor, J. E. (2011). Work-sharing during the Great Depression: Did the presidents reemployment agreement promote reemployment? *Economica*, 78, 133–158.

Taylor, J. E., Neumann, T. and Fishback, P. (2013). Comparisons of weekly hours over the past century and the importance of work sharing policies in the 1930s, *American Economic Review Papers and Proceedings*, 103(3), 105–110.

Taylor J. E. and Neumann, T. C. (2016). Recovery spring, faltering fall: March to November 1933. *Explorations in Economic History*, 61(3), 54–67.

Taylor, J. E. (2019). *Deconstructing the Monolith: The Microeconomics of the National Industrial Recovery Act.* Chicago, IL: University of Chicago Press.

Taylor, J. E. and Klein, P. G. (2008). An anatomy of a cartel: The national industrial recovery act of 1933 and the compliance crisis of 1934. *Research in Economic History*, 26, 235–271.

Thomas, W. (1928). The economic significance of the increased efficiency of American industry. *American Economic Review*, 18(1), 122–138.

Tryon, F. G. (1927). An index of consumption of fuels and water power. *Journal of the American Statistical Association*, 22(2), 271–282.

Tugwell, R. G. (1927). *Industry's Coming of Age*. New York, NY: Columbia University Press.

Tugwell, R. G. (1933). *The Industrial Arts and the Governmental Arts*. New York, NY: Columbia University Press.

U.S. Bureau of Census. (1914). Abstract of the census of the manufactures 1909. Washington, D.C.: Government Printing Office.

U.S. Bureau of the Census. (1923). Abstract of the census of manufactures 1919. Washington D.C.: Government Printing Office.

U.S. Bureau of the Census. (1949). Historical statistics of the United States 1789–1945. Washington, D.C.: Government Printing Office.

U.S. Committee of Industrial Analysis. (1937). The national recovery administration: Report of the President's committee of industrial analysis. Washington D.C.: Department of Commerce.

U.S. Department of Commerce. (1975). Historical statistics of the United States, colonial times to 1970. Washington, D.C.: U.S. Government Printing Office.

U.S. Department of Labor. (1966). Technical trends in major North American industries. Department of Labor Statistics No. 1474, Washington, DC.

Vedder, R. K. and Galloway, L. E. (1993). *Out of Work: Unemployment and Government in 20th Century America*. New York, NY: Holmes and Meier.

Wanniski, J. (1976). *The Way the World Works*. New York, NY: Simon and Schuster.

Weinstein, M. M. (1980). *Recovery and Redistribution under the NIRA*. New York: North Holland.

White, E. (1990). The stock market boom and crash revisited. *Journal of Economic Perspectives*, 4(2), 67–83.

Wright, G. (1990). The origins of American industrial success 1879–1940. *American Economic Review*, 90(4), 651–666.

Index